# High
# Steel

# High Steel

## THE DARING MEN WHO BUILT
## THE WORLD'S GREATEST SKYLINE

## JIM RASENBERGER

HarperCollins*Publishers*

HarperCollins books may be purchased for educational, business, or sales promotional use. For information, please write: Special Markets Department, HarperCollins Publishers Inc., 10 East 53rd Street, New York, NY 10022.

"Musee des Beaux Arts," copyright 1940 and renewed 1968 by W. H. Auden, from *W. H. Auden: The Collected Poems* by W. H. Auden. Used by permission of Random House, Inc.

FIRST EDITION

*Designed by Elliott Beard*

Printed on acid-free paper

Library of Congress Cataloging-in-Publication Data
Rasenberger, Jim.
  High steel : the daring men who built the world's greatest skyline / Jim Rasenberger.—1st ed.
    p.   cm.
  Includes bibliographical references and index.
  ISBN 0-06-000434-7
    1. Structural steel workers—United States—Biography. 2. New York (N.Y.)—Buildings, structures, etc. 3. Building, Iron and steel—New York—History. I. Title.
TH139.R37 2004
624.1'821'092273—dc21

                                        2003056622

04 05 06 07 08 ❖/RRD 10 9 8 7 6 5 4 3 2 1

# CONTENTS

# High Steel

Ironworkers atop the Woolworth Building, 1912. *(Brown Brothers)*

# Of Steel and Men

"... high growths of iron, slender, strong, light, splendidly
uprising toward clear skies. ..."

—WALT WHITMAN
"Mannahatta," 1881

O nly a poet—maybe only Walt Whitman himself, for that matter—
could have described the skyline of Manhattan in 1881 with such
delirious hyperbole. High growths of iron? The highest point on the
island in 1881 was the steeple of Trinity Church, built in 1846 and
rising 284 feet over Broadway. The vast majority of secular buildings
rose just four or five stories, and the tallest rose a mere ten stories.
Even these were remarkably chunky structures, built of thick
masonry or dense cast iron, hardly "light" or "slender." They soared
like penguins.

But if Whitman's description seems a bit overwrought by today's
standards, it was also prophetic. New York was on the verge of enormous physical change in 1881. The main evidence of this stood in
the East River, in the form of two stone towers rising from the cur-

rents, one near Manhattan's shore, the other near Brooklyn's. The towers were high, startlingly high, each looming 276 feet over the river; but it wasn't the towers that made the Brooklyn Bridge so remarkable. It was the great steel cables draped between them, and the steel beams suspended from the harp-like web of steel wires. This was the part of the bridge that really mattered, the part that made it a bridge, unleashed from earth if not the laws of physics: steel.

Americans did not invent steel, but steel, in many ways, invented twentieth-century America. Cars, planes, ships, lawn mowers, office desks, bank vaults, swing sets, toaster ovens, steak knives—to live in twentieth-century America was to live in a world of steel. By mid-century, 85 percent of the manufactured goods in the United States contained steel, and 40 percent of wage earners owed their jobs, at least indirectly, to the steel industry. Steel was everywhere. Most evidently, and most awesomely, it was in the cities, ascending hundreds of feet above the earth in the form of steel-frame skyscrapers.

The first skyscrapers began to appear in Chicago in the mid-1880s, a year or so after the Brooklyn Bridge opened to traffic. The new buildings turned the old rules of architecture inside out: instead of resting their weight on thick external walls of brick or stone, they placed it on an internal framework—a "skeleton"—of steel columns and beams. The effect was as if buildings had evolved overnight from lumbering crustaceans into lofty vertebrates. Walls would still be necessary for weather protection and adornment, but structurally they'd be almost incidental. The steel frame made building construction more efficient and more economical, and it had a less pragmatic—yet more significant—effect. It gave humans the ability to rise as high as elevators and audacity could carry them.

The steel-frame skyscraper was born in Chicago, but New York is where it truly came of age. By 1895, Manhattan's summit had doubled to 20 stories, then it doubled again, then again—all before 1930 and all made possible by steel. And as skyscrapers sprang up from the bedrock, new steel bridges reached out to Brooklyn, to Queens, to the mainland across the Hudson, connecting the city so seamlessly to the world beyond that New Yorkers would soon forget they lived on an island.

In 1970, the summit of the city rose one last time, to 110 stories, on the stacked columns of two identical buildings in lower Manhattan. A stone's throw from Trinity Church and a short stroll from the Brooklyn Bridge, the twin towers of the World Trade Center seemed to herald a remarkable new age of building. They were so high—ten times as high as the "high growths of iron" Walt Whitman admired in 1881—they literally disappeared, some days, into the clouds.

The astonishing ascendancy of New York City's skyline has been recounted before, often and well. Several of its icons—the Flatiron Building, the Woolworth Building, the Chrysler Building, the Empire State Building—have achieved a kind of celebrity usually reserved for Hollywood film stars and heads of state, while their architects and builders have basked in reflected glory. Strangely, though, one group of key players is usually neglected in the telling of the skyline's drama: the men who risked the most and labored the hardest to make it happen. Called ironworkers, or, more specifically, *structural* ironworkers, these are the brave and agile men who raised the steel into the sky: the generations of Americans and Newfoundlanders and Mohawk Indians who balanced on narrow beams high above the city to snatch steel off incoming derricks or crane hooks and set it in place—who shoved it, prodded it, whacked it, reamed it, kicked it, shoved it some more, swore at it, straddled it, pounded it mercilessly, and then riveted it or welded it or bolted it up and went home. That was on a good day. On a bad day, they went to the hospital or the morgue. Steel is an unforgiving material and, given any chance, bites back. It was a lucky ironworker who made it to retirement without losing a few fingers or breaking a few bones. And then, of course, there was always the possibility of falling. Much ironwork was done hundreds of feet in the air, where a single false step meant death. Steel was the adversary that made them sweat and bleed. It was gravity, though, that usually killed them.

This is the story of the ironworkers who built New York—and are building it still. Without idealizing them, it's fair to say that they are a remarkable breed. What makes them remarkable isn't just their daring or acrobatics; it's their whole way of life. History lives through them by way of their genealogies. Many come from a close-knit group of families, multigenerational dynasties of New York ironworkers. They are the sons and grandsons and great-grandsons of the men who built the icons of the past. They are the Montours, the Deers, the Diabos, and the Beauvais from the Kahnawake Mohawk Reserve near Montreal. They are the Kennedys, the Lewises, the Doyles, the Wades, and the Costellos from a small constellation of seaside towns in Newfoundland. They are the Collinses, the Donohues, the Johnsons, the Andersons, and the McKees, whose grandfathers immigrated to New York from Germany and Scandinavia and Ireland. When a young man from one of these families looks out over the skyline and says, "My family built this city," his brag is deserved.

Today's ironworkers are, in many respects, cultural relics. They live at odds with the prevailing trends of twenty-first-century American culture, or at least American culture as prescribed by glossy magazines and morning television shows. They drink too much, smoke too much, and practice few of the civilities of the harassment-free workplace. As gender roles become less defined, the ironworkers, virtually all of them men, continue to revel in a cocoon of full-blown masculine camaraderie. Education levels have increased across the board in America, but the education of most ironworkers stops at high school. Unionism is in decline, with just 11 percent of American workers still enrolled in labor unions at the start of the twenty-first century, but New York ironworkers remain avid and unabashed unionists. The labor force has turned en masse from manual work to high-tech, sedentary work in ergonomically correct settings, but ironworkers continue to depend on muscle and stamina and a capacity to endure a certain amount of pain. And as Americans become increasingly averse to risk, ironworkers continue to risk their lives every day they go to work.

On a cold afternoon several winters ago, I climbed out of a subway station at the corner of 42nd Street and Seventh Avenue and looked up to see a tall young man in a gray sweatshirt walking a pencil-thin beam hundreds of feet over Times Square. The economy was still booming, the World Trade Center was still standing. Christmas was a few weeks away. Down on the ground, Salvation Army bells jingled and people pushed along the sidewalks, dashing into the intersection. Up there, the young man seemed oblivious to all of this. He walked with a smooth stride, his arms loose at his side. For all the care he displayed, he might have been strolling down a country lane.

I never spoke to Brett Conklin that afternoon—I never spoke to him, in fact, until after he fell—but a few weeks later I saw him again, this time in a photograph. I'd written an article about ironworkers for the *New York Times.* The newspaper had dispatched a photographer to the building on Times Square where Brett worked, and when the article appeared it featured a large photograph of Brett on the front cover. The photograph shows a handsome young man, his hard hat turned rakishly backwards, standing on a beam at what appears to be the edge of the building. He's looking down with an expression that is—what?—fearless, contemplative, defiant. Or maybe none of those. It's an expression that I find impossible to read. I suppose what it is, really, is the expression of a young man whose life is about to change.

*Icarus high up on Empire State,* by Lewis Wickes Hine, 1931.
*(New York Public Library/Art Resource, New York)*

# PART I

# The Hole

In Brueghel's "Icarus," for instance: how everything turns away
Quite leisurely from the disaster; the ploughman may
Have heard the splash, the forsaken cry,
But for him it was not an important failure; the sun shone
As it had to on the white legs disappearing into the green
Water; and the expensive delicate ship that must have seen
Something amazing, a boy falling out of the sky,
Had somewhere to get to and sailed calmly on.
           —W. H. AUDEN

# ONE

# Some Luck

B rett Conklin was one of the lucky ones.
       Of the 1,000 or so structural ironworkers who worked in
New York City in the winter of 2001, most, like Brett, lived somewhere else. They lived at the far reaches of the city's suburbs, in
Connecticut or New Jersey towns where a man making a good middle-
class income could afford a patch of decent real estate. Or they lived
in Bay Ridge, Brooklyn, by the anchorage of the Verrazano-Narrows
Bridge, where several hundred Mohawk Indians boarded during the
week, four or five to a house. A few Newfoundlanders still held claim
to the old neighborhood around 9th Street in Brooklyn, while another
clan—the Newfies of Lindenhurst—maintained a well-kempt enclave
on Long Island. One man lived on a farm in the Berkshires that winter,
waking in the middle of the night to begin his star-lit drive to the city.
Two men drove all the way from Wilmington, Delaware, to Times
Square every morning, then back again every afternoon.
       Wherever an ironworker lived, chances were he came into Man-
hattan by one of its tunnels or bridges. The difference was enormous. A tunnel was dank, gloomy, infested. Entering New York by

tunnel was like sneaking into a palace through the cellar door: it lacked dignity. The proper way for an ironworker to enter the city was by bridge, swooshing over water, steel vibrating beneath him and gathering in the sky before him. The ironworker entering the city by bridge enjoyed a peculiar kind of pride. His work—or the work of his father or grandfather, of the generations of ironworkers that preceded him—lay before him and under him and vaulted over him. Every bridge and building represented a catalogue of friendships, marriages, births, falls, cripplings, and, in some cases, deaths. The relationship between an ironworker and the city's steel structures was intensely personal.

On the morning of February 20, 2001, as on most mornings, Brett Conklin had the good fortune to enter the city over one of the most spectacular bridges of them all, the George Washington, a 4,760-foot suspended span crossing the Hudson River between Fort Lee, New Jersey, and northern Manhattan. Shortly before dawn, his commuter bus, which he'd boarded 40 miles to the west, slowed for the toll, then shifted up and started across the bridge, and Brett could look up to see the two lacy steel towers, each taller than a 50-story skyscraper, and the four suspension cables draped between them, each weighing about 7,000 tons and still bejeweled, in the wintry gloom, with luminous green electric bulbs. Downriver a violet fog hovered over the tops of the buildings. Dawn was breaking. The newspaper forecast mild temperatures, rising to a high in the low 50s, mostly cloudy with a chance of dim sunshine. There was no mention of rain in the forecast.

Half an hour after crossing the bridge, Brett emerged from the Port Authority Bus Terminal and strode across Eighth Avenue. He was a striking man, six feet four inches tall, large-boned and well built, but with a soft, boyish face. Brett had recently moved in with his girlfriend but he spent a good deal of time at his parents' house, eating his mother's cooking, watching sports on television with his father and younger brother. He was, at 28, still very close to his family and proud of it. When his mother expressed reservations about his decision to go into ironwork six years earlier, he'd listened carefully, weighed her words, then made his own decision. Respectful but headstrong—that was Brett.

With his long stride, Brett covered the distance to the building on Times Square in a matter of minutes. He slipped into it through a side entrance on 41st Street. The building had reached 32 floors, just six floors shy of topping out. Upon completion, it would become the headquarters of Ernst & Young, the accounting firm, and take its place among five other skyscrapers to leap up in Times Square during the last two years, and among dozens to appear in Manhattan over the last five or six years. Like every other tall office building in New York, it would be supported almost entirely by structural steel.

Brett was lucky to be an ironworker in New York during one of the greatest construction booms in the city's history. The boom had been going strong since the mid-90s. Over the last few months, the stock market had shown signs of contraction, but nobody was too worried about that, not yet. Enough new office space had been conceived in the bull market to keep ironworkers in pay for years. Local 40's shape hall on West 15th Street, where union ironworkers went when they needed work, was as quiet as a tomb. If a man showed up, he was sent right back out that same morning. Virtually anyone with a book—that is, membership in the local—who was healthy and wanted the work could have it. Even members of out-of-town locals who drove into town to partake of the bounty—"boomers," they were called—went out the same day on a permit.

A fine bounty it was, too. $33.45 an hour, plus a generous benefits package, made New York's wage the highest an ironworker could earn in North America. In good times, a capable hand could work virtually nonstop, turning that $35 an hour into $1,400 a week, and turning that $1,400 a week into $65,000 or $70,000 a year. At 28, with a girlfriend but still no family to support and no college loans to amortize, this was a considerable sum of money. Indeed, Brett was doing better than most of his old high school friends who had college diplomas and white-collar jobs. What's more, the work he did was a good deal more exciting—more *satisfying*—than anything one of them was likely to find hunched over a computer in a fluorescent-lit cubicle inside one of these skyscrapers that Brett and his fellow ironworkers built. Sometimes on weekend nights Brett would come into the city with his old high school friends and point out buildings he'd worked on. "We'd see the steel and the rigs and the kangaroo cranes, and I was always, like, look at that, see, that's what I do. I was always real proud of being an ironworker. That's one of the things about it. It makes you proud."

Brett stopped briefly at the shanty, a small plywood cabin that squatted on the concrete floor of the building's basement. Inside, wooden benches ran along the walls and bare light bulbs dangled from the ceiling. On one of the plywood walls somebody had used a piece of chalk to draw an enormous pair of woman's breasts, probably to add some cheer, but there wasn't anything too cheery about a pair of disembodied breasts. Brett grabbed his gray hooded sweatshirt from a hook on the wall, then gathered his hard hat and a wide leather belt from the other hook.

Back upstairs, lines had already formed at the two construction elevators—"man-hoists," as ironworkers call them—that ran along the north side of the building. The wait presented an opportunity for a hundred ironworkers to huddle together and stamp their feet and stay warm by hurling insults at each other. Ironworker banter was relentless, and the men with the sharpest tongues dominated the lines for the hoist.

"Jesus, you look like shit, Johnny."

"I feel like shit. Last night was a tough one."

"But you always look like shit, Johnny. What happened to your eye, anyway? Your wife do that?"

"Naw, it was your wife. She likes it rough."

The accordion door screeched open and 20 men crushed in. The cage shot up the outside of the building, rattling like a can of nails. Fogged Plexiglas covered the metal grilling, a favor not to the iron-workers, who weren't likely to care, but to the other tradesmen and the dozens of other possibly acrophobic surveyors and inspectors and financiers who might visit the site of a building under construction. Accelerating upwards at the edge of a building in an open cage held to a building by a thin monorail was not an experience for the faint of heart.

The hoist stopped with an abrupt clunk on the 27th floor. This was as high as it went. The operator yanked open the gate, and Brett and the others filed out and walked across the metal deck to the ladders. They started up the steep rungs, a coil of men stretching out, then bunching together, then stretching out again. The higher they climbed, the shorter the coil, as men dropped out along the way. At the 28th floor, the welders peeled off, then the detail men turned away at the 29th. Brett kept climbing.

From the moment he steps up onto the corrugated metal deck, a visitor unaccustomed to the summit of a modern skyscraper-in-progress is likely to find the surroundings unsettling. This is especially true if he happens to be among the 23 percent of Americans who described themselves in a 1999 Harris Poll as "very afraid" of heights. The clinical term is acrophobia. In the hierarchy of American fears, according to the poll, only ophidiophobia—fear of snakes—ranks higher.

The novice visitor's first shock, beyond the inescapable fact of height, will be the slap of wind on his cheeks; no matter how tranquil the morning below, the air, lacking obstacles to drag down its velocity, blows hard at the top of a skyscraper. More disconcerting is the absence of walls and ceiling. Without these bearings, the novice's brain balks, shooting an urgent message to nerve receptors in his extremities. The gist of the message is: DON'T MOVE! But even as his legs refuse to move, he notices that they are in fact *moving*—or rather, the building itself is moving. Tall buildings sway slightly, and the stronger the wind, the more they sway. It's called deflection. The Empire State Building, extremely rigid by today's standards, deflects a couple of inches off its vertical axis in wind. Newer, lighter buildings deflect a good deal more than that, up to two feet off their vertical axes on upper floors. The height of the building, in feet, divided by 500 provides a good estimate of how far a modern building deflects at its top in peak winds. (A 750-foot building, then, deflects up to a foot and a half.) A certain amount of deflection is perfectly natural, even beneficial, for a tall building; better for a structure to bend like green wood than to snap like dry timber. Some buildings, though, over-deflect, a condition which can cause structural problems. In rare cases, it stresses joints and, over time, sheers bolts and welds. More likely, over-deflection will simply cause leaks in windows and disrupt elevator service by pushing elevator shafts out of plumb.

Over-deflection isn't primarily a structural concern; it's a human concern. If a building moves too much in the wind, people on upper floors start to feel dizzy and nauseated. The issue isn't how far the building sways in any direction or even how fast it sways—it's how quickly it *accelerates.* Just as in a car or on a train, humans feel movement inside a building when the building is speeding up or slowing down; it's acceleration that makes people's stomachs turn. By the time most buildings are ready for occupancy, they've accumulated so much bulk from their frames and walls and floors that they are fairly rigid. What deflection remains in buildings is then hidden by the walls and ceiling that surround the inhabitant and remove any visual and aural clues of movement. They fool the brain into a pleasant perception of stillness.

No such luck at the top of a skyscraper under construction. Rigid-making walls and floors are still many months away. So are ceilings. The building moves all too obviously and the sky gapes all too endlessly, and it all takes some getting used to.

When the novice finally works up his courage and manages a few tentative steps across the derrick floor, he will find it hard going. The term *derrick floor*, by which ironworkers refer to the ever-rising top floor of a skyscraper under construction, is a misnomer. For one thing, in this age of tower cranes, derricks are all but extinct. For another, the derrick floor isn't really a floor at all, but wide-wale corrugated steel decking. The troughs are ankle deep, perfect for receiving and molding the concrete that will eventually be poured into them but treacherous to walk on. To make matters worse, the decking is usually littered with debris—discarded bolts, scraps of wire, soda cans, chains. A first timer's instinct is to shuffle along slowly with eyes cast down, until suddenly he feels a shadow pass over and looks up to see a 15-ton girder swooping not 10 feet above him on the hook of a tower crane. Dark brown columns stick up from the deck like trees scorched by fire. Grids of beams link some of the columns, and men walk on the beams, while other men straddle them, working at the joints with torque wrenches and four-pound mauls called "beaters." The jarring sound of beaters whacking bolt heads—*chung! chung! chung!*—rings out over the steady blanketing hum of the crane engines. A pigeon alights, flaps its wings once or twice, then takes off again. Even pigeons seem to find the environment inhospitable.

And yet, it is breathtaking. The air is literally fresher, as gravity tends to keep heavy particles of pollution close to the ground. Some days the sky is a wide swath of blue and the top of the building could be hundreds of miles from the city, an alpine ridge populated by a strange breed of mountain men. Across the chasms, distant figures stand or sit in offices, but they look more like plastic dolls in a playhouse than real people. They do not seem to move much. Every now and then one of them turns and looks out vacantly at the ironworkers for a few moments, then turns away.

———

By 7:20 Brett was on the steel, climbing above the 32nd floor. The sun was making a lackluster effort to rise. The cranes hummed and the sound of steel meeting steel rang through the damp air. From where he stood, Brett could see most of the men up top. They were a fair sample of New York's ironworkers in the winter of 2001. On the derrick floor stood Joe Lewis, a stocky man with a heavy brogue. Joe was born and raised along the coast of Conception Bay in Newfoundland, a small speck on the map that had produced an extraordinary number of New York City ironworkers over the years. Joe's three sons were ironworkers and his brothers were ironworkers. His father had been one, too, until the work killed him.

On the other side of the building stood John Collins, a brash 40-year-old from a legendary family of New York ironworkers. His grandfather had worked on the Empire State Building; his father and seven uncles had worked on most of the big buildings of the last 40 years. John's father had recently passed away, but an 82-year-old uncle still worked iron in the summers.

J. R. Phillips and his cousin Jeff Phillips straddled the steel a few yards from John Collins. Both were fourth-generation Mohawk ironworkers on both sides of their families. Like their fathers and grandfathers, they made a weekly commute down to the city from a small reservation just north of the Canadian border, spent their days on the steel, their nights in Bay Ridge, then drove home to Canada every Friday afternoon.

Hanging off the side of building on a small wooden platform called a "float" was Joe Gaffney, a sandy-haired man of Irish and Norwegian extraction whose brothers and uncle were ironworkers. In the winter of 2001, Joe Gaffney's mother happened to be employed in an office on Sixth Avenue that gave her a perfect view of the Ernst & Young building. She kept a pair of binoculars in her desk and would occasionally check up on Joe, then immediately regret having done so. The sight of her son perched on a thin plank

Brett Conklin on the Ernst & Young building, January 2001.
*(Photo by Michael J. Doolittle)*

of plywood lashed to side of the building 300 feet above the ground—it was really more than a mother could bear.

Now and then, the superintendent of the job, Frank Lane, would climb up to the top and have a look around. Frank—one of the two men who drove in to Times Square from Wilmington, Delaware, every morning—was young for a superintendent, still in his early 40s. With long sideburns, a wad of tobacco tucked inside his cheek, and bulging biceps, Frank looked tough even for an ironworker. In fact, as superintendents go, he was a decent sort. Most of the ironworkers actually admitted to liking him.

Nearly everybody up here had some deep familial connection to ironwork, which made Brett an exception. There were no ironworkers in Brett's family. Once you were an ironworker, though, you *were* family. "We might get into it sometimes at a bar or something, but the next morning it's all forgotten," said Brett. "We look out for each other. You have to. Especially the guys in your gang."

## THE RAISING GANG

The gang is the essential unit of ironwork. The men are deployed in half a dozen different types of gangs, the task of each described fairly precisely by its name. Bolting-up gangs drive and tighten the bolts that hold pieces of steel together. The plumbing-up gang—there is usually one per job—traverse the beams, measuring and adjusting columns to ensure that they are perfectly vertical, or plumb. Decking gangs spread corrugated sheet-metal deck over completed rectangles, or *bays*, of steel made by the floor beams. Once a floor is set, other gangs follow to further secure it. This includes the welders, a few detail gangs, and the safety gang. The job of this last gang is to enclose hazards with steel cable, set nets on the outside of the building, and generally reduce the chances that a man will get killed.

A journeyman ironworker prides himself on his ability to work in any gang. No journeyman is above any job and no journeyman is below it. The wage is the same no matter what you do. All ironworkers are created equal.

In theory, anyway. In practice, one gang stands above the others. This is the raising gang. The five members of the raising gang—six if you count the foreman—are the men who actually erect the steel. They work under the cranes to set it, piece by piece, in the frame of the building. What they assemble is by no means complete. It still requires a great deal of labor to make it plumb and strong. But like an elite military unit, it's the raising gang that goes in first and captures territory. By the time the others arrive, the raising gang is off to claim the next level of altitude.

The two key men in a raising gang are the connectors. Working in pairs, connectors make the initial couplings of steel beams and columns as the pieces swoop in under the booms of cranes. They snatch the steel from the sky, "set" it in position, "hang" it with a high-strength bolt or two, then move on to the next piece as the other gangs—the bolter-ups, the welders, the detail men—come in behind to make the couplings permanent. The connectors are the alpha dogs of high steel. They are the most agile, the strongest, the most fit. Connectors routinely climb 30-foot columns, scooting up vertical trunks of steel using nothing but their arms and legs, much as a racoon pulls himself up a tree. Connectors also walk the narrow beams that run along the perimeter of the building, 30, 40 stories over the ground, or higher. By law, ironworkers are supposed to wear safety harnesses that are attached to the frame of the building whenever they work at a significant height above the deck or the ground, but connectors are an exception to this law. They move so quickly that tying-off would be impractical. This means they are always in danger of falling or getting knocked off. A piece of wild steel, a gust of wind, a missed bolt— it doesn't take much to send a man over. The connector's job is demanding, dangerous, and highly competitive. It is the job that every young ironworker wants. Brett Conklin had it.

Brett was born to connect. Height did not bother him. He didn't mind standing on a beam with the deck 30 feet below on one side and Broadway hundreds of feet below on the other: he *liked* it. Brett was also a natural and avid athlete. Football was the game he loved most. On weekends, he played linebacker on a flag football team in the Rockland County league. He was strong, aggressive, and agile, all necessary attributes of a connector.

The only thing working against Brett on the steel was his size. Connectors, like gymnasts, tend toward compactness. This gives a man the advantage of quickness and a low center of gravity, the better to stick to the steel. Brett compensated for his 6'4" frame with a fine sense of balance and good reflexes. As for his weight—205 pounds of himself, plus 40 or 50 pounds he carried in tools and bolts on his connecting belt—this was a lot to haul up and down columns all day long, but from the moment Brett became an iron-worker and set his sights on connecting, he trained himself to overcome his size with strength and technique. He climbed every chance he got in those early days, learning how to distribute his weight, how to let his legs do most of the work, how to angle his size 11½ boots between the flanges. "I just practiced, practiced, practiced," he said. "I became good at it, really good. Climbing columns was definitely one of my better points as a connector."

By the time Brett got to the Ernst & Young building, he was at the top of his game—"the total package," in the words of his connecting partner, Tommy Mitchell. He had experience, having connected for the better part of five years, but still held onto the enthusiasm of a young man doing something he loves. "The thrill of it," recalled Brett. "It was thrilling. All day long you're moving, working hard, learning something new. You work hard, and the day flies by. I loved that feeling. I loved to work hard."

He knew very well the work was dangerous. The chance of something going wrong seldom left your mind, and whenever it did, something would happen to bring it back to you. You'd be walking a beam and a sudden gust of wind would knock you off balance for a second, and when you got to the other side your heart would be racing and you'd think, *Well, that was close.* A few weeks earlier, a rookie crane operator, sitting in for the regular operator, had gotten a piece of steel caught on a safety cable that ran around the perimeter of the derrick floor. The operator, unaware of his mistake, kept booming up as the piece started to bend. A few seconds more and it would snap or slip out of the choker and possibly fall to the street. Without thinking, Brett ducked under the safety cable and leaned out over the edge of the building. The steel was whipping around, swinging at him like a club, but he balanced on a wide beam several hundred feet above 42nd Street and somehow managed to pry it free. The piece popped loose and sailed away. Only after he stepped back onto the deck did it occur to Brett how close he'd just come to falling.

Altogether, the Ernst & Young job had been safe. One man had broken his foot, another had crushed a finger. A Mohawk Indian named Jeff, who had been working in Brett's gang, had gotten injured when a piece of steel hit him in the chest. But within the spectrum of possible injuries that could befall an ironworker, these were all fairly run-of-the-mill; none were killers or career-enders. The only ironworker on this job who had spent any length of time in the hospital was a young connector known to his fellow ironworkers as Big Ben. Sometime after Christmas, Big Ben, who never smoked and took great care of himself physically and who was, as his nickname implied, famously strong, came down with cancer. It was just one of those things: you never knew.

Later, Brett would recall fragments of the event. They'd rattled around in his mind like pieces of a missing jigsaw puzzle. The gang spent the morning setting steel on the 32nd floor. They had just landed a column when a light drizzle began to fall. The rain was a welcome surprise, since it meant the day would probably be called and the men would get to go home early. It's one of the few axioms of ironwork: rain cancels work. Wet steel is too slick to climb or walk. Before quitting, though, Brett had one thing left to do. He had to scale the column to its top, 30 feet straight up, and unhook the line of the crane. It was an entirely routine procedure for a connector, one that Brett had performed hundreds of times. Brett grabbed hold of the flanges with his hands, dug in with his feet, and started to climb.

Joe Lewis was a few floors below when he heard the sound, a sickening *THUD*. It lacked the peculiar twang of falling steel and Joe knew instantly what it meant. "Ah, jeez," he said. "That's somebody just went down." By the time Joe got upstairs, ironworkers were gathered around Brett. He lay supine on the derrick floor. He'd blacked out for a few seconds, then come to. Somebody was calling into a radio for help. Brett lay there, stunned, looking up at the 30-foot column from which he'd just fallen.

*Don't move*, somebody said.

*You flipped over*, somebody else said. *You were coming down head first.*

Brett gasped. His back and chest felt scorched. He was sure he'd broken his back. The pain in his back was almost unbearable. He did not even feel his ankle.

When an ironworker falls up top, the fastest way to get him down is by crane. The crane's boom is rigged up to a seven-by-five metal bin with low sides, called a scale box. Usually, scale boxes are used to transport supplies from the street to the decks, but in emergencies they double as airborne stretchers.

Brett descended from the top of the Ernst & Young building in one of these. A few paramedics and fellow ironworkers rode down with him. Brett lay on his back, facing up. Later, he'd remember how the rain fell on his face, the way the cold drops pricked his skin. He'd remember the crowd gathered on the sidewalk and the faces of the ironworkers sticking out from the edge of the building 30 stories up, gazing down at him. The paramedics gingerly lifted him on a board, then slid him into the back of an ambulance. Then the doors slammed and the ambulance sped south down Seventh Avenue to the trauma center at St. Vincent's Hospital.

The rest of the day was a blurry nightmare of pain and upset. From a gurney in the hospital Brett called his parents. His mother answered. The moment she heard his voice, she began to cry. "It was horrible . . . horrible," Brett would recall a year later. He then repeated the news to his father.

That evening, with his parents at his side, Brett digested the preliminary test results. He had a collapsed lung, three crushed vertebrae, and a fractured spine. The worst damage was to his left foot, still too numb to feel. Apparently, the foot had taken the brunt of the fall. The bones were splintered, one of them spearing his ankle joint, and bone fragments were scattered throughout his foot. Over the next two years, Brett would undergo several operations to repair the foot. He would undergo hundreds of hours of physical therapy for his leg and back, then psychological therapy to deal with the trauma of having his young life permanently altered.

Ironworkers' injuries don't usually make the newspapers. The Sunday after Brett Conklin fell, though, a small item about his accident appeared in the *New York Times*. The reporter had visited Smith's, an ironworkers' watering hole on Eighth Avenue, on the very evening of the accident. There he'd found several ironworkers drinking and talking about it. "I looked up and saw him climbing the column," one of the ironworkers told the reporter. "I looked up again and saw him coming down."

"It was his own fault," said another. "It was too wet and he shouldn't have been messing around. The kid learned the hard way."

According to the article, Brett had tried an "old ironworker's trick" of sliding down a column headfirst. He'd been goofing around—"skylarking," in ironworker parlance—when he lost control. "He slipped, did a flip in the air and landed two floors below," wrote the reporter. "He missed falling through a hole in the steel, and death, by two feet."

By the end of the following Monday, virtually every ironworker in New York had either read the item or heard about it. Most found it infuriating and implausible. A certain amount of skylarking was probably inevitable, but anything that put a man in harm's way was looked upon severely by ironworkers. The implication that Brett had attempted a death-defying stunt on a damp day when he was almost guaranteed to fall seemed ludicrous.

No one knew exactly why or how Brett fell. Not even Brett knew. He wished, he once admitted, that the whole event had been videotaped, so he could watch it over and over and over again. He wanted to figure out what happened—how one moment he had been reaching up, the next falling upside-down toward the deck. As for the ironworkers in the bar, it was perhaps comforting to place blame on the injured man, to assume that he did something to cause his own injury. It meant you had control over your own destiny. *Poor bastard . . . but it would never happen to me.*

The truth was that bad things happened all the time, and not for any good reason, and they happened not just to the reckless and the stupid, but to the smartest, the quickest, the most experienced. Within six months of Brett's fall, Frank Lane, the superintendent, a man who looked like he could handle pretty much anything, had his legs pinned under a load of steel in Atlantic City, crippling him. Joe Lewis fell through a plank on a building on 59th Street and Sixth Avenue, destroying the nerves in his right arm and ending his ironworking career. Big Ben, the connector with cancer, got cured and came back to work. A few weeks later, a beam rolled over onto his leg and broke it.

## FALLING

Between 35 and 50 ironworkers die on the job in America every year. This is perhaps not a resounding number, given a workforce of approximately 50,000, but it's high enough to make it one of the most lethal jobs, per capita, in the country. (Only timber cutting and fishing rate as more lethal in a 1998 table compiled by the Bureau of Labor Statistics.) As for serious nonfatal accidents—that is, serious enough to put a man out of work for a period of time but not serious enough to kill him—the Occupational Safety & Health Administration (OSHA) estimates that American ironworkers sustain about 2,300 per year. This estimate is probably low. As OSHA itself has conceded, nonfatal injuries are difficult to track, since contractors are not legally obligated to report them. One good indication of the relative danger of the job is the fact that, nationally, employers pay an average of $41.24 in workers compensation per $100 of payroll for ironworkers, one of the highest premiums of any occupation in the country.

There are many ways for an ironworker to become injured. He can get hit by a piece of swinging steel or a dropped tool. He can inadvertently lop off his finger between two pieces of steel. He can lose his leg under a load. But the easiest way is by falling. Falling is the leitmotif of an ironworker's life. This is not to say he's doomed to fall—chances are he won't—but falling is a *possibility* that confronts him every time he steps out onto a beam or shinnies up a column. Falling is the thing he is always striving not to do, and the moment he stops striving not to do it, he puts himself in danger. Gravity lies in wait. All it needs is a false step, an ankle that turns in, a slight stumble, an instant of an imbalance or idiocy or just plain spaciness. Falls account for 75 percent of ironworker fatalities.

Other than skydivers, no group of humans has had more experience of falling from elevation than ironworkers. In New York City alone, hundred of ironworkers have fallen to their deaths and thousands more have fallen and lived. Thanks to reforms instituted by insurance companies and OSHA, ironworkers are much less likely to fall now than they were even twenty years ago. And those falls that occur are likely to be shorter and more survivable than the falls of previous eras. Still, ironworkers fall, and short falls are plenty dangerous. A study conducted in 2000 by the National Institute for Occupational Safety and Health (NIOSH) examined 91 fatal falls by workers, including, but not limited to, ironworkers. Half the fatalities occurred in falls under 30 feet. Nineteen fatalities—over a fifth—occurred in falls under 15 feet.

When a man falls from an earthly structure, even when he falls a considerable distance, the entire event lasts no more than a few seconds. A 50-foot fall will be over in about one and a half seconds. *One Mississippi Two Missi*—and it's done. Exactly how fast a man falls depends on a number of factors, including the position of his body, the clothing he wears, and how the wind is blowing that day. No matter how fast he falls, the rate of his acceleration will be 32 feet per second for every second of descent. He starts slowly, then speeds up very rapidly. Eventually, the gravitational force pulling him down will be matched by the friction of the air he is falling through, and then he will stop accelerating and maintain a fixed speed the rest of the way down. This speed is his *terminal velocity*—somewhere between 120 and 140 miles an hour. Unless it's a very long fall, the man will hit ground well before he reaches terminal velocity.

The important part of any fall, the part that can decide whether a man lives or dies, is that slender fraction of a second when there is still opportunity for a falling man to act, when his reflexes may work faster than his speed of descent and he may try to save himself by grabbing hold of something on the way down. They all try and many, amazingly, succeed. Good ironworkers are agile as cats; some are just as lucky.

In the late 1920s, an ironworker named Slim Cooper was driving a rivet on the 36th floor of the Grand Central Building on Park Avenue when the plank he was standing on gave way. Nowadays, floors are filled in as the building rises, so that if a man falls through the derrick floor he'll usually land on the floor below. But in the 1920s, buildings were open shafts for many stories below the working floors, making a fall inside every bit as lethal as a fall outside. Fortunately for Slim Cooper, a pair of parallel planks happened to lie across the beams directly below, on the 35th floor. As Slim plunged through the narrow breach between them, he flung his arms out. The boards caught him under each arm and held him there, his feet swaying over the open shaft until his gang could come and rescue him. "I meant to quit after that," Slim Cooper said later, "but I never did."

One man gets lucky, another gets unlucky. Seven men fell to their deaths during the construction of the Williamsburg Bridge at the start of the twentieth century. The last two of these, Harmon Hansen and Adolph Weber, fell in July of 1903. They were a hundred feet over land on the Manhattan side of the bridge when a wooden derrick they were using broke and plunged to the cobblestone street. In this case, their instinct to grab hold of something did them no good. They clutched the guy wire of the plunging derrick and it pulled them down with it. On the same bridge, two months later, a 25-year-old riveter named William Sizer was overcome by a dizzy spell and started to fall. He reached out and grabbed the nearest thing at hand, a keg of rivets. The keg came with him. Even as he began spinning head over heel, Sizer held onto the keg for dear life, letting go of it only an instant before slamming into the East River "headforemost," as the *New York Times* put it in the next morning's edition. A few moments later—headforemost—he popped back out of the water, bruised, bewildered, but very much alive. "I can hardly believe I fell from the bridge," he told reporters as he lay in Bellevue Hospital recovering from his 130-foot dive.

Why did William Sizer live while the seven before him died? One man falls 50 feet and walks away, another falls 10 and breaks his neck. In the late 1920s, Paul Rockhold fell from the 12th floor of an apartment building under construction on Riverside Drive. Around the fourth floor, he hit a plank of green wood and bounced, then went down another four floors and landed in a pile of debris. He spent eight months in a hospital but he lived. His explanation: "The devil wasn't out that day."

"You never can tell," an ironworker named Billy Beatty told a magazine writer in 1901. "I remember a man who was standing on a traveler [a kind of crane] up eighty-nine feet. The light of a line that was picking up a stick of timber swung over and took him off his feet, knocking them right from under him. But he came down square on those feet of his, let me tell you, after falling the whole eighty-nine, and the only harm it did him was to drive his hip up four inches. That was all."

Then there is the more recent story of an ironworker named Ray who fell back in the 1970s. Ray fractured his spine and was paralyzed for life. It was a hard fate, but at least he got a huge settlement from the insurance company. As his girlfriend was driving him to pick up the settlement check, another car cut them off. "His girlfriend slammed on the brakes, he went through the windshield and got killed," recounted Joe Lewis, the Newfoundlander signalman who worked in Brett Conklin's gang. "I mean, now that is bad luck."

The real question isn't why Brett fell but, rather, by what grace of good fortune he flipped and landed on his feet, instead of his head. He lived. He was not a quadriplegic. He had a family who loved him and a girlfriend who would stick by him through the grim times to come. For all that had happened, he was, he knew, lucky.

Among ironworkers the term for falling is "going into the hole." The hole is the foundation of the building, the mud pit from which it sprang. By the time a building starts to rise, the hole has been covered in cement and filled with ductwork and wires. It has become, in other words, a basement. But for ironworkers it is always more than a basement. It is the hard spot down there, the place in the earth from which gravity asserts its pull. Going into the hole doesn't require falling clear through to the foundation. It's a term used to describe any substantial fall. Sometimes the hole is just another word for the grave.

The largest hole in New York City in that winter of 2001 was about a mile north of Times Square, at the western rim of Columbus Circle. Since the mid-1950s, the site had been home to one of the most despised buildings in New York, an enormous white slab called the Coliseum. Now the Coliseum was gone, demolished, and in its place was a vast basin of dirt, 3.4 acres, 33 feet deep, 630 feet corner to corner. From this hole would rise a building as enormous, complex, and expensive as any the city had seen for decades. The twin-towered Time Warner Center would rise 750 feet and cost 1.7 billion dollars to build, the highest price tag for any building in the history of the city. Its 20 acres of tinted glass would enclose 21 million square feet of office, retail, and residential space, including the headquarters of the largest media conglomerate in the world, several television studios, a 251-room hotel, a 1,200-seat jazz hall, several suburban malls' worth of shops and restaurants, and 198 "super-luxury" condos priced between 1.8 million and 27 million dollars. The building had all the earmarks of an instant New York icon. Such a building required a title, a legend, and a clever copywriter had provided one: *"The Center of Everything."*

On the morning of February 20, 2001, several hours before Brett Conklin fell, a raising gang of ironworkers arrived for their first look at the hole from which The Center of Everything was to rise. The six men gathered at the western edge of Columbus Circle and looked down into it, and all of them thought the same thing: *That is one big hole.* With the exception of the 55-year-old veteran signalman, Chett Barker, none of them had seen a hole like this. Most of them hadn't been born when Chett got his first look, 31 years earlier, at the foundation for the World Trade Center. Nothing could compare to that, but this came close.

One of the men in the gang that morning was a 32-year-old blue-eyed Mohawk Indian connector named Keith McComber. Keith McComber's eyes weren't just blue; they were startlingly blue, pale and liquid and fringed with long lashes that gave his otherwise rugged features a sensitive, soulful cast. They were the eyes of a leading man or a poet. One afternoon about 10 years earlier, somebody on the reservation had called him Bunny Eyes and the name stuck. Over the years, Bunny Eyes had been shortened to Bunny. Now if you mentioned Keith McComber, no ironworker had any idea whom you were talking about. But everybody knew Bunny.

At lunch that first day, around the same time that Brett Conklin was arriving by ambulance at St. Vincent's Hospital, Bunny and the rest of the raising gang—who had not yet heard news of the fall—lined up on stools at the Coliseum Bar and Grill, a narrow bar on 58th Street. A few cardboard shamrocks were taped to the wall behind the bar in anticipation of St. Patrick's Day. Each had a name written on it and, beneath this, an inscription dedicating the shamrock to the Muscular Dystrophy Society. Bunny sipped his beer and eyed the shamrocks.

"How much for one of those?" he asked the bartender.

"One dollar."

"I'll take one."

He paid his dollar and wrote his name, his real name, on the green cardboard: "From the heart of KEITH comes this shamrock." The bartender taped it up over the bar with all the others. It never hurt to buy yourself some luck.

# TWO

# The Man On Top

## (1901)

A t the start of the twentieth century, the most remarkable hole in
New York City was a 35-foot deep gash on 23rd Street, where old,
meandering Broadway cut across the modern grid street of Fifth
Avenue and formed the hypotenuse of a narrow right triangle. The
wedge-shaped plot had been the home of a ticket booth for the Erie
Railway and, before that, a bare sliver of grass known as Eno's Triangle. Awkwardly shaped and minuscule—"a stingy piece of pie,"
somebody once described it—it was about the last place on earth
most people would have thought to build a 21-story skyscraper. But
that is exactly what the construction firm of George A. Fuller, in col-
laboration with the architect Daniel H. Burnham, proposed to do in
the summer of 1901.

The steel-frame building that began to rise from the hole the following autumn was officially named the Fuller Building, but no one
ever called it that. It was, and always would be, the Flatiron, so called
for its resemblance to a nineteenth-century clothing iron. "For many

reasons this building is unique," a sales brochure informed prospective tenants. "It is the cumulative result of all that is known in the art of building, and is equipped with every conceivable convenience that human ingenuity could devise. From a structural standpoint, it is the strongest building ever erected." It was also, much like the Time Warner Center 100 years later, the Center of Everything: "Situated in the very heart of New York City, its accessibility is exceptional: It is in close proximity to all the leading hotels, theaters, railroad stations, and ferries."

In fact, the Flatiron was located well north of the main business district of New York in 1901, but no matter: this would turn out to be one of its assets. No other tall buildings stood nearby to compete for height or attention. And attention is exactly what this building demanded. Curious and skeptical pedestrians paused and craned their necks to marvel at the strange steel sliver, and at the sight of its exterior walls going on nonsequentially, a few floors here, a few floors there, rather than from the bottom up, as walls had always gone. A decade after the first steel-frame skyscraper arrived in New York, the concept of walls as an *afterthought* was still difficult to grasp.

A photograph taken of the building as it went up (dated 1901 but probably shot in the early spring of 1902) illustrates the new "curtain wall" technology perfectly. The building's frame has reached the 15th floor in the photograph, giving it another six to go before topping out. Derricks poke out from the sides. Beams and struts lie in careful stacks on the sidewalk below, waiting to be hoisted. Stalk-like columns rise from the top. Most of the building is an open skeleton of dark oxidized steel, but along the bottom two floors and several middle floors white limestone panels clad the exterior, as thin and fragile-looking as bleached seashells.

At first glance, the building in the photograph appears empty and quiet, frozen in Sunday morning stillness. Closer inspection, though, reveals a dozen or so white-suited masons scattered along a scaffold on the eighth floor. Still closer inspection reveals a lone dark figure hunched over a column at the top of the building, standing along its southern edge. His back is to the camera, so it's difficult to infer much about this man on top, except that he is, in all likelihood, an ironworker: there's not much chance he'd be standing so casually on the edge of the 15th floor if he weren't. His name is probably Irish, or if not Irish then Scandinavian or German. "I never knew but one Italian iron man," a veteran ironworker told a magazine writer in 1901, "but he was a good one." He comes to this occupation from another line of work—few men, in 1901, set out to be ironworkers—but is still relatively young; old age is rarely achieved in a field where the average worker has a four percent chance of getting killed or permanently disabled every year that he works. His reward for his risk is about $4 a day and the awed expressions of men and women who pause on the street to look up and marvel at him.

"In the eyes of all men, not hidden in shops nor buried in the bowels of the earth, they are continually plying their muscular yet delicate and venturesome craft," declared one admirer in *Frank Leslie's Popular Monthly* in July of 1901. "Look up fifteen stories along the steel ribs of a great business structure just under way and the structural workers are like insects creeping over the great metal limb. . . . With but a plank, perhaps a beam of iron only, as a resting place between earth and sky, the workers are doing wonderful things, just how wonderful you must be up there to see."

For those already up there, the view was superb. It contained shards of the past and glimpses of the future, a mind-boggling collage of transformation. Far out in the waters of the harbor were the Statue of Liberty and Ellis Island, where nearly half a million immigrants would arrive within the year. Closer, to the east, was the Brooklyn Bridge, 20 years old and supporting tens of thousands of people a day. At the foot of the island, near the anchorage of the bridge, was Wall Street, where the New York Stock Exchange surged into record territory—an astonishing two million trades in a single day, then three million a few months later.

It was down there on Wall Street that J. P. Morgan had recently consolidated the largest single corporation in history, United States Steel. Largely formed around Andrew Carnegie's already enormous holdings of steel mills, railroads, and mines, and worth over a billion dollars, U.S. Steel instantly controlled 60 percent of the American steel market and 30 percent of the world steel market. In March of 1901, the cover of *Harper's Weekly* featured a drawing of the earth girded by a thick belt; Uncle Sam stood over the earth, pulling the belt tight. "A Steel Cinch on the World," read the caption. Lest anyone miss the point, an editorial in the magazine affirmed it two weeks later: "The United States has become the master of the world in making steel. It has no rival."

Most strikingly, what the man on the 15th floor saw from his perch of steel—steel, as it happened, that had been forged by U.S. Steel; the Flatiron was among the new conglomerate's first customers—were the high spires and towers, the domes and turrets, of brazen new buildings. This was a very different skyline from the one that made Whitman swoon 20 years earlier. Over 300 buildings rose nine stories or higher. Dozens rose 15 or 20 stories, and at least seven now soared above the steeple of Trinity Church. Joseph Pulitzer's World Building, at 309 feet, had been the first to overtake Trinity in 1890; the Park Row Building, its twin copper-roof cupolas reaching nearly 400 feet over City Hall Park, was the latest, completed in 1899.

"It is not easy to imagine the feelings of a New Yorker exiled for a period of ten or twelve years—no more—who is returning to his native land by one of the ocean steamships," the engineer William Birkmire had written a few years earlier. "As he looks about from the deck of the vessel as it steams up the bay, the first glance that he obtains of the lower part of Manhattan island will probably be, if he has not been forewarned, the greatest surprise of his life."

The buildings inspired a wide range of reaction, from awe to disgust. Mainly, they seemed to inspire anxiety. A public accustomed to stocky stone buildings remained skeptical that these high wispy things could stand. In 1888, during the construction of a narrow 145-foot-tall structure on lower Broadway called the Tower Building—generally credited as New York's first true metal-frame skyscraper—a leery crowd gathered in a gale at a safe distance, fully expecting to watch it topple. The building's architect, Bradford Gilbert, tried to reassure the crowd by climbing to the top with a plumb line. "When I reached the thirteenth floor, the gale was so fierce I could not stand upright," Gilbert later told the *New York Times.* "I crawled on my hands and knees along the scaffolding and dropped the plumb-line. There was not the slightest vibration. The building stood as steady as a rock in the sea."

Gilbert's demonstration notwithstanding, rumors about the instability of tall metal-frame structures had proliferated through the first decade of New York's skyscrapers. A tenant of the 20-story American Tract Society Building claimed that on upper floors clocks and watches lost time or ceased functioning due to vibration. A Boston newspaper warned that all buildings within the vicinity of skyscrapers were in mortal danger. Even the renowned architect of many of these enormous new buildings, George B. Post, publicly expressed doubts about their viability. "It may stand a short gust of wind blowing very hard, but if this were to keep up for any length of time, the cage might begin to sway," he told the *New York Times.* "Then matters would be serious. The rivets would be cut off and the oscillations would increase with each swing backward and forward, soon wrecking the building."

From Paris, meanwhile, came a prediction from a French savant with even more ominous implications for metal-frame structures: that the iron of the Eiffel Tower would spontaneously polarize, becoming, in effect, a 1,000-foot-high magnet sucking everything metal toward it. "All the houses in Paris will suffer from a St. Vitus's dance, and, gradually attracted toward the Champ de Mars, will finally find themselves stuck to the tower," reported the *Scientific American* in 1886, evidently more amused than alarmed by the prospect. "As for locomotives entering Paris, it will be found impossible to stop them at the various termini; they will rush through Paris, and dash themselves to pieces against the center of attraction."

A more recent and serious concern among many architects and physicians was that tall buildings would cause rampant spread of disease by casting streets in permanent midnight. "The results of bacteriological investigation show that the evil microbes flourish and increase in damp, dark places, but that sunlight destroys their life," stated an 1896 report by the New York chapter of the American Institute of Architects. "Our narrow streets, when lined with tall structures, will become unhealthy alleys. . . ."

The most pressing concern of many New Yorkers was simply that their old city was quickly vanishing beneath an alien new city of skyscrapers. A few years after the Flatiron topped out, the writer Henry James, returning to his native New York from a long sojourn in Europe, would despair at these "monsters of the market," as he referred to the tall buildings. "Where, for the eye, is the felicity of simplified gothic, of noble pre-eminence, that once made of this highly pleasing edifice the pride of the town and the feature of Broadway?" he would plaintively wonder of old Trinity Church. "The answer is, as obviously, that these charming elements are still there, just where they ever were, but that they have been mercilessly deprived of their visibility."

## CHICAGO

Whatever one thought about these new buildings, they were an authentic American creation. They were not an idea borrowed from across the Atlantic, from Henry James' beloved Europe, like so much American architecture and culture in the nineteenth century. They

Riveters on the Trinity Building, New York City, 1904. In the background is the steeple of Trinity Church, the tallest structure in Manhattan until 14 years earlier, now overwhelmed by the steel skyscrapers rising around it. *(Trade Catalog Collection, Northwest Architectural Archives, University of Minnesota Libraries)*

were as "indigenous as the red Indian," the British architect Alfred Bossom would later write. And they came not from the east, but from the west—from Chicago.

"In the early eighties . . . Chicago was like a young bustling giant bursting his clothes," wrote Paul Starrett, one of four brothers who would become legends in the skyscraper-building industry—and who all began their careers in Chicago. The city was the nexus of the expanding country; virtually every major rail line passed through it. Just a decade earlier, it had been leveled by a ferocious fire, but it had been reborn, more robust and brash than ever. By 1880, Chicago was the fastest growing city in the country.

The red hot center of Chicago was the Loop, a small patch of the sprawling city circumscribed by Lake Michigan to the east, the Chicago River to the north and west, and railroad yards to the south. Businesses pressed themselves into the confines of the Loop, and the more businesses that built and settled there, the more businesses that wanted—*needed*—to be there. The price of real estate escalated rapidly through the 1880s, from $130,000 to $900,000 per acre. For property owners, the rising price of real estate created an over-whelming incentive to add leasable square footage. Given the limits of available land, there was only one way to go: up.

The height of buildings had been pretty well fixed at six stories through the middle of the nineteenth century. This was a matter not of structural integrity but of human endurance, five flights of stairs being about as many as anybody could reasonably be expected to climb. This first problem of height had been solved by Elijah Otis's "safety elevator," first demonstrated in 1854 and now commonplace in 10- and 11-story office buildings and hotels around the Loop. But while Otis's elevators made new heights plausible, the new heights created a fresh set of problems. The "elevator buildings" were primarily constructed of masonry, supported by walls of stone and brick. The taller a masonry building grew, and the more weight its walls had to bear, the thicker those walls had to be, particularly near the base. Thicker walls meant less floor space and fewer windows. The last of the tall masonry buildings in Chicago, the 16-story Monadnock, completed in 1891, required walls six feet thick at its base. Since lower floors yielded the highest rents, the equation was financially untenable.

In 1883, a practical-minded architect with the ornate name of William LeBaron Jenney began planning the nine-story Home Insurance Building right in the heart of the Loop. Jenney, born in 1832, was one of the older architects in the city. He had employed and mentored many of the young Chicago architects whose reputations would eventually surpass his own, including Daniel Burnham and Louis Sullivan. He was respected and well liked—a natural "bon vivant," as Sullivan described him—but nobody thought much of his aesthetic judgment. Jenney had spent the Civil War as an engineer for Ulysses S. Grant, and later for William Tecumseh Sherman, rebuilding bridges for the invading Union army. He thought like an engineer. Pragmatics came before aesthetics, calculation before decoration.

As Jenney planned the building, he faced an architectural conundrum. On one hand, the building, to pay for itself, would have to be tall, at least nine stories. On the other hand, the president of the Home Insurance Company, J. J. Martin, insisted that the building have numerous windows to permit light and fresh air into offices. A normal masonry high-rise was out of the question. "How are you going to manage it?" wondered Martin. Jenney replied that he was going to go home and think about it.

In one version of the story, almost certainly apocryphal, Jenney arrived home, deep in thought, and came upon his wife reading a book. As she closed her book and set it atop a birdcage, Jenney's eyes narrowed on the birdcage. Seeing how the thin rods of the cage so effortlessly bore the weight of the book, he was struck by a vision of a building constructed like a cage, in which the weight of the building is removed from the walls and placed on a metal frame, and in which the walls are no more important structurally than the blanket laid over a birdcage at night. Eureka!

A hapless young Minneapolis architect named L. S. Buffington had a more sinister explanation for Jenney's epiphany: he believed that Jenney swiped his idea. Buffington had been dreaming of tall skeleton-frame buildings (he called them "cloud sketchers") as early as 1880 and had written and spoken of them well before the Home Insurance Building came into existence, although he never actually built one. As for where he got *his* ideas, he credited the French architect Viollet-le-Duc, who years earlier had envisioned a building remarkably like a skeleton-frame skyscraper: "A practical architect might not unnaturally conceive the idea of erecting a vast edifice whose frame should be entirely of iron, enclosing that frame and preserving it by means of a casing of stone."

Actually, Jenney's plan for the Home Insurance Building was neither an act of thievery nor a leap of genius. It was a simple step of logic. Iron columns and beams had been deployed architecturally since the middle of the nineteenth century, when cast-iron buildings first began to rise in New York City. In masonry buildings, cast-iron columns had been used to add strength to walls and piers, and wrought-iron beams had long served as lintels and girders. So the idea of using iron framing to support buildings was not new. What *was* new was the idea of supporting the building *entirely* with iron framing.

The idea owed something to earlier architecture, but it owed an even larger debt, often overlooked in histories of skyscrapers, to the railroad bridges of nineteenth-century America. Jenney's experience in the Civil War made him well acquainted with bridge-building techniques and almost certainly influenced his architecture. Bradford Gilbert, that fearless designer of New York's Tower Building, referred to his own metal-frame design as "an iron bridge truss stood on end." When steel-frame skyscrapers became common late in the century, it was bridge companies that fabricated the steel and oversaw their erection. Bridges, with a metaphorical aptness worthy of bad poetry, were what you crossed on your way to the modern city.

## FLYING TRAPEZOIDS

"It is a notorious fact that there is no country of the world which is more in need of good and permanent Bridges than the United States of America," wrote the American bridge builder Thomas Pope in 1810. Just four years after Lewis and Clark returned from their failed hunt for a water route across the continent, Pope foresaw that the future of the country depended not on navigating rivers but on spanning them. "Extended along an immense line of coast on which abound rivers, creeks and swamps, it is impossible that any physical union of the country can really take place until the labours of the architect and mechanic shall have more perfectly done away the inconvenience arising from the intervention of waters."

Nineteenth-century American bridge builders built more bridges than any country in the world. Before the end of the century, over 200,000 bridges would be erected in the United States, some 3,000 miles of bridge in all. Acknowledged masterpieces like the Brooklyn Bridge in New York and the Eads Bridge in St. Louis notwithstanding, the great majority of nineteenth-century American bridges were unlovely, workmanlike truss bridges, or what engineer Thomas Curtis-Clark referred to, in 1869, as "skeleton girder" bridges (anticipating the term for metal-frame building by about 30 years). A truss was essentially a brace, usually trapezoidal, that ran along each side of the bridge span to prevent it from sagging or collapsing. Each side of the truss was comprised of a top chord and a bottom chord—the principal horizontal girders—and, between the two, a lattice of diagonal cables or bars. The genius of a good truss was that it gave ample support without adding much weight. This was critical. The more something weighs the stronger it needs to be simply to hold itself up and—not incidentally—the more it costs to build.

As with most engineering, bridge building was the art of doing more with less, and a good truss combined strength with economy. But strength was difficult for early bridge builders to calculate. Unlike buildings, in which strains, absent earthquakes, were fairly constant and predictable (gravity pulling down and wind pushing sideways), even the simplest bridge faced complex strains in keeping its own dead load aloft. Then came the sudden intense impact of the live load—a 35-ton locomotive, for instance, trailed by hundreds of clattering tons of freight—and the bridge jiggled and danced on its bolts and pins, its iron pulled and pressed and wrenched, and then a few moments later it was all over. The live load was off to torture another bridge, and the dead load recovered, unbent, and attempted to resume its pre-assaulted state. Every time this happened, it became a little more arthritic, a little less like its old springy self. And then, one day, perhaps, it collapsed.

Bridges collapsed frequently in the late nineteenth century, 25 times a year on average in the 1870s and 1880s. Occasionally, a bridge collapsed spectacularly and with great loss of life, as occurred one snowy December night in 1876. Two locomotives, traveling front to back and trailed by 11 railroad cars, slowly started across a 13-year-old wrought-iron bridge in Ashtabula, Ohio. The first locomotive had just made it safely across when the bridge fell. The second locomotive and all 11 cars fell with it into the deep gorge below. Ninety-two people died, making Ashtabula the worst American train disaster of the century.

When a bridge fell, engineers flocked to its mangled remains, eager to learn what had gone wrong so they could avoid the fatal flaw in their own bridges. With every disaster they learned what worked and what failed. What were the tolerances of cast or wrought iron? Which arrangements of chords and diagonals gave strength to a truss and which did not? The bridges schooled American engineers, providing them an opportunity to experiment with new structural forms and to gauge the strength of materials, like iron, that would play such an important role in the development of skyscrapers.

Iron was still something of a mystery metal when the first iron bridges began going up in the middle of the nineteenth century. The material had been in use in various forms for thousands of years but until this moment nobody had ever asked much of it structurally. The oldest form of iron is wrought, which humans began using in substantial quantity around 1200 B.C. Wrought iron is the reduction of iron ore heated at very high temperatures. Cast iron came later, in the fourteenth century. The main difference between wrought and cast iron is the amount of carbon that binds with the iron during smelting. Wrought iron has very little carbon; cast iron has a great deal of it. Wrought iron is softer, more pliable and flexible. Cast iron is hard and brittle; it is easily cast in shapes—hence its name and prevalence as an ornamental metal—and bears up well under great weight. Under the wrong conditions, though, cast iron buckles and breaks. In the parlance of engineers, wrought iron performs best under *tension*—as, for instance, a floor beam—while cast iron performs best under *compression*, as a column. Nobody really understood these distinctions when builders began putting up iron bridges. And when the transition to steel began in the 1870s, nobody understood much about it as structural material either.

Steel had been around almost as long as iron. The *Oxford English Dictionary* cites a reference to steel—"style"—in *Beowulf*, from the year 725. Chaucer used the word, which he wrote as "steell," in 1380, though it's not clear that his steell was the same thing as our steel. The word generally connoted a superior form of wrought iron into which some carbon had seeped during the smelting process to give the iron more hardness. Steel's carbon content, about 1.5 percent, is higher than wrought iron's but lower than cast iron's.

Most early structural steel was crucible steel, a laboriously manufactured high-carbon version. James Buchanan Eads insisted on crucible steel in parts of his great bridge over the Mississippi River at St. Louis, completed in 1874. Eads's steel supplier was the Keystone Bridge Company, a subsidiary of Andrew Carnegie's burgeoning empire. Carnegie still had doubts about the future of the product that would transform him from a rich Pittsburgh businessman into one of the wealthiest men in the world. But in 1868, he took a trip to Britain and witnessed a demonstration of a new invention called a Bessemer Converter. The trick to economically turning molten "pig" iron into steel, an Englishman named Henry Bessemer had discovered, was to blow air through it as it heated. The air burned off excess carbon 10 times faster than any previous method and used less fuel to do it. For the first time in history, steel could be manufactured quickly, cheaply, and in vast quantities. Carnegie needed no more convincing.

Steel was slow to win acceptance as a sound or practical structural material; early on it was used mainly for rails on railroad tracks. But gradually engineers came to recognize its superiority to both wrought and cast iron. Steel combined the best of both metals—the flexibility of wrought iron and the brute bearing strength of cast iron—and was at least 20 percent stronger than either. New methods of production would soon make it a good deal stronger.

Like iron, steel first proved itself on bridges. The first all-steel bridge went up in 1879 in Glasgow, Missouri. That same year, Washington Roebling changed the specifications for the floor beams and trusses of the Brooklyn Bridge from wrought iron to steel. (Ten years earlier, his father, John Roebling, had decided to use steel in the bridge's suspension cables.) Steel's migration from bridges to buildings was a simple step, pushed by the hand of Andrew Carnegie. The market for steel rails was drying up in the late nineteenth century. Carnegie, with his extraordinary nose for progress, anticipated skyscrapers as a new market for his Bessemer Converters before most people had any idea what a skyscraper was.

William LeBaron Jenney once again played the role of pioneer. His plan for the Home Insurance Building originally called for a structure of cast-iron columns and wrought-iron beams. But after ground broke on May 1, 1884, Jenney received a letter from Carnegie, Phipps & Co. inviting him to try its new steel beams. Jenney agreed to place steel in the top three floors, marking the first use of structural steel in architecture. When the Home Insurance Building topped out in the winter of 1885, the steel skeleton-frame skyscraper—all nine stories of it—was born.

## CIRCUS ACTS

As iron and steel came of age on nineteenth-century bridges, so too did the trade of ironwork. Long before the men who practiced it called themselves ironworkers, they were "bridgemen," and bridgemen they remained long after they turned their skills from skeleton-girder bridges to steel-frame buildings. The two types of structure were so similar that the skills and constitution a man required to build one applied equally well to building the other.

Early bridgemen lived hard itinerant lives. The bridges they built were often in the middle of nowhere, or near some no-luck town looking to the railroad for salvation. They camped at the site or, if they were fortunate, found a room in a nearby boarding house. The work itself was difficult and perilous, but also sometimes thrilling. From these remote towns the bridgemen frequently picked up starry-eyed farm boys as new recruits. "Here is how we get 'em," an engineer explained some years later. "A big railroad bridge is being built over a river. The boy from the farm comes to watch it. He sees the men climbing out over the water, using ropes for staircases, taking all kinds of daredevil risks. And pretty soon his jaws fall open, and he says to himself that this here game beats the circus all to hollow. . . . He watches his chance; he gets out there himself, learns how to tie ropes and sit on air. In a few months, he is one of the gang. And then good-bye to the farm. It's the roving life after that, from Maine to the Rockies."

The bridges were usually prefabricated in shops, then shipped in sections to the site for assembly. The bridgemen fastened the sections by pounding long iron "pins" through matched eyeholes, then bolting them tight. It was called the "pin-connection method" or simply "the American method," and with it American bridgemen could raise a bridge faster than anyone on earth, often within a matter of days. Speed mattered. It mattered because the railway was spreading over the country like wildfire, making the demand for bridges relentless. It mattered, too, because truss bridges were generally erected over rivers. A temporary wooden scaffold, or "falsework," would be driven into the river's bed to take the weight of the iron until the bridge's superstructure was assembled and self-supporting. Compared to the lazy old rivers of England, America's waterways tended toward the violent and the unpredictable. Bridgemen lived in constant fear of ice flows or "freshets" suddenly gushing down from mountain melts and whisking away the falsework and the bridge and, potentially, the bridgemen themselves.

A few of the iron spans these early bridgemen built remain aloft, crossing over Laughery Creek near Aurora, Indiana, and over the McKenzie River near Springfield, Oregon, and over the Susquehanna River in Ouaquaga, New York, and elsewhere. The great majority are gone, though, made obsolete by steel and concrete and the decline of the railroad. Records of early iron bridges seldom mention the bridgemen; they give an impression, almost, of bridges erecting themselves. But at least one engineer's account of an iron bridge, built in the spring of 1873 over the Missouri River (at St. Joseph), suggests the urgency and danger nineteenth-century bridgemen encountered.

> It was now April 20. Bad weather almost constantly, the river gradually rising to its June flood—the dangers daily increasing rather than diminishing, and the hardest span of all yet to raise. . . .

Two sets of falsework had already been swept away by flooding. As soon as the third falsework was complete, the bridgemen hurried to raise the iron:

> It was all transported from shore, a distance of about eight hundred feet, and hoisted into place and coupled in about thirty-six working hours. The sight of the turbulent water surging and boiling around the piles below, like a fierce monster hungry for its prey, was emi-

nently suggestive, and every man worked with a will, and the result was that the span was put in place quicker than any similar piece of work was ever done before. Everyone drew a long breath of relief when it was finally pronounced safe.

Not all early bridgemen toiled in anonymity. The Brooklyn Bridge, because it was the longest and highest bridge ever built, and because it linked the two largest cities in the country, was a frequent subject of newspaper and magazine coverage during its construction. Most of the reports focused on the work of the chief engineer or the politicians and financiers behind the bridge, but the bridgemen, too, made occasional appearances in the press. As a rule, they earned these appearances by dying in a manner the papers deemed newsworthy.

Exactly how many men died while building the Brooklyn Bridge is uncertain (David McCullough, author of the definitive history of the bridge, estimates between 30 and 40) but there is no question the job was very dangerous. Much of the danger belonged to the caisson diggers, the laborers who descended into dank, dark pressurized chambers beneath the riverbed to excavate the foundations for the bridge's towers. Many of these men became gravely ill from the poorly understood effects of sudden depressurization, "the bends," when they climbed out of the caissons at the end of a shift. Once the stone towers were complete, though, the bridge presented a different, more obvious kind of danger: falling. Now came the time for the bridgemen to take over; for what David McCullough refers to as the "circus acts."

Working almost 300 feet over the river, crowded together atop the towers, these men stood higher than the vast majority of Americans had ever ventured. This was a strange and alien world where a man could feel, in the words of Master Mechanic E. F. Farrington, foreman of the bridgemen, "as completely isolated as if in a dungeon." Years after the bridge was complete, Farrington wrote of standing atop the Brooklyn tower one foggy morning and seeing the city nearly vanish. "The spires of Trinity in New York, and in Brooklyn, and the tops of masts of a ship in one of the dry docks, with the roof of the bridge towers, were all that were visible of the world below. . . . Rising through this misty veil was the confused crash and roar of busy life below."

The Brooklyn Bridge, like most long spans, was a suspension bridge. Its roadbed would hang from giant cables anchored into massive stone blocks on either shore and draped, in a sort of inverse arch, between the towers in the river. First, the bridge's four cables, each containing 3,515 miles of thin steel wire, had to be spun out. This was done by sending wheels of wire back and forth between Brooklyn and Manhattan thousands of times, threading the wires through sheaves, then corseting them together until, at last, they made a cable about 15 inches in diameter.

It was fast, precise work, and to do it a man had to be nimble-fingered and surefooted. Above all, of course, he had to be fearless. "No man can be a bridge-builder who must educate his nerves," Farrington wrote in his memoir of the bridge. "It must be a constitutional gift. He cannot, when 200 feet in the air, use his brain to keep his hand steady." Many of the men were, like Farrington himself, former sailors. Sailors had experience clambering about at height, having scaled the hundred-foot masts of square-riggers and schooners. They understood rigging, the arts of rope knotting and hoisting. They adapted well, in part, because the machinery of bridge building derived from sailing vessels. The derricks that bridgemen used to lift steel had evolved from the boom and mast of ships; indeed, the terminology was the same. The horizontal arm of a derrick was its "boom," the vertical pole its "mast." The rigging required to lift iron and steel—the blocks and tackle—were nearly identical to the rigging on a ship. And, of course, the kind of man who willingly cast his lot to the high seas was a good candidate for the perils of bridge building. Both careers demanded a certain willingness to die.

One of the former seamen under Farrington's supervision was a swashbuckling young rigging foreman named Harry Supple. The former seaman got his name in the papers not once but three times. The first time was after a derrick fell and he was among the injured. The second time was for a daring whooshing ride he took in a boatswain's chair along the wire from the top of the New York tower down to the anchorage. "Stupendous Tight-Rope Performance," ran the headline in one newspaper.

The third time came two years later, in 1878, when he was working atop the Brooklyn anchorage, helping to feed steel wire into the sheave of a spinning wheel. The wire suddenly snapped, whipping out with a crack and a hiss. It knocked Harry Supple off the tower to the Brooklyn pavement 80 feet below. He lived a few hours, then passed away.

## NEW YORK

The building of the Brooklyn Bridge was a distant memory by the turn of the century. So was Jenney's Home Insurance Building in Chicago, 16 years old in 1900. Skyscrapers had moved out of their infancy and into their rowdy adolescence, and New York was where they came to spend it.

New York was by far the largest city in the United States in 1900, and the richest. It was also the fastest growing, experiencing the same kinds of real estate pressure that drove Chicagoans skywards in the 1880s; in fact, by 1903, office rents in New York would be four times as high as in Chicago. The combination of limited land and ready money made New York's destiny as skyscraper capital of the world practically inevitable.

Chicago's politicians had already forfeited the chalice in any case. In 1893, they passed an ordinance banning buildings over 10 stories, having come to believe that tall buildings were destroying their city. A year earlier, New York's leaders had arrived at the opposite conclusion. They jettisoned the city's more conservative zoning laws and embraced the principle of metal-frame construction for the first time.

Builders knew where the action was at the end of the nineteenth century. They arrived in New York in droves, many of them the same men who had recently helped create the skyline of Chicago. The George A. Fuller Company, for example, came from Chicago. So did Daniel Burnham, the most celebrated architect of his time. The bridgemen came, too, flocking east from all over the country to apply their skills and daring to the skyscrapers.

Once here, the bridgemen quickly melded into another group of tradesmen, housesmiths, who were already working the territory. The term "Housesmith," soon to vanish from the American lexicon, referred to skilled mechanics who set iron fixtures, like railings and stairs and lintels, in masonry buildings. Housesmiths also worked as joiners on cast-iron buildings and other proto–metal frame structures. By the end of the nineteenth century, housesmiths had moved into the burgeoning market of structural iron and steel erection. They had become, in effect, the more urban and domesticated version of bridgemen. Perhaps they lacked a bridgeman's experience with dizzying height, but they were trained in riveting and fabricating iron. They were also, significantly, experienced in the internecine labor politics of New York City, having chartered a union called the Housesmiths Mutual Protection Association way back in 1864.

Now, 30 years later, ceding to the influx of bridgemen, the housesmiths' union reorganized under a new name: The United Housesmiths' and Bridgemen's Union of New York and Vicinity. This organization then combined with five other local unions to charter the ambitiously named International Association of Bridge and Structural Ironworkers. In deference to its pioneering status as a union town and birthplace of the skyscraper, Chicago was designated Local 1. New York became Local 2.

## ROUGHNECKS

They called themselves roughnecks. Other trades called them "the roughnecks up above yuh." The Irish were "harpies," the Swedes and Norwegians were "squareheads." A veteran who knew his way around the steel was a "fixer," while a man new to the trade was a "snake," not because he was necessarily venal but because he was somebody you wouldn't willingly trust with your life.

Unlike more established trades, in which members entered as teenaged apprentices then worked their way up to journeyman status, ironwork tended to attract fully grown men who had already tried their hands in other lines of work. Some had farmed, others had been on the railroad or in factories. Many, like their predecessors who built the Brooklyn Bridge, were former seamen, particularly the Norwegians and Swedes. Mixed among them by 1901 were "a few Canadian Indian half-breeds, who are highly esteemed for their endurance and skill," according to *Frank Leslie's Popular Monthly*. These men almost certainly hailed from Kahnawake, the Mohawk Indian reservation near Montreal that would still be supplying ironworkers to New York a century later.

Although the distinction between housesmiths and bridgemen was officially defunct by 1901, two separate strains continued to run deep through New York's roughnecks. The "Homeguard" were staunch members of the local union, true New Yorkers who would travel for work if required but preferred to stay put and reap from the harvest of steel. The "Floaters" were a different breed. Floaters were afflicted with a bridgeman's wanderlust. They rambled between bridges and buildings, between states, often traveling great distances from job to job. A floater would work on a skyscraper in New York, then jump a boxcar and ride the rails out to San Francisco for another job, then stop off on his return to join a gang on a backwoods bridge in the "jungles"—his word for just about anywhere that wasn't New York or Pittsburgh or Chicago or San Francisco.

One young man, Billy Beatty, bragged that he'd already been to 27 states and territories in his five-year career. A few men had recently returned from Egypt, where they'd helped build a bridge across the Nile. Other gangs had traveled to India and Cuba, while another was about to depart for the jungle, the *real* jungle, to raise steel viaducts in Uganda.

*The Bridgemen's Magazine,* founded in July of 1901, served as a job bulletin and gossip rag for the floaters. Locals around the country wrote in to let floaters know if they were needed, and floaters wrote back to say where they were and where they were headed. Thus, members of New York's Local 2 learned that "Cork" Manning "came into the burg with some other human flotsam and jetsam about two weeks ago, but may be drifting Southward. . . ." In the same issue, a man called "Munch Chunk" wrote in to let his fellow bridgemen know he'd just arrived at Niagara Falls from New York City, having helped himself to his own "private railway car, N.Y.C. & H.R.R.R., No. 62,064." He'd gone north to build a bridge with Billy Beatty and a man called "Goose." How, Munch wondered, could he and his fellow floaters like "Bughouse" Murray and "Kid" Finnegan and "Boxcar Slim" and "Jimmy the Bum" and "Skipper" Hicks—how could they get their hands on *The Bridgemen's Magazine* since they were never in one place long enough to receive any mail?

"The calling is one that hardly attracts the home-loving married man," is how a report by the U.S. Commission on Labor Relations described the bridgemen's trade some years later. And once a man had succumbed to the calling, he was "not likely to develop in a high degree the social habits that tend to ideal citizenship." On the contrary, he tended to be "shiftless," "irresponsible," and "reckless."

Most floaters would probably have agreed with the description. But the founder and editor of *The Bridgemen's Magazine,* James L. Kelly, endeavored to cultivate the image of a somewhat more civilized bridgeman: a roughneck who appreciated the finer things in life. To this end, among the union news and editorial tracts, Kelly never failed to include a sample of poetry and high thoughts:

> *What was the song we sang together,*
> *You and I in long-lost June?*
> *Something to-day in the dreamy weather,*
> *Brings back a strain of the tune. . . .*

began a poem in one issue, while in another, Mr. Kelly considered

> How often have bridgemen, when working out in the "jungles" thought of Washington Irvin's [*sic*] tribute to the lark, which revels in the brightest time of day, in the happiest season of the year, among fresh meadows and opening flowers; and when he has sated himself with the sweetness of the earth, he wings his flight up to heaven as if he would drink in the melody of the morning stars.

When the bridgeman was done thinking of lost tunes and larks, he could further broaden himself with curious facts and helpful bromides:

> Avoid alcoholic drinks if you want to insure yourself in these torrid days against heat prostration. Alcohol in any form is first a stimulant and then a depressant. It overworks the heart for a time, and then there is languor due to lack of material on which to labor.

> The best way to get out of debt is to pay out.

> The dome of the United States Capitol is 287 1/2 feet high. The weight of the iron alone in the dome of the Capitol is 8,909,200 pounds.

> The Lord made woman—but she made herself into a lady.

On the subject of women, George O'Kane, who called himself Doctor O'Kane and frequently wrote to the magazine from New York, believed that bridgemen would be better off if they were more willing to "try the saving grace of matrimony." Nor would it hurt to dress a little better while they were at it. "There is a large class of bridgemen who work steadily, dress respectably and are a credit to the organization and the community in which they reside," wrote Dr. O'Kane. Another class, however, dressed and behaved like bums. "We heard some of the latter uncharitably criticizing the former the other day, calling them dudes and other things. We look at the matter differently and think that diamonds never flashed from a fitter repository than a UNION bridgeman's bosom."

The promise that bridgemen, even floaters, were capable of cultivation was confirmed in the winter of 1903 when Munch Chunk (whose real name turned out to be William Woodring) wedded a charming young widow at the Little Church Around the Corner, at Fifth Avenue and 29th Street. The service was followed by a lavish champagne reception at the bride and groom's home at Park Avenue and 112th Street. "All the roughnecks were invited to attend," reported *The Bridgemen's Magazine*, "and Mr. and Mrs. Chunk were sorry they had laid in such a large stock of the flowing beverage, as the invited guests did not leave until everything was cleaned up." That was two days later. Evidently, these roughnecks truly did appreciate the finer things in life.

The start of the twentieth century was a good moment in the history of New York's ironworkers. The ruinous strikes that would begin in the spring of 1903 were still in the future. Peace reigned. The wage, $4 for an eight-hour day, was a good one at a time when factory workers averaged less than $8.50 per week. True, ironwork tended to be irregular, but for the moment there was more work than there were men to do it. The George A. Fuller Company alone was running about 15 steel jobs in Manhattan in 1901, with several others soon to break ground. All around the city, derricks were swinging, rivet guns were clattering, and steel frames were rising. On the East River, where the Williamsburg Bridge was about to overtake the Brooklyn Bridge as the longest suspension bridge in the world, bridgemen stood on black-ribbed girders and catcalled down to the hoist operator hundreds of feet below. *"Yeow-yeow-yeow!"* they called, then the operator shouted back *"Hey-y-y!"* and then everybody cried, *"Ho-hoo-ho-hoo,"* and the load started to rise. Meanwhile, work was getting under way on the Manhattan Bridge, another long suspension bridge over the East River, and would soon commence on a great cantilever bridge between Manhattan and Queens. There was so much demand for structural steel work in Manhattan that the steel companies could not keep up with it, and some jobs—the Flatiron among them—temporarily suspended construction while waiting for more steel to arrive.

The basic customs of the work were in place by 1901. The steel was hoisted from the street by wooden derricks that were secured to the top of the building by guy wires. The derricks rose as the buildings rose, but their steam-powered cable drums, and the men who operated these, remained below on the ground. The ironworkers topside communicated with the operator by bell lines that ran to the basement: two yanks meant the operator should pay out the cable and let the load down; four yanks meant he should reel it in, and up. As a load began to rise from the street, a man or several might jump onto it and hitch a ride to the top, one hand fecklessly grasping the cable as the ground receded. A "bullstick" man would pivot the derrick by throwing his weight into a long lever, and the derrick's boom would swing in over the scantily planked floor.

When it came time to hang steel, the "setters," as connectors were then called, slipped in the first bolts, then the rivet gang moved in. The "heater" stood over a small coke forge propped on a few pine planks laid across beams. He barbecued a rivet to a white glow, then plucked it from the coals with tongs and flung it, fast and hissing, 20,

30, as far as 50 feet, to wherever the gang happened to be working. His "catcher" snatched the rivet from the air with a funnel-shaped cup, its mouth no wider than a salad plate. The catcher withdrew the still red-hot rivet with his tongs and plugged it into the rivet hole. Now the "bucker-up" held the blunt head of the rivet flush against the column or beam with a steel bar, while the "riveter" stood on the other side of the connection and pressed the barrel of a pneumatic hammer against the shank of the rivet. He pulled the trigger and the piston fibrillated—*br-r-r-r-r-r-ip!*—smashing the semi-molten metal into a button flush against the steel. All of this happened with great speed and deafening clamor—heat, toss, insert, smash, then move on across the steel to the next rivet hole. A good gang could do a few hundred rivets a day. A thousand a day was not unheard of.

All of this assumed, of course, that nothing went wrong. But things did go wrong. Sometimes the heater threw a wild one. Sometimes the catcher missed and the rivet seared his skin (you knew a catcher by the scars on his forearms) or plummeted through the frame of the building like a meteorite. The gang would shout a warning to those working below and, inevitably, everyone would do the one thing a person should never do when a hot rivet is plummeting toward his head: they looked up.

It did not take a full rivet to injure a man. As the pneumatic guns pounded the rivets into their holes, cinders frequently flaked off and dropped. "I had the strangest experience once," a young ironworker told *Frank Leslie's Popular Monthly*. "I happened to have my mouth open and the red-hot burr flew right in my throat. It burned the roof of my mouth badly, and then dug into my right cheek somehow. But the doctor at the hospital could never find the bit. They thought it must have worked out in some way and that I must have swallowed it."

Of greater concern than rivets or cinders was the ever-present danger of falling. There were no safety harnesses, no fall nets, no safety wires around the perimeter of the working floor in 1901. A law passed 12 years earlier required contractors to spread wooden planking below the men as they worked. This would have done little to keep men from going over the side of the building but it might have protected men from going into the hole on the inside—if, that is, contractors had obeyed it. They did not. As construction photographs of the Flatiron and other steel-frame buildings clearly illustrate, planking was spotty, allowing plenty of man-size gaps between timbers. If a man slipped, he could go many stories before hitting something solid.

The danger was reflected in the carnage. At the start of 1902, *The Bridgemen's Magazine* noted that Local 2 had buried two men a week for the previous six weeks. Meanwhile, of 1,000 members in Chicago's Local 1 that same year, 103 were injured, 15 more were permanently disabled, and 18 died: nearly a quarter of the union's members injured or killed in a single year. A few years later, Chicago would record 83 injured, 17 permanently disabled, and 23 dead. Altogether, about two percent of ironworkers died and another two percent were permanently disabled each year in the early twentieth century. In other words, of every 100 men in a local, 40 were likely to be dead or disabled within a decade, 80 within two decades. Not even the luckiest man could hope for a long career on steel. "We do not die," went an ironworkers' slogan of the time. "We are killed."

"We are only too well justified by the facts in making the statement that a man, on the day he starts in the structural iron industry, signs his death warrant," wrote the president of Local 2, Robert Neidig, in 1903. "It is a sad, gruesome, and only too truthful fact that no ironworker is considered to die a natural death unless he gets killed. One of our members that lives to be old and dies in his bed is looked upon as a curiosity by the vast majority whose crushed and mangled remains are laid beneath the sod before the hand of Time has had a chance to touch one hair with silver." In February of 1903, Local 2 raised its initiation fee to $100, exactly the amount the union paid out for funeral expenses when a member died. "All we are asking of these candidates," wrote Neidig, "is to give us enough money for decent interment."

No workers' compensation existed in 1901, so if a man died, his widow, if there was one, made do with the $100 from the union and perhaps a small settlement from the builder. As a rule, builders were not generous with settlements, on the grounds that the sort of man who went into ironwork knew what he was getting into so hadn't much right to complain when he died. "The men are fully aware of the risks they run when they undertake the work," one builder told the *New York Times*. "If the man has not a cool head and is subject to giddiness in working at dizzy height, he takes an unjustifiable risk in accepting such a job. . . . It would be a benevolent and philanthropic thing, no doubt, for employers to provide for families of their work-men who are killed as a result of their own carelessness, but on the other hand I don't see that it would be just to compel them to make such provisions."

A great many of the city's early skyscrapers were built by life insurance companies. Metropolitan Life, New York Life, Manhattan Life, Washington Life—their buildings were among the tallest in the city. Here is one telling irony of the ironworker's plight: none of these companies would have provided him with life insurance. He was not, actuarially speaking, worth the risk.

As soon as the scaffolding came off the Flatiron, crowds would gather at the intersection of Broadway and Fifth Avenue, some to admire the new building, others to ridicule its bizarre mile-high pie-slice shape. From certain angles, it would appear as sharp as a blade or as unsupported as a stage flat—a sheer wall with nothing behind but air. Sightseers would gather to watch it topple in the wind, but they would be disappointed, for the building would turn out to be every bit as strong as its promotional literature had promised. The wind would not bother the building nearly so much as the building would bother the wind, causing powerful and perilous downdrafts. A boy would be blown off the curb into Broadway and killed by a cab. Women who walked near the building would risk immodesty as drafts lifted their petticoats, revealing a glimpse of Victorian knee.

Among those drawn to the base of the new building would be a young and soon to be celebrated photographer named Alfred Stieglitz, whose moody, snow-swept photographs would help establish the Flatiron as the most recognizable building in the country. In 1904, he would write about the Flatiron in a letter to his father: "It appeared to be moving toward me like the bow of a monster ocean steamer—a picture of a new America still in the making."

And what of the man in that earlier photograph—the nameless man on the 15th floor with his back to the camera? Impossible to say. But if this building was an ocean liner, then he'd ride it into the future. If this was the new America in the making, he'd be among those making it. Because the new America was going to be made of steel.

The Flatiron, still in the making, 1902.
*(Brown Brothers)*

# THREE

# The New World

## (2001)

Two weeks after they arrived at Columbus Circle to build the Time Warner Center—two weeks after Brett Conklin's fall 17 blocks to the south—the raising gang was high over the hole, enjoying a mid-morning coffee break on the machine deck of crane number 2. Last night a dusting of snow had fallen over the city, but the sun had come out strong and the sky was brilliantly blue and the snow was mostly gone. The men sat on the deck, smoking and gazing out at the multi-million-dollar view of Central Park. When their cigarettes burnt down, they flicked them over the edge and the butts fluttered 110 feet to the mud at the bottom of the hole.

Since that gray February day they first came—it was early March now—the men had been setting up kangaroo cranes. This was the first step in any major steel job in New York; until there were cranes, there could be no steel, and there would be no cranes until the raising gang assembled them, piece by piece, like giant Christmas toys. The gang had already completed crane number 1, to the east. Crane number 2 was well on its way, soon to be joined by number 3 and number 4, which would serve the southern tower of the building. For the next month, a temporary crawler crane in the hole would feed the raising gang prefabricated components of the cranes and the men would bolt these into place: box-shaped sections of the tower, one stacked upon the other like milk crates; then the rubella, a turntable-like collar on which the crane would pivot, or "slew"; then the machine deck, the drums and engine, the operator's cabin, the mast, and finally, the lacy 180-foot-long boom.

The cranes were called kangaroos not because they resembled the eponymous marsupial, but because they were first manufactured in Australia. If they resembled any living thing, it was the ornithological species that shared their name: *cranes.* They rose on a single spindly leg, absurdly top-heavy, graceful and agile but also slightly ludicrous. What kept them from keeling over were the four 12-ton counterweights that hung from a rack under their rumps. As the crane's boom reached out and dipped to take a load, the counterweights, in a small miracle of weight distribution, slid in the opposite direction. As the boom lifted and strained under the load, they slid further out; as it rose, pulling the center of gravity toward the crane, the counterweights moved back home.

Before that miracle could occur, though, the raising gang would have to install the counterweights. At a nod from their foreman, the men slowly stood, their break ended. The connectors, Jerry Soberanes and Keith McComber—the blue-eyed Indian the others called Bunny—slithered through the hollow center of the rubella, then ducked under the machine deck and wriggled between the diagonals of the latticed tower. They hung onto the outside of the tower, a hundred feet over the hole, and waited. A moment later, the first of the counterweights swept in on the boom of the crawler crane. Along the bottom of the counterweight, welded to it, ran a slender horizontal terrace of grilled wire, just wide enough to accommodate a man's boot. The counterweight was still a yard off the stern when

Jerry stepped across the open air and onto its terrace. The counter-weight, with Jerry aboard and clinging to it, swung gently away from the tower, then gently back. Now it was Bunny's turn: he reached a foot out over the gap and stepped on beside Jerry. They stood there on the narrow ledge a hundred feet over the hole, swaying in the breeze.

A few minutes before noon, the raising gang started down a narrow metal ladder through the interior of the crane's tower. When they reached the bottom, they stepped out onto the mud, a treacherous topography of half-frozen divots and crags concealed under a few inches of boot-sucking paste. Bunny and Jerry led the way to the dirt ramp at the southwest corner of the hole. Like most connectors, they were fit and agile and didn't have much trouble high-stepping through the mud. Their wrenches and connecting bars clanged in the scabbards of their connecting belts, and with a little imagina-tion—a pointed helmet instead of a hard hat, a long yellow beard instead of a clean-shaven face, a rocky beach instead of mud—they might have been Viking warriors arriving home after a season of berserking. They had the weary look of men returning from difficult work.

They walked shoulder to shoulder, side by side, matching strides. Bunny and Jerry had never connected together before this job but already they'd acquired the complementary rhythm of old partners. This would stand them in good stead. Over the next sev-eral months, nearly every move one of them made would depend on the timing and skill of the other. So, sometimes, would his life. Connectors routinely step out onto beams held aloft by a bolt on one end and the tapered end of their partner's spud wrench on the other. They make the step based on nothing but a slight nod from the partner's head, the nod that says: *It's in the hole, trust me.* Trust is everything.

For some reason, connecting, like love, tends to attract opposites.

Bunny and Jerry's differences began with their backgrounds. Like many of the Mohawks, Bunny was a fourth-generation ironworker on both sides of his family. Ironwork ran deep in his blood. His father was an ironworker. His brother had been an ironworker, too, until a few years ago when his leg got caught and mangled under the counterweight of a crane. Bunny's cousins were ironworkers. His wife's family, too—they were all ironworkers.

Bunny had intended to become an ironworker since he was a boy. More precisely, he'd intended to become a connector. He remembered the respect people accorded his uncles, Robert and Gerald McComber, who connected together for many years. "I'd always heard stories about them, how good a name they had," he said. "It gave me a goal. I wanted to live up to the name." At 18, Bunny purchased a union book from the Montreal local and started booming down to New York as a journeyman. A few years later, he transferred into No. 361, the Brooklyn local to which most of the Kahnawake Mohawks belonged. He was connecting by the time he was 21. Now he was 31, an old hand. To his colleagues, Bunny gave off an air of cocky assurance. He was known as a talker, a boaster, a swaggerer, a young man who thought he knew pretty much all there was to know about ironwork. Which was a pretty fair description of most connectors.

Not, though, of Jerry Soberanes. Jerry had a wry smile but didn't say much, at least not when he first met you. His trajectory into ironwork had been more like Brett Conklin's than Bunny's. A friend's father was an ironworker and steered him into it. A daredevil kind of kid, Jerry had started connecting soon after he finished his apprenticeship. Now, at 31, he cruised the steel with the unflappable cool of an airline pilot in a storm. A fallen beam, a surprise gust, a near miss—nothing much got a rise out of Jerry. He'd smile and shrug and keep working, and wouldn't mention it unless somebody asked. Then he'd say, "That? Nah, that wasn't too bad. Coulda been worse."

Trekking through the mud behind Bunny and Jerry were Matt

Kugler, the tagline man, and John White, the hooker-on. Matt, at 29, was the youngest of the gang. His father had been an ironworker, which was reason enough for Matt to try something different. He served three years in the Marines, then realized he wanted to do what the old man did after all. He still looked like a marine. He had the broad square shoulders, the ramrod bearing, the crewcut, the biceps, the tattoos. Before this job was over, some of the ironworkers would nickname him Rambo. It wasn't just the way he looked; it was his attitude about ironwork. He was so gung-ho you weren't sure sometimes if he was kidding. "Let's go build this thing," he'd announce. "I'd like to build this thing myself. Christ, give me a chance, I'll build the whole goddam thing, I swear it!"

John White was the least likely man to be in a raising gang. He was an apprentice, and it is rare for an apprentice to gain admittance to a raising gang. But John White was not your average apprentice. He was 35, which made him the second oldest man in the gang. Until a few years earlier, he'd built racecars for a living. He'd never met an ironworker and had only the vaguest inkling of what one did when he took the apprenticeship test on a whim. He passed with flying colors, enrolled, and two years later he'd worked his way, against all odds, into a raising gang. He loved the work and planned never to leave it.

The fifth man down, Chett Barker, didn't even bother trying to keep up with the other four. He was 55 years old and, like most ironworkers over 50, even those who have never been seriously injured, he was hobbled. Most of his joints were arthritic. His legs bowed slightly, an orthopedic anomaly common to veteran ironworkers whose knees have grown to accommodate the steel flanges that so often come between them. His face was youthful but shot through with blasted capillaries from days spent straining in wind and cold and sun. Chett's career had begun with his apprenticeship 37 years earlier on the Verrazano-Narrows Bridge, the last great bridge job in New York—and 60 feet longer, Chett liked to point out, than the

Golden Gate. "People should know that," said Chett, "because it's the goddamned truth."

Chett lurched slowly through the mud. As a young man, after his apprenticeship on the Verrazano, he had served a tour on the front lines in Vietnam with the First Air Cavalry. Between the war and work, he had seen more than his share of death and injury. His own father, a bridgeman, fell badly three times, nearly dying the third time. Chett, at 55, could hardly walk, but things, he knew, could be worse.

Chett was still only halfway to the ramp when Bunny and Jerry climbed out over the rim of the hole onto the street and stamped their boots. An attractive young woman stood near the gate, waiting to cross the street. Bunny took a step toward her and lifted his arm. When she saw the hard hat, she scowled, but then she saw the smile, the dazzling blue eyes, and accepted the proffered arm. Bunny escorted her to the opposite sidewalk, tipping the brim of his hat as they parted. As the woman walked off, Matt, who'd never met Bunny until two weeks ago, chuckled. "Bunny," he said to no one in particular. "What a fuckin' piece of work."

The men had been coming to the Coliseum Bar and Grill for lunch since that day Bunny purchased his shamrock two weeks earlier. The bartender had already committed their tastes to memory, and now, as they filed in and straddled stools along the bar, their beer bottles were open and down on cardboard coasters before their elbows touched wood. Chett shuffled in and sat down next to Bunny. The bartender set him up with a shot and a chaser.

The Coliseum was narrow and low-ceilinged, down a few steps from the sidewalk. This was a bar entirely lacking attitude or gimmick: no light-stained wood or fancy sconces, no amber beers from the Pacific Northwest. What it did have were shamrocks two months of the year and Christmas lights year round, two televisions, one jukebox, an oak bar worn smooth by decades of touch, and a capable Irish bartender named John. In all likelihood, the Coliseum was doomed to the same fate as its demolished namesake across the street. Rents in the neighborhood were already skyrocketing in anticipation of the $1.7 billion Time Warner Center. It was difficult to see how a no-nonsense watering hole like this one fit into the new picture. For the moment, though, the Coliseum had hit upon a piece of luck: ironworkers.

It's arguable whether bars were good for ironworkers, but there was no doubt that ironworkers were good for bars. At every job site, the same thing happened: a certain bar was anointed, then colonized. From the bar's usual noontime clientele of two or three old men sipping alone, the population of the place suddenly swelled, at 12:05 P.M., to dozens of ironworkers, laughing and swearing and bellying up, drinking one, two, maybe a third for the road—and then, suddenly, 20 minutes later, they were gone and the two or three old men were sitting there in the quiet under a haze of smoke. Those were a lucrative 20 minutes.

For the moment, the men of the raising gang and the three old men at the bar were pretty much it. A young family of tourists— dad, mom, adolescent son—quietly ate hamburgers over at one of the vinyl-covered tables by the wall, having somehow chosen the Coliseum, of all places in Manhattan, for lunch. The boy glanced over at the raising gang. His mother spoke quietly to him and he turned back to his food.

"A raising gang is like a wheel," Chett was saying as he sipped his beer. "You got five men, six if you count the operator—"

"Seven if you count George—"

"Why would anyone count George?"

George was the foreman of the gang. The men called him King George. He'd grown up in the same New Jersey town as Matt and Jerry. They were old friends. But George was their foreman—their *pusher*. "We grew up with the guy," said Matt. "You'd think he'd let us go five minutes early for lunch. No way. He's by the book." George also happened to be younger than any of them, even younger than Matt, and happened to be married, by all accounts, to a beautiful woman. So he deserved what he got when he wasn't around to defend himself.

"—six guys, three of them up in the sky, three down on the floor, and the boom keeps moving. I'm talking to the operator—"

"Tommy—"

"A *wheel*?" This was Matt, grinning. "What the fuck is Chett saying down there—?"

"So I'm talking to Tommy on the phones," continued Chett, "he's way up in the operator's cab. He booms down to where the steel is shook out and lowers the hook. John wraps the choker around the piece we're lifting. I tell Tommy, '*Boom up*,' he booms up, and Matt bears down on the tag line so it don't hit nothing on the way up. It's got to come up level and straight, 'cause if it doesn't it could snag up on something and pop the choker—"

"—Somebody gets hurt."

"Somebody *definitely* gets hurt. So it goes up straight, then I tell Tommy to swing over to where Bunny and Jerry are waiting, then 'Boom down, boom down,' and I bring it right into their hands, on a dime."

"We hope."

"They hope. Or I might just tell Tommy to knock 'em off the side, depending on how they're treatin' me. Their lives are in my hands." Nobody laughed at this. It was true. "And then it goes around all over again. Like a wheel."

"Wow. That's deep," said Matt. He chuckled. "Like a wheel. I gotta think about that one."

"Let me tell you something," said Chett. "Most of these guys I don't know. George I know, he was on a gang with me once, but most of these guys, like Bunny—I never met Bunny before. But I've worked with a lot of raising gangs, and you know something?"

Chett paused. He took a sip. The other men waited for the punch line. Chett put his beer down. "These guys are good," he said simply. "This is a good gang."

How good was mostly theoretical at this point. The truth was they wouldn't really know until they started setting steel. Putting up tower cranes was interesting and challenging, but it wasn't what raising gangs are about, which is setting steel. Then a good raising gang starts to move like a wheel, like clockwork, like a machine—like a well-oiled cliché. The hooker-on finds dead center with exactly the right choker, not an eighth of an inch too thick or too thin. The boom of the crane dips and lifts, the choker pulls snug over the flanges, the piece jumps up, the tag-line man bears down and it levels off into a smooth, easy rise. It swings a hundred feet overhead, then starts down again, dipping right into the gap between the columns. The holes practically align themselves. *Zing*—the first connector makes his hole with a connecting bar. *Zing*—the second man makes his hole. In go the bolts; a few flicks of the wrist and they're tight. "Hot Wrench," they call a connector who's in a groove like this; he's moving so fast, goes the joke, that sparks are leaping off the metal, his spud wrench is conducting heat, he is *on fire.*

It made no sense, really, to be in a raising gang. Every union ironworker officially earned the same wage. When times were good, like now, men in raising gangs took in a little extra under the table—contractors were willing to pay it to secure good gangs—but the money hardly justified the additional danger and hard work. Men who chose to be in the raising gang chose it because there was no other life, because they thrived on the hard work, the pace, the thrill, and the competition.

Raising gangs, and the men who joined them, were naturally competitive. Contractors used this disposition to their advantage. In the old days, they'd put an Indian gang on one derrick and a gang of Newfoundlanders on the other, just to promote a little fighting spirit. It made the men work harder and the building went up faster. Again, this made no real sense from the ironworker's point of view—the faster the building went up, the sooner the ironworker was out of a job. But they did it anyway. It was more important to be good than to be employed.

"Who's gonna set the first two floors, who's gonna be first to jump their rig, who's gonna be last? Everything's speed, timing, speed, timing," Bunny explained. "There's ways you do things that'll save you seconds, and at the end of the day, it'll end up being minutes, maybe half an hour. Then you'll be ahead of the game the next morning. You're constantly trying to save time and bank time." One of the attractions of this job at Columbus Circle was the promise of four raising gangs instead of the usual two. "When we get four cranes going, oh, God, that's gonna be a blast," said Bunny. "That's when we'll know if we've got a good gang that can work together."

Working well together wasn't just a matter of speed. It was also a matter of trust. Each man here would at some point hold one of the other four men's lives in his hands. Everyone knew it. If John calculated the tolerance of the choker incorrectly and the cable snapped, somebody might die. If Matt lost control of a piece of steel, somebody might die. If Chett failed to stop the crane from booming up, or down, or if Bunny or Jerry made one of the countless small mistakes that connectors occasionally make—there were so many ways for these men to injure each other. Trust was everything. Trust was why raising gangs were often made up of brothers and cousins and old friends. Trust is what brought George, Jerry, and Matt into this gang. They'd grown up together; they knew and liked each other. Trust was what Bunny didn't quite feel at the start of this job, having never connected on an all-white gang before. When you were with your own people, your kinsmen, you naturally tended to feel the trust. When you were with people you hardly knew, it came harder. Trust, and the need to feel it, partly explained what these five men were doing in the Coliseum at quarter past noon on a Tuesday, and why ironworkers, on the whole, spent a good deal of time drinking together in bars. They were building the camaraderie they needed to do their job.

"The consumption of alcohol is an intentionally enacted ritual, which reinforces an occupational community's basic assumptions and strengthens members' communal bonds," wrote the sociologist William Sonnenstuhl in his 1996 study of "occupational drinking cultures." As defined by Sonnenstuhl, an occupational drinking culture is a closely knit group of men brought together by work that is physically demanding and dangerous, such as longshoremen, coal miners, and railworkers. Sonnenstuhl focused on tunnel workers— sandhogs—but his conclusions apply equally to ironworkers. Both trades are dangerous and both put great value on feelings of kinship among members. And both have tended to consume great quantities of alcohol. "The drinking rituals," concluded Sonnenstuhl, "underscored the duties they owed to one another."

"This is a good gang," said Chett one last time. He drained his beer and paid up. "I need some time to get back." A few minutes later, at 12:29, the others set their bottles on the bar and hopped off their stools. They filed out into the sunlight.

"Let's build this thing," said Matt.


## THE BUILDING

The building they meant to build was a Siamese twin, joined-at-the-hip structure. It was huge and mind boggling, if not downright schizophrenic. I'm an office building! I'm a hotel! I'm an apartment building! I'm a Center for the Performing Arts! *I'm the Center of Everything!*

First and foremost, the building would serve as corporate headquarters of Time Warner—or AOL Time Warner, as the company called itself back then. Including offices and studios for various branches of the entertainment and news divisions, the company would occupy about 854,000 square feet of space, most of this on the lowest 10 floors of the building. The merger of AOL and Time Warner in January of 2000 had spawned the largest media company in the world, instantly worth 342 billion dollars. These conjoined towers would represent more than office space: they would represent corporate dominance. That was the idea, anyway, back in that heady time, before the conglomerate foundered and jettisoned AOL from its name.

For the moment, the business of AOL Time Warner—communications—was the red-hot center of the American economy, very much as steel had been a hundred years earlier. "Global media," said Gerald Levin, then CEO of Time Warner, "will be and is fast becoming the predominant business force of the twenty-first century." AOL Time Warner, much like that corporate behemoth of a century earlier, U.S. Steel, aspired to vertical integration of its industry, only now the plan had a new name: "synergy." Instead of iron ore, the raw material would be human ideas. Rather than manufacture and ship steel ingots, the new company would produce and distribute "content" in the form of images, words, and sounds. But the goal was the same: to control the product from one end to the other.

The parallels between Big Steel and Big Communications went only so far. Steel, for one thing, was manifestly physical. You could see steel rising, you could actually watch it transform real space from your vantage on an actual street corner. You could, if you got close enough, reach out and touch its rough skin. The business of AOL Time Warner, by contrast, was largely invisible. Ghostly integers whipped through fibers and cables. Apart from the glow of television sets and computer monitors and glossy magazines, there wasn't much that was tangible about it.

The world had become a far more conceptual place than it had been a hundred years earlier. As a result, it demanded a better-educated worker. In 1901, fewer than 13 percent of Americans graduated from

high school, while only one in 50 graduated from college. Seventy percent of the workforce was devoted to manual labor. A century later,
the numbers told a very different story. Almost 90 percent of young
Americans were high school graduates, and a quarter were college
graduates. The majority of the workforce, nearly 60 percent, was
engaged in occupations that required little, if any, physical exertion.

For all these changes, the Time Warner Center would be built
much as the Flatiron had been built a hundred years earlier. There
would be differences—bolts instead of rivets, kangaroo cranes
instead of derricks—but still the work would involve men braving
heights to join steel. The white-collar college-educated workforce
that would eventually sit in the building's climate-controlled,
ergonomically correct workstations while sipping lattes from the
place across the street—the place that may once have been the Coliseum Bar and Grill—would owe its habitat to ironworkers whose
education had ended, in most cases, with high school graduation.

It was a nice irony, except that it wasn't completely true. The
ironworkers, as it turned out, wouldn't actually build all of the Time
Warner Center. They would not even build half of it. Most of the
building was not going to be steel. It was going to be that other
material, despised and reviled by all self-respecting structural ironworkers: *concrete.* The ironworkers would only go as high as the 23rd
floor on the north tower and the 24th floor on the south tower, and
then—*concrete.* Here was the largest steel job New York had seen in
years and it wasn't even a steel job. If there was any dark lining in the
silver cloud in the great boom of 2001, this was it: *concrete!*

The New York offices of the Cantor Seinuk Group, structural engineers for the Time Warner Center, were located on the third floor of a
17-story building on the east side of midtown Manhattan. The building was typical of the steel-frame, wedding cake–shaped towers of the
1920s. It rose eight stories, then "stepped back," ascending in ever-
smaller boxes. It was a functional building if not an especially imagi-

native one, a straightforward steel-frame high-rise conforming to New York City zoning laws and building codes of its time. The skeleton design was so simple a first year engineering student could probably pull it off.

The firm's offices were plainly tailored, lacking the architectural flourishes one might expect to find in, say, an architect's office. As a rule, engineers don't like to spend more money than is strictly necessary; miserliness is practically part of the job description. Over the receptionist's desk hung the one decorative extravagance in the lobby, a four-by-six-foot collage displaying Cantor Seinuk's many projects, including a stadium in Phoenix, a high-rise in Israel, a riverfront complex in London, and dozens of skyscrapers in New York.

On a stormy March morning two days after the raising gang convened in the Coliseum Bar and Grill, Ysrael Seinuk, the leading partner of Cantor Seinuk (Cantor having departed some years earlier) stood by a round table in his office, looking crisp, trim, and a good 10 years younger than his 69 years. Outside, the rain stopped and started again, washing dirt over the windows. Pedestrians hurried along on the street. The wind turned umbrellas inside out. It was on days like this that the works of engineers were tested.

"If we had used steel instead of concrete, that building would have been another forty feet higher," said Seinuk, speaking in a clipped Cuban accent and gesturing through the window to the top of the Trump World Tower, the firm's latest achievement. "Those forty feet would have been nothing but a big sail on a day like this."

He was pointing to the top of a new building looming to the east, a brown glass sliver. As architecture, the building was perhaps of dubious distinction, but as engineering it was noteworthy. Seventy-two stories tall and just 25 yards wide at the northern and southern walls, the building's height-to-width ratio placed it among the slenderest high-rises in the world. And it was made of reinforced concrete.

By conventional definition, a skyscraper is a tall building supported by a steel frame. "By skyscraper is meant a building that exceeds in height the practical limit of solid masonry construction," is how a 1939 report on the origins of the skyscraper put it. "The absolute and first essential in the structural creation of a skyscraper is the metal (ferrous) skeleton." But looking up through Seinuk's window at the glass façade soaring into the fog, there was no denying that the building was a skyscraper, even if it was made primarily of concrete.

Ysrael Seinuk understood the potential of concrete as well as any engineer in New York. He attributed this to his Cuban education. In the early 1960s, when Seinuk, a Jew, immigrated here to escape the grip of Fidel Castro, America was still a country built largely of steel, and steel is what American engineers knew best. At the same time, Seinuk and his fellow Cubans, having no steel industry to speak of, were making a virtue of necessity and learning to stretch concrete to its limits. "In Cuba we were using eight-thousand PSI concrete; here they weren't using anything over four thousand," said Seinuk, referring to the pounds-per-square-inch standard of measuring concrete's strength. "We had completed in Cuba three hundred thirty-three–foot post-tension single span bridges. And the largest in the United States was a hundred feet."

All this had changed over the last 40 years. American concrete was now as strong as any in the world. The concrete in the new Trump building was 12,000 PSI, and 16,000 PSI concrete was at hand.

Concrete has many advantages over steel as a structural material. For one thing, it significantly lowers the distance between floors, so that a 70-story concrete building will be shorter, much shorter, than a 70-story steel building. Floors in concrete buildings are six-inch thick slabs laid flat on concrete pillars. Even after wiring and ceiling fixtures are added to the bottom of the slab, and after floorboards or carpet are added to the top, the total space between ceiling and floor will be eight or nine inches. Steel beams, flange to flange, are generally eight or nine inches deep by themselves. On top of these come corrugated sheets filled with cement, and below go ceilings.

Altogether, the space between a ceiling and the floor above is about 15 inches on a steel-frame building, or seven inches more than it would be for concrete. A small difference in itself, perhaps, but multiplied by 70 stories this comes to about 40 feet. That's 40 fewer feet of façade to cover the perimeter of the building; 40 fewer feet of wires and pipes running inside the building; 40 fewer feet to brace against wind pressure; several million fewer dollars spent on construction.

There are other advantages to concrete. It goes up faster than steel, typically three floors a week compared with steel's pace of one or two floors. And during construction, it's easier to manipulate—to mold, to modify—than steel. A single imperfectly fabricated piece of steel can turn into a contractor's nightmare, holding up the building's erection as ironworkers burn or pummel it into place. No such problems arise with concrete. It is cast on site in plywood forms. Mistakes can be fixed with a hammer, a sheet of wood, a few nails.

No wonder concrete has taken such a large bite out of the construction market in recent decades. Until the middle of the twentieth century, tall buildings in America, office and residential both, were inevitably steel. Concrete structures seldom exceeded 20 stories until 1960. By the mid-1970s, though, the architect John Portman, among others, was designing huge opulent reinforced concrete hotels in places like Las Vegas and Miami. And by the 1980s, any large residential building or hotel built in America was likely to be concrete.

Given all of concrete's splendors, wasn't steel doomed? Seinuk frowned. "Of course not. That is silly—silly talk. There are buildings that want to be concrete and you have to do them in concrete, and there are buildings that want to be steel. If you try to do a building that wants to be steel in concrete, it's going to be very foolish."

Steel buildings are more difficult to build than concrete buildings, but, once completed, they are far more pliable. They are easier to renovate, an important advantage in buildings that will see many tenants with different space requirements over the course of their lives—office buildings, for instance. Bashing a hole through a floor or trying to move a column is an expensive and elaborate procedure in a concrete building but is easily achieved in a steel building. Also, steel is better suited to longer spans, the kind of long spans you are likely to encounter in office building lobbies and television studios. And because steel, at 50,000 PSI, is still much stronger than concrete, steel columns and beams take up less space than concrete structural members.

"The building always tells you what it wants to be," said Seinuk. "Whoever designs the building trying to tell the building what it wants to be is going to have a very expensive design." The Time Warner building, then, would be concrete where it wanted to be concrete and steel where it wanted to be steel. And where it wanted to be steel was on the bottom.

Determining precisely how the steel would be arranged was a task that fell to Mr. Seinuk's partner and second-in-command, Silvian Marcus. Like Seinuk, Marcus was a Jewish émigré from a communist regime, in Marcus's case Soviet-dominated Romania. Also, like Seinuk, he had been at the firm for a long time, almost 30 years. Otherwise the two men could not have been more different. Whereas Seinuk was trim, elegant, and reserved, Marcus was rumpled and sleepy-eyed. He gave the impression of a large but kindly bear awakened from a nap: a grumpy mensch. When the phone rang, he picked it up, closed his eyes and held the receiver an inch or two from his ear, as if he knew it could only transmit a headache. Suddenly, his eyes would widen and twinkle, and he'd break out in delighted laughter, tickled by something. In the spring of 2001, nothing tickled Silvian Marcus more—or caused him more headaches—than his design for the Time Warner Center.

This was the most complicated building Marcus had ever engineered. As Marcus was fond of pointing out, it really wasn't one building but half a dozen different buildings pressed together, each having a different function and different structural requirements. The most obvious distinction, of course, fell between the parts of the building that were steel and those that were concrete. The towers, which contained the hotel and the condominiums, would be made of concrete. (They would be topped by a steel crown, so ironworkers would, in the end, have the last word on the building.) Beneath the towers, steel would rise only as high as the 23rd floor. But those 23 floors would consume almost twice the amount of steel required by a typical steel-frame skyscraper, and its arrangement would be at least twice as complex.

The difficulties began with the columns. The function of columns is to transfer the load, or weight of the building, to the ground. In most buildings, this is accomplished by vertical columns running in a straight line from the top of the building to the bottom. The path of transference is clear and well marked. Not so in the Time Warner Center.

"Because of the way the building functions, a column cannot go straight," said Marcus. "He has to move and change places every few floors. After he finishes his function on a particular floor, then he's going to a different usage, where the column layout doesn't fit him anymore. So we have inclined columns, hanging columns, columns that terminate all of a sudden. This makes the building totally different than a conventional building." The shopping arcade needed one column layout, the offices another. The television studios for CNN required very long spans, 40 to 65 feet, uninterrupted—and unsupported—by columns. Amidst all of the canted columns and strangely transferred loads, just a dozen columns would run straight up from the bottom of the building. Marcus called these columns "boomers." They were enormous, between 30 and 45 tons apiece, and very important. It was their job to support the enormous trusses that would top the steel section of each tower.

The trusses were the most audacious part of Marcus's design.

They would support not only the concrete columns rising up from them, but also a number of steel columns, called "hangers," hanging down from them. The trusses would serve, too, as the central system of wind-bracing for the concrete towers, acting like huge outriggers to prevent them from swaying. No one, as far as Marcus knew, had ever asked quite so much of a truss before.

No one had ever asked quite so much of a steel fabricator either. In a conventional wedding-cake or glass-box skyscraper, where floors replicate each other as they go up, many pieces of steel are the same, so that a beam on the fifth floor is interchangeable with a beam on the ninth floor. That would not be the case in this building. Nearly every piece of steel, all 18,000 of them, would be unique. The steel design alone would generate about 26,000 shop drawings to specify the shape of each piece of steel, about four times the usual number of shop drawings for a skyscraper. The drawings took up so much space that Cantor Seinuk had rented a room in Long Island City to store them all.

Why so much complexity? The short answer is economics and computers. Building owners wanted flexible, multi-use, tenant-pleasing spaces, and they wanted to build them as cheaply as possible. This is how they made their profits. Architects and engineers naturally wanted to satisfy their clients. Computers helped them do this by allowing them to measure loads and strains before any material was raised. They gave engineers freedom to experiment and innovate in ways that would have been inconceivable back in the 1920s. But if computers were facilitators to innovative engineers, they were also enablers to capricious and needy clients. The more complicated a building could be, the more complicated, inevitably, it *would* be.

Trying to keep track of all 18,000 pieces of steel, to make sure that each piece did what it was supposed to do, was enough to keep Marcus awake at night. Everything had been thoroughly considered and calculated, run through the computers and simulators, double- and triple-checked by hand. But only one test really counts for a design that has not been tried before, and that test must wait until the building begins to rise: Will it work? Will it function? Will it stand? These questions were not academic. Three weeks earlier, a steel truss had collapsed during the construction of a convention center in Washington, D.C. The accident occurred at 11:30 at night. Twelve hours earlier, or twelve hours later, it would have killed dozens of ironworkers.

A structural engineer is an odd creature who must temper the hubris of a Master Builder (how would he or she dare build without it?) with the self-doubt of a neurotic. Lying in bed at night and brooding over grim hypotheticals—*what if we got it wrong? what have we failed to consider?*—is what drives engineers to design sound buildings. The moment an engineer stops doubting the design, he or she puts the structure, and human lives, at risk.

Marcus was confident his building would function exactly as he meant it to, but he also knew he carried an enormous burden of responsibility to the men who would erect it and the tenants who would someday inhabit it. "It's a pressure that you go to sleep with and you wake up with," he explained. "It's not the life of one person, but of so many people. Take a doctor, a surgeon, a very responsible position. But if he makes a mistake, he kills one person. If I make a mistake, or one of my assistants or colleagues makes a mistake that it's my responsibility to be sure he will not make, then my life ends with a question mark.

"I pray, although I am not a religious man, for everything to be O.K.," said Marcus. "Because there are so many things, so many complicated things. We check and re-check. But we also need to be lucky."

## FOUR

# The Walking Delegate

## (1903)

I'm a peaceful, law-abiding, simple citizen—that's Sam Parks. I've been played for a rowdy, but the tag don't fit and I don't pose for that picture. Of course, if there's a fight, I don't run away. No man has got any business in the labor movement that gets cold feet as soon as there's a scrap.

—SAM PARKS

... the shameful truth must be confessed that relief can come only from the capture and impounding of Sam Parks as one would a mad dog.

—HENRY HARRISON LEWIS
*Harper's Weekly*, October 17, 1903

Lutheran All-Faiths Cemetery lies on a bluff in Middle Village, Queens, about four miles east of Manhattan. The cemetery grounds cover 225 acres and contain the remains of roughly half a million dead. A hundred years ago, the cemetery was surrounded by open farmland. Today, shopping outlets and gas stations encroach at every end and jets from the nearby airports roar overhead. Still, it is a pleasant, almost pastoral place, wooded with elms and oaks and cedars of Lebanon, smelling of cut grass and damp earth. Here, among the Teutonic names—the Grimms and Geissenhainers and Knolls and Schoensiegals—an Irish-born ironworker named Sam Parks lies in eternal rest.

Or maybe he doesn't.

"There is no one named Sam Parks in our files." The woman behind the desk of the cemetery office declares this with a finality that brooks little discussion. She has been to the files—twice—and she is certain that no Parks, Sam or otherwise, was buried in Lutheran All-Faiths Cemetery. Not in 1904; not in any years around it. "If he was here, we'd have a record. And there is no record. *Who did you say he was?*"

Sam Parks was an ironworker who rose to become one of the most powerful, beloved, and reviled figures in New York City at the start of the twentieth century. He was a union walking delegate for Ironworkers Local 2 who managed in a few years to take control of the entire building industry in New York City and dictate its operation. With a few choice words—*Hit the bricks, boys!*—he could shut down construction in the city, putting tens of thousands of men out of work and bleeding millions of dollars of capital from the booming building industry. Hundreds of newspaper articles were devoted to him during his brief reign, along with feature articles in many of the leading magazines of his time. The fierce attention continued unchecked through his death in the spring of 1904, when 1,500 mourners marched in his funeral procession and 10,000 spectators crowded the streets to glimpse his hearse. The procession wended a circuitous route around the Upper East Side of Manhattan, arriving at a pier at the foot of East 92nd Street. From here, Parks' casket was ferried across the East River, then taken by carriage to Middle Village, and there interred—according to the newspapers—in Lutheran Cemetery.

Then the articles ceased. Sam Parks promptly vanished into an oblivion so thorough that not even his grave—not even a *record* of his grave—survives.

## WAR

Samuel J. Parks was born in County Down, Ireland, in the early 1860s. Around the age of 10, he emigrated to Canada, and by 14 he was working in the northern forests as a lumberman. He crossed the border into the United States and worked variously as a river-driver, a coal-heaver, and a sailor on the Great Lakes. He also spent time in western railroad camps. It was here, probably, that he first acquired the trade of bridge work. He later worked as a bridgeman in Wisconsin, where he earned a reputation as a riveter of Bunyanesque prowess. It was said that Sam Parks could drive more rivets per hour than any bridgeman alive.

Sometime in the early 1890s, Parks moved to Chicago. He went to work on the skyscrapers that were rising from the prairie city, but by the time he left a few years later, he'd gained something more important to him than employment: an education in union politics. Chicago was the labor capital of America, boasting more unions, and more powerful unions, than anywhere in the country. The only way to deal with employers, the labor bosses of Chicago believed, was to be stronger than they were. Parks learned this lesson well.

The contempt that labor unions and employers felt for each other in late-nineteenth-century America is difficult to appreciate today. Labor and capital were engaged in a sustained class war, and "war" was no metaphor. On one side of the divide, riotous workers armed with fists and cudgels and dynamite fought for better working conditions, better pay, and shorter hours. On the other side, businessmen who controlled America's largest assets—railroads, oil wells, coal fields, and, of course, steel plants—did everything in their power to stamp out agitation that might diminish profits and productivity.

The employers had the upper hand in most disputes. They were often supported by local and federal government, which supplied them with police or military protection. In the courts, the Sherman Anti-Trust Act, intended by Congress to limit corporate monopolies, was more often applied against unions. Even lacking government help, employers, particularly large corporations, were better positioned to wage war than workers. They had the financial resources to survive long strikes, and they had a pool of hundreds of thousands of immigrants arriving in the country every year from whom they could draw fresh workers to replace strikers. Many businesses hired small armies of Pinkerton "detectives" to provide additional protection against proletarian incursions.

Nowhere was the deck more unevenly stacked against workers than in the steel industry. The kind of corporation that Andrew Carnegie and his fellow steel magnates envisioned controlled every aspect of production and distribution, much of this carried out by subsidiaries. The concept of total control was called "vertical integration," and the steel-frame skyscraper was its soaring triumph. From the raw iron ore deposits of the Mesabi Range in northeastern Minnesota, Big Steel's reach extended to the coalmines that supplied the coke needed to fuel the furnaces that converted the iron ore into steel. It included the plants along the Monongahela River near Pittsburgh, where the ore was melted down, swept clean of slag, and molded into steel ingots. It included, too, the plants where the steel was fabricated—soldered, hole-punched, riveted—and many of the rail lines that ran between its various components. Finally, it extended to the building contractors and ironworkers who erected the steel columns and beams that had begun their journeys as bits of earth.

Ideally, the workers would fall in with the program as easily as the ore gave itself up from the ground. In the words of Frederick Taylor, the renowned efficiency expert who spent much of his career in the steel industry, the perfect laborer was "merely a man more or less the type of the ox, heavy both mentally and physically"—all the better to behave exactly as told, and to do so without complaint.

Much to the dismay of employers, workers refused to play their assigned role. They wanted to earn more money while working fewer hours, in better conditions. When, in the summer of 1892, Carnegie's second-in-command, Henry Clay Frick, told unskilled workers at a plant in Homestead, Pennsylvania, that he intended to *lower* their already meager wages, they responded in an altogether un-oxlike manner. They struck.

Frick immediately fired all 3,800, then surrounded the plant with a barbed wire–trimmed fence and shipped in 300 armed Pinkertons to protect strikebreakers. As the Pinkertons arrived by barge on the night of July 5, 1892, gunfire broke out between guards and strikers. Nine workers and seven guards were killed, and 163 more seriously injured, before the skirmish ended. Six days later, the governor of Pennsylvania came to Frick's aid, placing Homestead under martial law and effectively terminating the strike. Frick reduced the mill wage by half and brought in replacements.

"Our victory now complete and most gratifying," Frick cabled Carnegie, who had removed himself to his estate in Scotland. "We had to teach our employees a lesson and we have taught them one they will never forget."

He was right. There would be no more union activity at Homestead for another 44 years. An executive at U.S. Steel, which took over the Homestead plant in 1901, later expressed management policy even more bluntly than Frick: "I have always had one rule: if a workman sticks up his head, hit it."

The steelworkers had been subdued. The ironworkers were another story—a story in which Sam Parks would play a large role. Sam Parks had his own policy: he hit back.

Sam Parks.
*(Courtesy of Wirtz Labor Library,*
*U.S. Department of Labor)*

## SAM I AM

In a 1902 photograph his power is evident. His face is sharp-boned, his hair slicked back, his moustache dark and thick beneath his prow nose. His expression is flat but his eyes glimmer with intensity. As you stare at them, they stare right back, seeming to take your measure and find you lacking. Even those who despised Parks acknowledged the remarkable force of his character. "In many ways he is a leader of men," said New York District Attorney William Jerome, the man who would devote himself to putting Parks in jail. "He has personal magnetism and the power to convince others that his word is law. He has physical bravery, daring, and a dashing style of leadership. He is a brute, his language is foul, and the man is personally offensive to decent people, but his shrewdness is beyond question."

Parks had arrived in New York in 1895 at the invitation of the George A. Fuller Company, the builders of the Flatiron. He had worked for Fuller in Chicago, and when the company opened an office in New York, it asked Parks to come east and work as a foreman. The exact nature of Parks' relationship with Fuller would later become a subject of speculation. For the moment, Parks was simply another ironworker, albeit a gifted one.

William Starrett, of the legendary Starrett family of builders, recalled working with Parks in New York in the 1890s. Starrett was a young man at the time, recently embarked on a lustrous career that would lead, in time, to the Empire State Building, and he had been given his first opportunity to supervise a steel erection job. Steel was starting to rise from the hole, but young Starrett, anxious and inexperienced, still had no foreman to run his riveting gangs. Just then, "a long, lanky Englishman tapped me on the shoulder," Starrett recalled years later in his memoir (apparently confusing Parks' Irish brogue for an English accent). "It was Sam Parks, that debonair Robin Hood of the building industry. . . . Sam produced a pair of overalls, and within an hour his bellowing voice resounded in that deep excavation, and I knew that I had a leader."

Parks didn't do much in the way of hands-on ironwork after the Starrett job. He'd found his true calling in the work of the union. Just before Parks' arrival in New York, structural ironworkers had reorganized into the Housesmiths' and Bridgemen's Society. Its members were still bloodied by the strike they'd lost a few years earlier. And they were still making between $1.75 and $2.50 for a 10-hour day while their Chicago counterparts were making $4. Parks was their man.

Within three months of his arrival in New York, Parks managed to get himself elected as walking delegate. The job of walking delegate, common to trade unions at the end of the nineteenth century, was to patrol the job on behalf of the union; to ensure that the men were being treated fairly and that no scabs were sneaking onto union jobs; to find work for the idle; and to provide a decent burial for the dead. In theory, it was useful and reasonable to have such men to act as watchdogs and facilitators. In practice, the position was a breeding ground for the kind of corruption in which Parks would soon come to specialize.

Parks at once dedicated himself to "organizing" Local 2. Another walking delegate, named Ely, later described Parks' remarkable efficacy in the early days of his tenure: "I was organizing on the East Side, but I could make no headway at all. I met Parks who had just started in to organize the West Side and he offered to change places with me. I agreed, and in about six weeks he had the entire East Side organized. Every Friday over three hundred dollars was coming in at the meetings of the union for initiation fees. I met with as little success on the West Side as on the East Side, and Parks changed off with me again. In six or seven weeks, he had the West Side as thoroughly organized as the East Side. How he did it, I don't know."

How he did it, according to Parks' own account, was with his fists: "In organizing men in New York I talked with them at first nice and pleasant, explaining how they could be better off in a union. Bosses began to learn that I was about and pretty busy; and they had men stationed around to 'do' me. But they could not keep me off a job. I sneaked up ladders and elevator shafts, stole up on beams, waited for the men on cellar doors where they ate their dinner. Some did not believe that unions would be good for them; and I gave them a belt on the jaw. That changed their minds."

Parks once claimed to have gotten into as many as 20 fistfights in a single day's work. "I like a fight," he said. "It's nothing after you've risked your life bridge-riveting at three dollars a day."

Parks soon surrounded himself with an entourage of like-

minded lackeys. His group called itself, with grim irony, "the entertainment committee" and convened at a saloon near the union hall,
on the northeast corner of Third Avenue and 59th Street. Owned by
a man named Bernard Lynch, the saloon served as unofficial headquarters of the Parks faction in the union. And to ensure that their
faction was the *only* faction, they used the back room of Lynch's
saloon to "entertain" men who hadn't gotten the full thread of Parks'
argument. If a man had the temerity to stand up at a union meeting
and question one of Parks' proclamations, they might just attack
him on the spot. The union meetings at Maennerchor Hall on East
56th Street frequently degenerated into brawls. One method of
intimidation favored by the entertainment committee was to knock
a man down, then stand on his face. Eye gouging and rib cracking
were also in bounds. In one instance, members of the committee
allegedly ripped the flesh off the face of a recalcitrant unionist, scar-
ring him for life.

Parks' tactics were brutal but effective. Union membership
swelled from several hundred to 1,500, then to 3,000, then to
3,500, and as it grew so did the union's power over builders in the
city. The more ironworkers who came into the union, the fewer
non-union men employers could call upon in the event of a strike.
And if contractors tried to remedy a strike by importing non-
union men from outside New York, as they often did, Parks' men
would pay the unfortunate imports a visit and "entertain" them
vigorously.

Parks liked ordering strikes almost as much as he liked hitting
people. At any given moment he had up to a dozen jobs tied up
around the city. Parks demanded better working conditions and better wages, and he seldom negotiated on his demands. His dim view
of negotiation was represented by his prized bulldog, a fearsome-
looking creature named Arbitrator. The name was both a joke and a
threat. Arbitration, to Parks, was something that came at the end of
a leash and had big teeth. Parks had no interest in achieving peace

with employers, an opinion he made clear in a short essay he published in *The Bridgemen's Magazine:*

> . . . since the sun first arose on a newly erected world there has always been a battle between the strong and the weak, a struggle for mastery between the bulldogs of war and the craven worshipers of the white-winged dove, and it always ended the same way. The worshipers of the bulldogs of war, making the earth re-echo with paeans of victory, while the worshipers of the bird of peace humbly bowed their necks, permitting the collar of bondage to be clasped thereon. . . . God helps those that help themselves.

Parks' bias against compromise would have disastrous long-term consequences for the ironworkers. In 1902, he fought and killed a proposed agreement between the international union and American Bridge Company, by far the largest employer of structural ironworkers in the country. The agreement offered better terms for ironworkers than any they'd received—or would again for decades to come.

In the short term, though, Parks' tactics paid off splendidly. Builders yielded to his demands. There was so much money to be made in the skyscraper boom they could ill afford to lose time on an ironworkers' strike. Because the steel frame preceded the rest of the building, ironworker strikes devastated employers. Stopping the steel, Parks understood, was the surest way to a builder's wallet. He succeeded in raising the prevailing union ironworkers' wage in New York to $2.50 across the board by 1898, to $3.20 by 1900, to $4 in 1902. "By then," Parks later boasted, "we had them all. Why, for 1903, they went to $4.50 without a murmur." He promised to raise the wage to an even $5. "And then we'll stop," he added drily. "Capital has some rights."

His fellow ironworkers may have disagreed with his tactics, but they couldn't argue with his results. The more Parks pushed around builders, and the more the builders capitulated, the greater Parks grew in the estimation of his fellow ironworkers. He was "Fighting" Sam Parks, "The Bismarck Among Bridgemen." When he told the men to walk, they walked. "His four thousand ironworkers," observed *McClure's* magazine, "obeyed like children."

Parks' power expanded still further after the Housesmiths' and Bridgemen's Union joined the Board of Building Trades, an alliance representing 39 separate trades in New York. Parks quickly worked his way up to become its president. He now held sway over not only 4,000 or so ironworkers, but also 26,000 other building tradesmen, all of whom, it was said, were prepared to strike at his command. Nobody had ever wielded as much power in the building trades. And nobody had ever been as willing to abuse it.

On an afternoon late in the winter of 1902, Sam Parks met with a man named Neils Poulson, president of Hecla Iron Works, in a small unfinished room in the Flatiron Building, still under construction at the time. The men met to discuss a strike that Parks had called on Hecla six weeks earlier. Since Hecla was supplying ornamental iron for the Flatiron, the George A. Fuller Company, the building's general contractor, was eager to get the strike settled and so had arranged this meeting. Poulson told Parks he'd lost about $50,000 due to the strike, and that the strike was wrong and unjust. "I also told him the way the men were picketing the works and slugging the people at work was illegal," Poulson later recounted. According to Poulson, Parks responded, "I don't give a damn for the union or the law." The only way the strike would end, Parks insisted, was if Poulson paid him $2,000. "I want the money, and the strike won't stop till it comes. . . . Don't you forget I am Sam Parks." Another newspaper gave the quote a more Seussian turn: "I'm Sam Parks, I am."

Exactly when Parks began grafting is unclear. Perhaps he had been doing it all along. Certainly by 1901 it had become a serious habit. Pay up, he would tell a contractor, or he'd pull the men and stop the job. Or, more effectively, he'd call a strike first, then demand a few hundred or a few thousand dollars to call it off. "Seeing Sam Parks" was a common phrase in the building industry, and everybody knew what it meant. If you intended to put up a steel building in New York, you'd better pay Parks. Otherwise, you'd have no ironworkers to build it.

Graft was a profitable calling. On his modest salary of $48 a week, Parks began to collect diamonds, including three large stones mounted on a gold ring he wore on his right hand. He also wore a thousand-dollar sealskin coat, according to one account, and no longer made his rounds on foot but in a hansom cab, accompanied by his bulldog. The legend of his quickly accumulated wealth grew in the telling. He was said to live in a luxuriously appointed home, where oil paintings festooned the walls and champagne flowed freely. His wife was said to spend her days shopping at department stores and having her nails manicured and her hands massaged, while Parks sauntered around town squeezing more graft and adding to his fortune of several hundred thousand dollars. Some of this was true, much of it was not.

For the most part, the employers paid up without a fight. Keeping Parks happy was worth a few thousand dollars when millions were at stake. In any case, hardly anyone begrudged a man a little graft in turn-of-the-century New York. Boss Tweed had been dead over twenty years, but Tammany Hall, and the Tammany way of doing things, still prospered in New York City. The muckraker Lincoln Steffens, writing in *McClure's* magazine in November of 1903, estimated that the Tammany machine pocketed millions of dollars a year in graft. Steffens quoted the ex-chief of police, William "Big Chief" Devery, who once admitted that the police alone took in over three million dollars in one year during his short reign. Devery wasn't confessing; he was bragging.

Graft flourished exceptionally well in New York's booming building industry. Poorly paid inspectors from the Department of Buildings routinely made side deals with builders to let violations pass for a fee. (The customary fee was one-half of what the builder would have spent to repair the violation.) What the builder saved, the inspector made, and everybody was happy. Paying graft to unions was accepted practice, too. In many cases, builders initiated payments to union representatives, bribing walking delegates to strike competing firms. In Chicago, always the leader in such matters, they had a fancy term for these collusive payoffs: "trade agreements."

The George A. Fuller Company seems to have profited most handsomely from hardball tactics. Just five years after opening an office in New York, Fuller had grown into the dominant construction contractor in the city. Fuller grew in part because it could deliver buildings faster than any other general contractor. But how did the company manage this? To most people in the building industry, the answer was obvious: Fuller greased the most palms. Few failed to notice that unions, and most conspicuously the ironworkers union, seldom struck Fuller buildings. And no one missed the coincidence of the astonishing rise of the George A. Fuller Construction Company and the timely arrival of Samuel J. Parks in New York City. Many assumed that Parks was on Fuller's payroll from the moment he entered the city—that he'd come to the city expressly to do Fuller's bidding. The truth is probably more complicated. Parks did favor Fuller, going so far as to contribute a gushing letter to *The Bridgemen's Magazine* complimenting Fuller for its "spirit of amity." No doubt the compliment had been purchased. But Sam Parks carried water for nobody. He had too much pride for that. Indeed, in the end, it would be pride, not greed, that destroyed him.

An iron contractor named Louis Brandt recalled going to visit Parks in the summer of 1902 with a payment that the walking delegate had demanded to settle a strike. This was typically how it worked: Parks summoned a graftee to his row house on East 87th Street off Lexington Avenue, named his price, then dismissed the man. "Come," he would scoff if one objected to the payment, "we are not children."

Brandt had arrived on this summer day to give Parks $300 in cash. Parks told him to set the cash on a small table. As soon as Brandt put the money down, a young girl walked into the parlor, picked up the stack of bills, and walked back out without a word. It was a strange detail, particularly in light of the fact that Parks had no children of his own—who was this girl?—but it spoke volumes, somehow, of Parks' contempt for Brandt and his ilk. Parks treated them as if they *were* children. These were men of means and education. They were men of achievement. They could understand Parks' inclination to line his pockets—they were businessmen, after all—but they could not abide his contempt.

"That man Parks is a duffer," a Chicago union boss would later tell the *New York Times*. "There are a hundred men in this town who have forgotten more about working the graft than he will ever learn. . . . Those who know how to make the unions profitable as business propositions do not have to be ballroom bullies. Parks is entitled to what he got—not for what he did, which is all right, but for the way he did it, which was all wrong." In other words, if Parks had treated the businessmen with a little more polish and respect as he reached into their pockets, he might have gone on with the graft as long as his brief life permitted.

Strangely, for all of his alleged greed, Parks didn't seem to care much about money in the end. What drove him was a more subversive and heedless urge. He voiced it in a peculiar little essay published in *The Bridgemen's Magazine* in the late winter of 1903, shortly before his troubles began. The piece contains a stark, almost apocalyptic vision of a corporation like U.S. Steel usurped by a band of roughnecks.

> The Billion-dollar Steel Trust seemed to own the earth and hold first mortgage on the neighboring planets. . . . But while at the zenith of ambition and when it seemed impossible for anything earthly to shake their power, along comes an ungodly people, illiter-

ate descendants of Tubal Cain, the man that stood before Solomon and demanded his rights; uncouth workers of iron, who invaded the sanctuary, hurled the gilded heifer from the altar and sacrilegiously substituted a figure made of solid unpolished steel, mounted to the image of a Walking Delegate.

It's worth considering that Parks probably did not "write" these words, nor any of the words he published in *The Bridgemen's Magazine*. He was an unschooled man and—according to one of his obituaries—as illiterate as the descendants of Tubal Cain. He was also, as he had known for some time, a dying man, suffering from tuberculosis. Given the disease's long incubation, Parks might have contracted the bacterium before coming to New York. He was, in any case, seriously ill by 1902.

Tuberculosis is a slow, wasting disease that exhibits itself as fever, fatigue, and persistent, wracking cough. These days, strong antibiotics render tuberculosis curable, but at the start of the twentieth century it was the leading cause of death in America. The term "consumption," as it was commonly known, described the course of the unchecked disease; it appeared to consume a body from the inside out. In its most common pulmonary form, bacterium devoured the tissue of the hosts' lungs, causing them to cough up blood. The most obvious effect the disease had on Sam Parks, at least in the early stages, was that it made his skin sallow and his cheeks sunken. But it also seemed to fuel him with a kind of reckless, feverish energy.

In the spring of 1903, Parks began acting like a man possessed. He launched a scorched-earth campaign against the steel-erection companies, ordering strikes with even greater abandon than usual. By late spring, he'd ordered a total of 2,000 strikes. In April, the United Building Trades, under Parks' direction, threatened a general strike in all building trades, pulling 60,000 men from work. The demand: 10 to 20 percent increases across the board, or else a complete shutdown of the building industry in New York. It was a threat so broad, so *unreasonable*, that it demanded a reaction. It got one.

## SUMMER OF SAM

Early in the morning of June 8, 1903, more than a year after his meeting with Sam Parks in the Flatiron, Neils Poulson, president of Hecla Iron Works, paid a visit to the office of the district attorney of New York, William Travers Jerome. Accompanying Poulson was the vice-president of Hecla, Robert McCord. Poulson and McCord presented the D.A. with a cashed check made out to Sam Parks for $2,000. The check was enclosed in an oak frame, glassed on both sides, so that Parks' endorsement could be clearly seen on the back. The check had been written to Parks, the men told Jerome, as payment to call off the strike against Hecla in April of 1902.

Poulson and McCord could not have found a more attentive audience for their story than William Travers Jerome. The district attorney was that most rare of turn-of-the-century New Yorkers, a genuine reformer. He'd made his name as an investigator for the Lexow Committee in 1894, snooping out corruption in the police force and Tammany Hall. Behind a well-groomed moustache and wire-rimmed glasses, he kept his expression tight-lipped and severe. Jerome had had his eye on Sam Parks for some time, and when the men from Hecla called on him on this early summer morning, he began taking sworn affidavits on the spot.

The meeting with Jerome had been carefully orchestrated. After years of infighting, the builders of New York had reached the limit of what they would endure from Parks. That spring, every major building contractor in New York, with the exception of Fuller, had formed an alliance called the Building Trade Employers' Association. Pooled together, the assets of its members added up to more than $500 million. Its explicit vow, as voiced by its president, Charles Eidlitz, was to fight Sam Parks to the finish, however much money or effort the fight required. They would hire detectives and lawyers to investigate Parks and his cohorts, then hand over the evidence, pre-packaged, to District Attorney Jerome. The presentation of this elaborately framed check was merely an opening salvo.

Parks' first arrest came at three o'clock that same afternoon. When police took him into custody at a saloon on East 54th Street, Parks seemed more amused than concerned. "I am glad that I took off my diamond stud before I left home as I have found myself in the hands of the police," he joked. "My only regret is that I did not also leave my rings." When told that his bail was expected to be steep, he brushed aside any worries. "Well, it can't be too high for me." Police escorted him to the Criminal Courts building downtown, then across the Bridge of Sighs for an overnight stay at the Tombs.

Parks' bondsman arrived the following morning in the voluminous form of William K. Devery—the very same "Big Chief" Devery who'd once bragged about his prodigious grafting in the police force. Devery was one of the most colorful and crooked figures in turn-of-the-century New York, which is saying a good deal. He was an oversized man, fat, garrulous, and somewhat buffoonish, a big cigar forever stuck in the corner of his mouth under a walrus moustache. During his short but profitable tenure as chief of police, Devery enjoyed getting drunk and driving around in a hack, throwing money out the windows. He was gone from the police force by 1901, and out of favor with Tammany as well, but still very much a presence in New York politics. Now railing against the corrupt machine of which he had been such an illustrious participant, he'd launched a race for mayor of New York City. It was Devery's hope that his friend Sam Parks, who had already arranged his honorary induction into Local 2, would deliver the labor vote. Devery, in return, had promised Parks the powerful position of Manhattan borough chief.

"I've got the sugar right here," Devery announced to the press as he arrived to bail out Parks. Devery dug his hand into his pocket and pulled out a roll of thousand-dollar bills. "I'm ready to bail him out every time he's arrested! I'll put up the cash for him if I have to fill up this room to the ceiling."

Five thousand dollars later, Devery and a liberated Parks emerged from the City Chamberlain's office. A crowd of supporters erupted in cheers. "I am glad to help this man, because he is the friend of labor, too!" Devery exclaimed, mounting a nearby bootblack's stand. "He has gotten higher wages for the ironworkers, who have to risk their lives twenty or thirty stories up in the air without any law to protect them!" Devery then invited everyone in sight to a corner saloon for a few drinks. "I will stick by him," he said of Parks after standing a second round for the house. "He's a sticker and I'm a sticker and I get stuck on stickers."

"I am not downcast in my predicament," Parks told reporters as he left the saloon later that afternoon. He had been quiet and subdued since his release, and now he wanted to go home. "I have been through many hard squeezes, and I will come out all right."

The following day found Parks arrested on two new counts of extortion. Two days later, he was arrested on a fourth count, this one brought by a skylight manufacturer from Hoboken, New Jersey, named Josephus Plenty. Throughout June, new details of Parks' corruption were daily fodder for the press. "There seems to be no limit to the number of charges," D.A. Jerome told reporters. "If the laboring men knew the facts, Parks would not be trying to get out of jail on bail, but would be glad enough to avoid his associates wherever he might be kept."

Jerome underestimated the ironworkers' fidelity. A faction in the union did oppose Parks, but the majority of members rallied to his support, and the more charges that were leveled against him, the more they rallied. In the middle of June, they renominated Parks as walking delegate at a raucous meeting at Maennerchor Hall, then reelected him on June 22. Three days later, in a remarkable display of influence, Parks led 40 walking delegates from various building trades on a parade through midtown Manhattan, shutting down one job after the other. It was, according to a headline in the *New York Herald*, "Parks' Tour of Triumph."

The triumph was brief. In the heat of July, as construction stood frozen by Parks' edict, a grand jury indicted him on all four counts of extortion. He was arrested again later that month, this time for assaulting an ironworker at a union meeting.

One morning in early August, Parks went to buy a horse, in hopes that "fast driving" would revive his failing health. At the very least, a gallop through Central Park might stir a breeze to cool his tubercular fevers. "You don't know who I am," said Parks as he approached the owner of the Ben Hur Stable on East 25th Street, a man named Doc Field. "I am that notorious walking delegate that you have been reading about in the papers. I'm Sam Parks."

"Never heard of you," replied Doc Field. "I never read anything but the racing news."

By the end of summer, even the likes of Doc Field would be familiar with the saga of Sam Parks. Two days after his visit to the stable, Parks was convicted of assault. Before he could be sentenced, he returned to court, on August 12, to face one of the extortion indictments that had been brought against him in June.

The trial took just over a week. A team of prominent lawyers, led by a former magistrate named Brann, defended Parks, who carried himself with "impudent swagger" and a sneer on his pale face throughout. Ironworkers were gathered at the courthouse when the verdict came late on the evening of the 21st. As Parks stood, gripping the railing in front of him, the foreman stood and pronounced him guilty. Parks swayed slightly, then immediately recovered his composure. "With the old time swing of the shoulders," reported one newspaper, "he passed down the aisles, stopped for a moment to smile at friends among the spectators, and then waved his hands with the air of one who merely says 'good night.'"

For all of his public bravado, Parks sank into moroseness the moment he entered his old cell in the Tombs. He refused to receive visitors, with the exception of William Devery, who later issued a statement on his behalf. The statement condemned the D.A. and the employers. It also faulted the press for its misleading portrayal of Parks as a crook. And it included an epitaph that Parks had written for himself: "Here lies the friend of labor, crushed by capital." Those who wished to see Sam Parks as a martyr didn't have to wait long for more evidence of persecution. The same day Devery released that statement, the D.A. announced five more indictments against Parks, bringing the total to eight outstanding charges.

When Parks entered the courtroom for sentencing on August 26, the press noticed a deterioration in his condition. His complexion appeared a "ghastly hue." His eyes were sunken, his cheeks were hollow, and beads of perspiration gathered on his brow. The judge took the bench and announced the sentence: two and a half years in Sing Sing.

Local 2 happened to be meeting that night. When word of the sentence got back to the hall, the ironworkers exploded in an uproar. "It's a lie!" somebody shouted. Less vocally, though, some dared to welcome it as good news. "There will be many happy homes in New York tonight," one ironworker told a reporter from the *Daily Tribune.* "Some of us have been out since April, and the feeling has been among many of us that if Parks was out of the way work would start up at once."

Parks' wife, Dora, happened to be visiting him at the Tombs when guards came to remove him. She had spent most of his trial ill in bed, too anxious to appear at court. Now she broke down and threw herself onto her husband, weeping. He held her in his arms and soothed her and told her to be brave. After he was gone, she became so distraught that two prison attendants had to escort her home. It was all over for Sam Parks. Or so it seemed.

## HIS LAST RIDE

The headlines must have seemed a cruel joke to his adversaries: "CROWDS CHEER PARKS BACK FROM SING SING; *Wild Ovation for Walking Delegate Released on Bail.*" Like a creature in a horror movie, assumed to be slain and dispatched to hell but suddenly jumping from the shadows for one last scare, Parks was out of Sing Sing only a week into his sentence. His attorneys, asserting that negative press ruined Parks' chance for a fair trial, won a Certificate of Reasonable Doubt from a sympathetic judge. Parks was granted a new trial. In the meantime, he was free.

A large and rambunctious crowd gathered at Grand Central Terminal to welcome Parks back from Sing Sing. No one recognized him as he stepped off the Albany Special. His hair had been shorn, his moustache shaved, and he'd lost considerable weight in the week he was away. His face, according to the *Times*, "was absolutely without color." But then somebody saw him—"Here he comes—there's Sammy!"—and the crowd erupted in "wild shouts of exultation." A man in a white cap pressed a bouquet of roses into his hands. Parks put them to his nose, sniffed, and smiled.

A few days later, a reporter paid Parks a visit at his home, a six-room flat over a drugstore. He found the walking delegate lying in his bed in a small room looking gaunt and weak. Parks' eyes only lit up when he railed against the D.A. and the press for piling up on him. "Everything in this city goes to extremes," he complained. "They either slobber over a man or are ready to crucify him." The opulent lifestyle usually ascribed to Parks was nowhere in evidence. The apartment was small and simply decorated with cheap prints instead of oil paintings. Dora Parks was not out on the town shopping or getting her nails manicured. She was cleaning house in a plain dress with the sleeves rolled up, looking "fagged and tired."

On September 7, less than a week after his release from Sing Sing, Parks mounted a white mare at the corner of 59th Street and Fifth

Avenue. Rather than rebuff Parks after his conviction, the Board of Building Trades had chosen to honor him as Grand Marshal of its annual Labor Day parade. Parks wore a white cowboy hat and a gold-trimmed sash. Against the dazzle of his costume, his eyes appeared flat, his face haggard, his broad shoulders stooped. He was battling seven indictments, with many more promised by the D.A. He was in the later stages of tuberculosis and probably suffering from fever, nausea, and an overwhelming urge to lie down. And yet here he was, leading a parade down Fifth Avenue. Whatever else you thought of him, you had to admire the man on the white horse for his endurance.

If one of the mysteries of Sam Parks is why he self-destructed—why he let his contempt get ahead of his reason and greed—the other mystery is why the ironworkers stayed loyal to him for so long. It was a mystery that perplexed the D.A. and the press. After all, the ironworkers who were called to strike on Parks' behalf were his real victims. They lost their jobs. Their families were reduced, in some cases, to living on bread and tea. And yet they stuck by him through that long summer. Why?

The solution to the second mystery may lie in the solution to the first. They loved him for his recklessness. They loved him for his unreasonableness, and they loved him as unreasonably as he behaved. He was a dying man with little to lose, and so, in a sense, were they. None of them had a very good chance of seeing their hair turn white. They were all living on the edge, acting now, considering consequences later. Sam Parks wasn't smooth or silver-tongued as was, for instance, Devery. He was all raw bones and sharp edges. They stuck with him because he was an unpolished roughneck overflowing with a quality they understood even better than endurance: audacity.

As it turned out, however, there were limits to the ironworkers' loyalty. Somewhere in that week between Parks' release from Sing Sing and his march down Fifth Avenue, the ironworkers, if not yet Parks himself, seemed to realize those limits. The parade, as the *Times* put it, was a "fizzle." Less than 9,000 men showed up to march, far fewer than the 50,000 that some union officials had predicted, and significantly fewer than the 25,000 who had marched the previous year. Many of the sympathetic trade unions that had supported Parks and the ironworkers through the summer now chose to stay away. More pointedly, many ironworkers stayed away, too. Only about half the members of Local 2 bothered to show up, a clear indication that support for Parks was rapidly eroding.

A few days after the parade, as if to drive home the point, Frank Buchanan, president of the International Association of Bridge and Structural Ironworkers, announced his intention to suspend Local 2 from the union, a move he blamed largely on Parks' corruption. The *New York Times* responded to Buchanan's move with a hopeful editorial under a pithy headline: "EXIT PARKS."

Not quite. In late September, with a final astonishing burst of energy and spite, Parks boarded a train to Kansas City to attend the seventh annual convention of the ironworkers union. He left vowing to win reinstatement of Local 2 and, while he was at it, to unseat President Buchanan. "I'm a long way from being down and out," he told reporters. "I'm just about waking up." Arriving in Kansas City, Parks immediately took control of the convention with his booming voice and swagger. He demanded reinstatement of Local 2, and the delegates promptly obliged.

Back in New York, news of Local 2's reinstatement stunned the Employers' Association. "There is no use predicting," said one member. "Parks has gone so far that you cannot say what he will do next." A theatrical manager from Syracuse was so impressed by Parks' resurgence that he immediately cabled Kansas City to offer him a speaking engagement of 20 nights, at $500 per night. Parks said he'd think about it, then turned his attention to defeating Buchanan.

Just as it looked as if Parks might prevail and take control of the entire international union, his luck turned sour. Buchanan won reelection on the first ballot by a vote of 43 to 40. "I lose," whispered Parks.

Whatever manic energy had driven him to Kansas City suddenly dissipated. "I'm getting old," the 40-year-old walking delegate told reporters upon his return to New York. "I've had enough of it." Parks

Sam Parks, September 7, 1903,
at the head of the Labor Day parade.
*(New York Public Library)*

finally seemed to accept what others had long foreseen: he was beaten. And now, following several false finales, the real one came swiftly. On October 1, in an interview with *Harper's Weekly*, D.A. Jerome promised to have Parks back in Sing Sing within six weeks. Parks returned to court on a new graft indictment in late October. The jury took 11 minutes to reach a guilty verdict. "Parks received the verdict with an effort to display stolid indifference," according to the *Times*, "but a tremor ran through his frame and his face was an ashen hue. . . ." The judge sentenced him to two years and three months of hard labor, to commence November 6. The district attorney kept his promise with a few days to spare.

The press that had followed Parks everywhere he went for the past five months was there in the smoking car aboard the train to Sing Sing. Parks sat next to a deputy sheriff and lit a cigar. He told the reporters he planned to serve his sentence as a model prisoner and swore that when he came out at the end of his two-plus years he would be done with union politics forever. He took a pull on his cigar. "Boys, I'm up against it. Let me down as easy as you can."

## THE WAGES OF SIN

The official history of the International Association of Bridge, Structural and Ornamental Ironworkers, published on the union's hundredth birthday in 1996, absolves Sam Parks of his sins. "Whatever might be said of Sam Parks," it states, "he was a man of his time, who was dedicated to the well-being of his fellow New York Ironworkers. He may have wanted a full wallet for himself, but he wanted his friends to earn sufficient wages to take care of their families adequately."

That is a bit of a stretch. Parks did increase the wages of New York's ironworkers for a few years, but on the whole, he probably hurt them more than he helped them. A few weeks after Parks' return to jail, the *New York Times* estimated that he'd cost the city's ironworkers about $3 million in lost wages and cost New York's tradesmen as a whole somewhere between $30 and $50 million. Less quantifiable was the toll his belligerence took on the reputation of the union ironworkers. Employers would have nothing more to do with Parks' old union, and by late autumn, Local 2 was effectively finished. In January of the following year it officially dissolved and divided into four smaller unions, including Local 40, Manhattan's current local, and Local 31, the predecessor to Brooklyn's current Local 361. Despite these changes, relations between ironworkers and employers would remain sour for years to come. It's a legacy, no doubt, that would have pleased Sam Parks.

On the morning of May 4, 1904, Dora Parks boarded a train at Grand Central Terminal to Ossining, New York. It was a Wednesday, visiting day at Sing Sing, and she never missed an opportunity to see her husband. He had been failing steadily since he entered prison the previous fall and had recently been moved from his cell to the prison hospital. By the time Dora arrived, around noon, he had been dead five hours. She took what was left of his wasted body home with her on the 6:20 to Grand Central. She was a fragile, anxious woman, moved easily to tears by his ordeal. Now that it was over, it must have seemed like more than she could bear. It was: She would be dead, too, within a year.

"What sympathy the news of his death excites belongs wholly to those of his immediate family, who are disgraced by his career, without responsibility for it," stated an editorial in the *Times* the day after Parks' death. "The wages of sin are paid in full at last."

Dora was the Lutheran in the family, and it was a Lutheran funeral she gave her husband. The Reverend Henry Hebler of Zion Lutheran Church—Dora's church—presided over a small service inside the rooming house into which Dora had recently moved. Then the front door opened and the mourners walked out into the sunlight and the crowd. Many of Parks' old friends were there, and so were some of his old enemies, including President Buchanan of the international union. "Good bye, Sam, old boy," one man murmured as the velvet draped casket passed by. "Bad as you were, you did more for us than any other man." One estimate put the crowd of onlookers at ten thousand. A photograph in the *New York Herald* shows a crush of people in the street, dozens deep around the casket.

"All along the line of march, the sidewalks were crowded with sightseers, and women and children occupied every window," reported the *New-York Daily Tribune* in the next day's edition. At the pier at the foot of East 92nd Street, as police held back the crowd, pallbearers transferred the casket from the hearse onto a ferry, then embarked for the opposite shore of the East River. The funeral party continued on by carriage, reported the *Tribune*, "to Middle Village Lutheran Cemetery, Long Island."

A year after Parks' death, a writer named Leroy Scott published a short, melodramatic novel titled *The Walking Delegate* based closely on Parks' reign in New York. The novel ends with a spirited scene in the ironworkers' union hall. Parks' fictional doppelganger, Buck Foley, knows the police are closing in on him and jumps up onto a piano to make a gallant farewell speech. "What's past—well, youse know. But what I got to say about the future is all on the level. Go in an' beat the contractors! Youse can beat 'em. An' beat 'em like hell!" As police escort him away, he turns back to the men with a final wave. "So-long, boys," he shouts. Suddenly, just when it seems like the jig is up for Buck Foley, his roughneck allies rush the police. In the melee, Buck breaks free, slips away, and vanishes forever.

The story of the real Sam Parks doesn't end quite so dramatically, but it does end with a mystery. Why isn't he where he is supposed to be? Where did his body go when it floated away from the crowd on the pier? It's almost as if Sam Parks, in death, pulled off a final act of defiance and vanished, like Buck Foley, into the night.

# FIVE

# Mondays

## (2001)

H e stood on a concrete slab near the center of the hole and turned his blue eyes toward the cloudless sky and the 45-ton column slowly drifting across it. Bunny wasn't the only one looking up. A small crowd of officials from Bovis Lend-Lease, the general contractor, had donned sparkling white hard hats and descended the narrow metal stairs into the gloom of the hole, and they stood near Bunny—but not too near—gazing up at the huge dark chunk of metal hanging from the boom of the kangaroo. Crowds always turn out for the heavy picks, drawn by the ever-miraculous sight of something huge lifted and moved, and perhaps by the remote possibility of witnessing something truly astonishing: a 45-ton spear plummeting from the sky.

The column was among the dozen or so "boomers" that Silvian Marcus and his team of engineers had designed to bear the brunt of the towers' prodigious dead load (the thousands of tons of steel and concrete and drywall and glass and pipe that would go into making it), plus its relatively light live load (the hundreds of tons of office workers, hotel guests, apartment dwellers, pets, plants, and attendant vermin that would eventually occupy it) and the variable lateral load (wind), and then transfer all this weight and pressure to the schist bedrock below. Bunny stood on the spot where the bottom of the column would land, marking it with his body and occasionally gesturing to Chett Barker, the signalman. His eyes squinted and blinked. He was tired, operating on two hours of bad sleep snatched in the back seat of a Crown Victoria. His T-shirt bore the logo of a restaurant with a slogan inscribed beneath it: "JUST EAT ME."

It was a Monday morning, mid-April, almost two months since Bunny and Jerry and the rest of the raising gang first arrived at Columbus Circle. All four cranes were up, their cables threaded through the sheaves at the tips of their booms, their drums greased and spinning, and steel was finally starting to rise on the north side of the hole. To the ironworkers, the columns were a hopeful sight. Girders would soon link them, then beams would cross between the girders, then corrugated decking would cover the beams, and then they would be on their way out of the hole, and everybody else— other tradesmen, safety inspectors, contractors—would be below. Which is the way ironworkers like it.

There were about 50 ironworkers at Columbus Circle at the moment. Soon there would be double, then triple that number. The ironworkers were pretty easy to spot among the other tradesmen. They tended to keep to themselves, which made them seem more somber (false) and more arrogant (true). Even when they mingled with the others, they stood out. Their faces were broiled and wind-whipped. Their clothing was rust-stained and tattered, its fabric rubbed away by the rough skin of oxidized steel. On their hands, they wore thick cowhide gloves, gauntlet-cuffed. Most of the other tradesmen wore heavy boots with chunky heels, the better to keep their feet from getting pierced or crunched. Ironworkers preferred lightweight flat-sole boots, on the theory that heels were prone to catch on flange-edges and could send a man tumbling.

And then there were the hard hats. The other trades wore bright, clean, bulb-shape hard hats. Ironworkers' hard hats were generally battered and brown. Many were encircled by wide brims, as on a pith helmet, and nearly all were covered with fading decals publicizing the ironworkers' interests and affiliations—jobs they'd worked on, bars they frequented, sports teams they favored. The hard hats of the Mohawks featured a round decal showing the sharp profile of a man surrounded by bright yellow rays of the sun: the Iroquois warrior symbol.

A number of these warrior symbols were conspicuous on the hard hats of the ironworkers standing in the hole near Bunny that Monday morning in April. Of the 50 ironworkers on site, a third were men from Kahnawake, the Mohawk reservation near Montreal that had been supplying New York with ironworkers for nearly 100 years. This group included a second raising gang that had arrived a few weeks earlier. Because it was Monday, they were all, like Bunny, operating on two or three hours of bad sleep.

For the Mohawks, Mondays began late on Sundays, just before midnight, when the ironworkers kissed their wives good-bye, looked in one last time on their sleeping children, and stepped out into the dark. In twos and threes, they loaded into cars and drove out through the quiet streets. A loose convoy of big American sedans— "boomers," as some of the men called them—accelerated down the two-lane stretch of Old Malone's Highway, then sped south, the lights of Montreal fading behind them. They hit the U.S. border around 12:30. The night-shift patrol knew the Mohawks by sight, knew they did not carry passports, and knew they didn't need them. *"Onen,"* some of the border guards would call to them as they waved the men through. It was the Mohawk word for good-bye.

They stopped once or twice along Interstate 87 to change drivers. The pockets of their jackets bulged with sandwiches their wives had prepared for them earlier in the night, and somewhere along the way they pulled them out and ate them, quietly munching in the dark. They tried to sleep, but it was a dank, restless sleep of cheeks pressed against windows and necks cranked at odd angles—the kind of sleep it's almost better to do without. By dawn, they were awake at the George Washington Bridge. By 6:15 they were at the job site, stretching out their cricks, looking around for a pay phone to call home and wake up their wives and children, already missing them with a peculiar mix of exhaustion and loneliness. Then they grabbed a cup of coffee and headed for the shanty to get ready for work—for the five long days until Friday night, when they'd pile back into their cars and drive home to Kahnawake for the weekend.

It must have been a Mohawk who nicknamed the 12-pound maul ironworkers occasionally haul out: it's called a "monday." A few dozen swings of a monday could make your muscles scream with exhaustion. The only thing more excruciating than swinging a 12-pound maul was swinging a 12-pound maul on a Monday morning after two hours of bad sleep in the back seat of a Crown Victoria. Mondays sucked.

Bunny stuck out his hand, palm down, and fluttered it. The column slowly descended. When it was a yard or so above his head, he stepped aside, then turned back to grab its flank. Jerry grabbed the other side. Together, pushing and pulling at the steel, they guided the column down onto the footing, matching the eight holes of its base plate with the eight holes of the billet plate on the ground. The moment the plates were flush and the holes clear through, they screwed in the foot-long pins that anchored the column to the concrete footing below. Then Bunny grabbed hold of a flange, dug his toes in, and started to climb.

## BEATING THE WOW

The frame of a steel building is made of two basic structural components: *columns*, the vertical pillars that bear the building's weight and
transfer it to bedrock, and *beams*, the horizontal supports that link
the columns and carry the floors of the building. Cross-sectionally—
that is, from the perspective of somebody looking straight down
their shafts—most columns and beams resemble a three-dimensional uppercase I. They are comprised of two parallel plates called
"flanges" (the horizontal lines of the I) conjoined by a perpendicular plate called the "web" (the vertical line).

Plenty of other steel structural shapes have been tried over the
years—the rounded pipe of the old Phoenix column, for instance, as
well as various T's and L's—but the dual-flange/single-web form of
the I is by far the most common. There are many good reasons for
this, the most important being the high strength-to-material ratio
the arrangement provides. The I-shape puts the most steel exactly
where the piece needs to be strongest. Step onto a beam, the greatest
stress will be on the top of the beam, which will squeeze together
under your weight (compression) and at the bottom of the beam,
which will pull apart under your weight (tension). The center of the
beam will experience very little stress. Most of the steel, then, is concentrated on the top and bottom of the beam in the form of flanges,
while little is wasted on its center.

Another advantage of I-shapes: they're easy to join to each other,
much easier, say, than rounded tubes. The multiple flat faces press
flush against each other and give engineers options when they're trying to figure out how to assemble the thousands of members of steel
that go into buildings.

One consideration that did *not* determine the evolution of I-
shapes is how ironworkers would climb them and walk them. This
part ironworkers figured out for themselves.

Climbing a column is about as close as most people can get to scaling a sheer wall. The common method calls for an ironworker to approach the column from the outside of one of its flanges and hook his fingers around its edges—the flange is between an inch and two inches thick—then place the bottoms of his feet against the inside wall of the *opposite* flange. Now he's hanging there, pressing with his feet, pulling with his arms. If it looks uncomfortable, that's because it is. He starts to climb. His left foot rises and his right hand rises; then his right foot rises and his left hand rises. From this position, he scoots up, his hips swinging side to side. His arms and feet appear to take the weight, but in fact most of the weight is on the backs of his calves. His foot makes a lever, pressing his calf into the inside of the near flange. Using this method, a good climber hardly needs his arms. At any point he could let go and hold himself to the column with his lower legs.

There are other, less conventional ways to climb. Some ironworkers press their knees and shins against the outside of the same flange they're grasping with their hands, and then shinny up it. This looks a bit like a baby crawling up a wall. A few connectors prefer this method, though it's difficult to say why, as it has a tendency to shred the skin off a man's shins. In both cases, the trick isn't strength—many a musclebound hulk has tried and failed to climb a column—but weight distribution, finding the right balance between the push of the legs and the pull of the arms.

Ironworkers, particularly connectors, fly up and down columns all day. They speak of climbing thirty-foot columns as if it were no more difficult or dangerous than, say, walking up a flight of stairs. In fact, climbing columns is very difficult and very dangerous. Descending a column is slightly less difficult but slightly more dangerous. The position is the same, with the ironworker's hands cupping the near flange and his feet pressed against the inside wall of the far flange, but now instead of using his feet to climb, he uses the rubber soles of his boots as brakes to slow his descent. It's a controlled fall.

Joe Emerson, a connector at Time Warner Center,
climbing a column.
*(Photo by Michael Doolittle)*

On a breezy afternoon early in May, Bunny and Jerry finally climbed above the rim of the hole. The rest of the gang stood on the corrugated derrick floor 30 feet below. Columns and beams lay on the floor in more or less the same configuration they would later assume in the frame. Earlier in the morning, the gang had "shaken out" the steel, arranging it on the derrick floor so as to make setting as efficient as possible. As Jerry and Bunny hoisted themselves up to perch on their respective columns, they could see the other raising gang to the west, shaking out their own loads of steel on the deck. David "Chappie" Charles, the foreman of that gang, was shouting something at Chad Snow, the connector, and Chad was shouting back at Chappie, and everybody was laughing.

Bunny envied the men in Chappie's gang a little. It was easier working with other Mohawks. You knew each other from home; you knew how the other men worked, and you knew their quirks of personality and wasted little time in cultural translation. But it was also true, as Chad Snow once remarked, that you pushed yourself harder when you worked with other Mohawks. In a Mohawk gang, your pride was on the line; you cared what your fellow Mohawks thought of you in a way that you did not of non-Indians. "They're not expecting you to be the best you can be," said Chad of the latter. "You can float a little. But if you work with guys from home, everybody expects you to be the best. You want to make them proud."

There was no time for Bunny to consider such distinctions at the moment. He knelt on the top of his column and looked down. Below, Matt Kugler and John White were preparing the beam. Matt hooked his tag line into a bolthole at one end. Standing a few feet back, John scanned the length of the beam, eyeballing its center and estimating the gauge he'd need for his choker. A choker is a wire cable with an eye on each end. It wraps around the steel like a noose, one eye slipping through the other, the open eye then looping onto the crane hook. Of the two sins a hooker-on must never commit, the first is hooking the steel off center, in which case the piece will rise lopsided and might slip out of its noose. The second is using the wrong gauge of choker. Too thin, the choker will snap. Too thick, the noose won't close tightly around the steel. This was a fairly heavy beam, so John grabbed a ⁵/₈" choker, then leaned over the center of the beam and looped the cable around it. He pushed the one eye through the other, and pulled hard. The noose tightened. John slipped the open eye over the hook of the crane and nodded to Chett.

"O.K.," said Chett into the yellow squawk-box, "load up real slow."

A hundred feet over their heads, the sheaves at the end of the crane's boom began to turn. The choker pulled snug, biting into the steel. John stamped down on it and rode the beam a few inches, trying to get the choker to bite harder, then hopped off. The beam popped up, see-sawing in its sling. It was Matt's to handle now.

Matt's job was arguably the most difficult and thankless in the gang. The tagline man keeps the steel steady and steers it away from impediments—columns, other beams, ironworkers—in its flight path. Running tagline is like sailing a kite on a blustery day, only the kite weighs several tons. The crane operator controls the broad outlines of the steel's route but he can't check the small unpredictable motions that make a piece of steel potentially lethal: the see-sawing, the yawing, the spinning of a line un-torquing itself, the sudden swing of a piece caught broadside by a gust of wind. Steel moves through the air like a drunken giant, resolute, inexorable, and dangerous. A drifting five-ton beam can take out a brick wall, much less flick a connector off a column. In Newton's second law of motion, the acceleration of an object ($a$) is determined by the force ($F$) exerted upon it relative to its mass ($m$): $a = {}^F/_m$. In this case, $m$ was a 10,000-pound steel beam. Matt's unenviable job was to be $F$.

Matt glanced up, trying to steer the metal while taking long steps across the cluttered deck. Tagline men have little choice but to keep their eyes up, on their errant charge. If they aren't careful, they're liable to walk right off the edge of the deck or, at the very least, bang their shins and twist their ankles. Too careful, though, and they lose track of the steel and, inevitably, it hits something, and everybody yells. Everybody realizes that tagline is a difficult and thankless job, but they yell just the same. A few days earlier, an apprentice had filled in for Matt and accidentally let a large girder slice inches over the hard hat of a bolter-up and slam into a column, sending a spine-tingling shiver through the metal of the entire building.

"Jesus," said Bunny.

"Whoa—that was close," said Jerry.

The bolter-up put his hand on the top of his hard hat as if to make sure his head was still there. Down on the deck, the apprentice grinned sheepishly.

"Watch it, asshole!" somebody shouted. "Christ! You are useless!"

Now Matt let the rope go and the piece flew high over the deck, then started down. Chett spoke softly to the crane operator in the radio. "Nice and slow, that's it, down . . . down . . . load down . . . a hair more. . . ." When the piece dangled almost within reach, Jerry made a downward clockwise motion with his left index finger, then reached up and pulled his end in with his right hand. He brought the web of the beam flush against a plate, so that the holes in each lined up. From his belt he pulled a two-foot-long tapered bar—a connecting bar—and stabbed the skinny end through the matched holes. This held the beam and column in alignment while he dug into his bolt bag and fished out a bolt. With a few spins of the wrist, he removed the nut. He stuck the bolt into the hole, then tightened the nut by hand. On the other side, Bunny straddled the beam and "made" his hole with the tapered handle of his socket wrench. He was still tightening his nut when Jerry stepped out onto the beam. As Jerry started across it, the beam wobbled slightly. This was a fairly wide beam, a header, so the wobble was slight, but thinner pieces could start to oscillate side to side, alive with harmonic vibration.

Ironworkers call this motion the "wow" of the beam. If a man feels a wow coming, he'll try to stay ahead of it, and get across the beam before it has a chance to build. This is why you sometimes see an ironworker running, actually running, across a thin beam to get to the other side. He's trying to beat the wow.

Along with climbing columns, walking steel is part of the job description. In fact, it is a prerequisite. Anyone hoping to become an ironworker in New York City has to pass a physical aptitude test that includes climbing a 15-foot column, walking across a narrow beam, then sliding down the opposite column. The test tends to weed out the frail and the fat. It also weeds out acrophobes. Why an acrophobe would apply to be an ironworker is a mystery, but it happens occasionally.

Once out at a job site, a few apprentices take to walking steel as if they'd been hatched on the edge of a cliff. Most, however, need a few months to adjust. "Ye, gods!" wrote the builder William Starrett in 1928. "If there ever was an experience to bring to the human body its sense of helplessness and despair, its agonies and terrors, it is the sensation felt by one who has not had training when he suddenly finds himself out on a narrow beam or plank, high above the ground and unprotected by a hand-hold of any kind."

Two things have to occur inside of a young ironworker before he will manage to walk high steel competently. The first of these is psychological; the second is physiological.

Psychologically, the apprentice must learn to control the natural fear that Starrett described. Exactly how afraid he feels initially is probably genetically determined, at least in part, but it's also changeable. Studies suggest that even severe acrophobes can be successfully treated by exposure therapy, in which they are exposed to ever-increasing heights and slowly become accustomed to them.

An ironworker's apprenticeship is a crash course in exposure therapy. Ideally, the novice starts working in the hole, near the ground, straddling the beam and scooting along on the bottom flange—"cooning" the beam, as it's called. Then he works up his courage and steps onto the top flange of a wide beam, a header perhaps, and tries a few baby steps, then a few more, and gradually it takes. Or doesn't, in which case he might reconsider his career choice.

In the meantime, physiologically, the apprentice is daily improving his balance. Balance is an extraordinarily complex reflex system involving three of our senses—sight, sound, and touch—all of which play critical roles in navigating us through space. And then there is the all-important *sixth* sense located in the "vestibular apparatus" of our inner ear. The vestibular apparatus is a labyrinth of tiny curved canals filled with liquids and gels, and lined with microscopic hairs. What the vestibular apparatus "senses" is gravity. Depending on how the liquids and gels pool and slosh inside these canals, we are able to distinguish up from down and acceleration from inertia; we are able to dive into swimming pools, ride bikes without training wheels, and walk across dark rooms confident that our feet are on the floor and not on the ceiling.

As we navigate the world, or even just lay in beds, our brains busily collate input from our vestibular apparatuses with input from our other senses, with yet *more* input from nerves that control our muscles and joints (neck and ankles provide especially useful data) and assorted *other* inputs (the concentration of blood in our bodies), then instantly compute all of this into a three-dimensional matrix through which we ever so blithely saunter. At least, that is, until we find ourselves swooning on an eight-inch-wide beam 200 feet over the sidewalk.

To what extent is balance innate and to what extent is it learned? According to Dr. Bernard Cohen, a neurologist at Mount Sinai hospital in New York and a specialist in balance disorders, "this is a very basic question we don't have an answer to yet." What Dr. Cohen and his colleagues *do* know is that the balance system is highly flexible and adaptable. Which brings us back to ironworkers.

In 1909, *The Bridgemen's Magazine* published the speculations of an engineer on the subject of ironworkers and heights: "If it were possible for the average man to so concentrate his vision on the beam upon which he stands, that he could see nothing else than the beam, there would be no danger of falling. The moment he would catch a glimpse of the abyss on either side he would be gone." The key to balancing up there, thought the engineer, is "concentration of vision." Dr. Cohen agrees that changes in visual perception must somehow account for humans' ability to adapt to life in high place, but won't speculate much beyond this. "There can be a very powerful adaptation of the vestibular-ocular reflex, the interaction between the ears and the eyes. You can change how your eyes move depending on experience and circumstances. But exactly what goes on with them, I don't know."

Whatever the precise mechanics of adaptation, it is, in the end, difficult, if not impossible, to separate the physiological from the psychological. Fear makes people woozy and disoriented, and this, in turn, makes people more afraid. The biofeedback loop is a dog chasing its own tail. But this dog, to swap aphorisms, is one that can learn new tricks. With the exception of those who are clinically acrophobic or extraordinarily clumsy, most people could learn to walk steel beams high in the sky if only they were willing to apply themselves to it as diligently as ironworkers do. That, of course, is a very big if.

For some ironworkers, cooning remains the preferred method of transit long into their careers. It is safer, and if you aren't in any particular hurry, it's a perfectly adequate way to get around. Welders and bolter-ups, for example, can spend hours working on one bay of steel; they hardly ever *need* to walk on top of a beam. Most do anyway. Cooning is awkward and uncomfortable. Also, like "seagulling" (walking with your arms stretched out), it's faintly ignominious.

Connectors have no choice but to walk on top. They move

quickly when they set steel, from point to point, traversing the grid. They can pass whole days with nothing wider than six inches—the width, say, of a hardcover book—beneath their feet. Some days, and these are generally bad days, they set hollow square-shaped beams called tubes. The only way to walk a tube is on top; there is no bottom flange to drop down to if things get hairy.

Jerry walked steel as he did most things, without much fuss. His limbs were loose, his toes turned in slightly, his speed moderate but steady. When he came to a corner, he stepped across it onto the perpendicular beam, and continued along. Bunny walked with more crispness, an almost martial precision. He carved his corners sharply and cleanly, paused a moment to give each new beam a quick scan, then started across it. Every man finds his own way. There is nothing in the apprentice training manual about walking steel. Some men walk with measured deliberateness, heel to toe, heel to toe, as if counting their steps. Others scurry across as if chased by the devil. New ironworkers often walk duck-footed, trying to maximize their lateral support. One veteran connector working in New York in the summer of 2001 leaned forward and bent his knees, contorting his body into an italicized S. He might have passed for an old woman with scoliosis but for the fact that he darted across the beam with astonishing speed. He brought to mind a python striking prey.

Once an ironworker has learned to walk steel, he has to perform another kind of balancing act: finding the happy medium between comfort and fear. He must be comfortable up there to do the work, but it is possible, and risky, to be *too* comfortable. There are stories of men so relaxed they fell asleep while sitting on beams hundreds of feet over the ground.

No one at Time Warner Center ever fell asleep, but an agile ironworker did once stop in the middle of a beam to light a cigarette, cupping the match from the wind gusts blowing off the river. Another man counted a wad of cash on a narrow beam. Two others stopped to share a joke, no more than a 10-inch width of steel underfoot—and a concrete floor 30 feet below—then, laughing, passed each other and continued on their separate ways. A young ironworker sprinted across a beam, taking the whole length of it in three or four strides, then leaped over a two-foot-wide gap onto the deck. He grabbed a tool and ran back exactly as he had come. He would either make a great ironworker or a dead one.

According to John McMahon, who ran the Institute of the Iron-working Industry in Washington, D.C., until his retirement in the spring of 2001, it wasn't the young rookie ironworkers who suffered the most accidents; it was the good experienced men. "We used to keep track—we don't anymore—but we used to get all the reports that came in on the guys getting killed. And it would be amazing. You would think it would be either the apprentices or the old guys, but it's not. It's the guys who are at the absolute peak of their game, guys thirty to fifty, that's when most them get hurt. You think, now *how* could this be? These guys are physically fit, they're alert, they're strong. I guess it's a case of maybe taking things for granted. They forget to remember just how dangerous it is up there."

Forgetting to remember: this was the easiest way to get injured on a building. You might be walking along the decking at the top of the building and forget to remember the two-foot-square hole cut in the corrugated metal. Or you might be laying out sections of deck-ing to cover the beams and joist, a fairly simple procedure that caused an enormous number of accidents. A decker would set down a section of deck, then take a step back, forgetting to remember that he was working along the leading edge. ("Leading edge" being the term for that place where the metal ended and the open air began.) It was, strangely, deckers who suffered the highest rate of fatalities among structural ironworkers. Why? McMahon's theory is that decking gives men a false sense of security. They're more inclined to worry about falling when they're walking a thin beam than when they're standing on a sheet of corrugated metal.

The history of ironworkers is replete with tales of men who died because they forgot to remember. Like the man working high on a tower of the George Washington Bridge in the early 1930s who burned through most of a steel beam with a blowtorch, then stood up and stepped out onto the very piece he was cutting off. It snapped, he fell, the end. Where was his mind the moment before he made that dreadful choice? What was he thinking? What did he think the moment after?

The right to space out is one most people take for granted. If an office worker sitting at his desk happens to lose himself for a few moments in a dreamy reverie, it's no great matter. No one *dies*. Ironwork isn't like that. The construction site of a steel-frame building is a three-dimensional field of hazards. Hazards come from above, from below, from every side, and a man up there has to stay alert to these hazards many hours a day. Spacing out can be lethal.

High in the annals of the lethal space-out is the perplexing case of Charles Bedell, a gifted young Yale-educated engineer who oversaw the erection of steel on the Williamsburg Bridge. He had been with the bridge from its start four years earlier and he knew every piece of steel in it. He was a measured and conscientious man by nature, the last person on earth you'd expect to lose himself in a passing thought. One lovely sunny morning near the end of September of 1900 Bedell made his usual rounds of the bridge. He paused for a moment near the Brooklyn anchorage. He could see his office a hundred feet below. A month earlier, Bedell had been standing down there, on the street, when an ironworker fell and died at his feet. The event had shaken the engineer profoundly. Now, as Bedell stood on the bridge, whittling a stick and thinking about—*what?*—a 150-ton "traveler" crane crept up behind him, groaning and creaking on its tracks. A man did not have to be particularly light-footed or on the ball to avoid getting hit by the traveler. The crane operator saw Bedell standing there but assumed the engineer knew the crane was approaching and was just taking his sweet time getting out of the way. Only when it was too late did the operator realize Bedell wasn't planning to move. He shouted a warning. Bedell swung around and saw the crane bearing down. He lifted his right arm as if to grab the boom of the crane, then reeled back. He tumbled over the side of the bridge to his death on the street below.

Connectors were less likely to forget the danger than other iron-workers, because the danger was all too obvious. They had only to glance down to remember it. Most had fallen, and those who had not knew there was always a fair chance they would. Jerry had not fallen, but Bunny had. Chad Snow, the connector in the other gang, had fallen three times. No one stood around and thought about falling—you'd be finished if you did—but you took precautions. On windy days, you put extra bolts in your bolt bag to lower your center of gravity. When you were walking the outside of the building, you leaned in slightly, away from the street, and readied yourself to drop to the lower flange if need be. "You always look for a way out in case something goes wrong," said Bunny. "It becomes second nature. If a person doesn't do it, and something happens, they panic. Or they just stand there and they get hurt." A little bit of fear wasn't only nat-ural, it was necessary. "You gotta be completely nuts if you don't have fear," said Bunny. "If you lose your fear, you put yourself in danger, and everyone around you."

Unlike most young men who became connectors, Bunny had been a timid child. "I was kind of a scared kid. I didn't like to leave my parents. I hated to go away on trips." He first experienced heights as a teenager when, like nearly every other adolescent boy on the reservation, he ventured onto the Black Bridge, an old railroad bridge that crossed the St. Lawrence River onto Kahnawake, and climbed up into its superstructure. Ever since 1886, when the con-struction of this bridge introduced the Mohawks to ironwork, Indian boys had been going out on it to cheat death; climbing the bridge was an unofficial rite of passage. As teenagers, Bunny and his friends would run along the beams and scale the top chords, often at night, hollering and tossing empty beer cans down into the fast black water of the St. Lawrence hundreds of feet below. Every now and then, inevitably, a boy would fall. While this sent a chill through the others, it didn't stop them from going back. It was all right to be afraid. Being afraid was the point. You were afraid but you dealt with the fear and you did it anyway. It's a lesson many of these boys would take with them when they followed their fathers into iron-work.

"To tell you the truth, I still get nervous sometimes," said Bunny. "It does strange things to your mind. Every day I go to work, I look around and pick a person and think, what would he look like if he fell? Stupid things like that. But then you gotta push it out and get to work. You can feel afraid, but you still gotta do the job."

He was quiet for a moment. It was a Monday evening and Bunny was getting ready to turn in early. At work that afternoon, he'd seemed flip and carefree and a little cocky. Not tonight. "I just hope that if I fall, I go on the outside," he said. "It's longer that way, but it hurts less when you land."

"Will somebody kill the damn bird already?"

Sweat dripping from his face, his T-shirt drenched, Matt squinted up at an eighth-floor balcony across 58th Street, where a mechanical macaw perched on the railing. The bird was a fake, plumed with synthetic feathers and wired with a continuous loop soundtrack: *caw-cawcawcaw-caw!* The owners of the balcony only wanted to keep the pigeons away. Inadvertently, they were driving the iron-workers to madness. The cranes' engines whirred, the jackhammers split the sidewalk, the impact guns of the bolter-ups filled the air with their savage rattle, but the sound that pierced through all of this—the sound that drove the men crazy—was the fake macaw squawking on the railing across the street.

It was June, and summer was upon the city with all its heat and filth and irritants. The corrugated metal of the derrick floor reflected the sun's rays onto the men, retaining enough heat to cook through the soles of their shoes. When a breeze came, it carried the sweet sticky odor of port-a-pottys through the building. At lunch, the ironworkers sought the shade of Central Park, or a front stoop, or the air-conditioned chill of the Coliseum Bar and Grill.

The summer was off to a poor start. A few weeks earlier—on a Monday, as it happened—a young ironworker named Ron DiPietro had gone into the hole at a job on 56th Street, where ironworkers were erecting a skyscraper for the Random House publishing company. He'd fallen two stories, hit something, then fallen three more. He'd survived the fall, but barely. Now, a month later, he remained bedridden, still unable to walk.

Ron's fall hit close to home at Columbus Circle, not simply because it had occurred a few blocks away, but also because many of the men now working at Time Warner had recently arrived from the Random House job and knew Ron well. Ron himself had been due to transfer over to Time Warner within weeks. His gang would still come, but now it would come without him.

The worst thing an ironworker can do after a colleague falls is to dwell on it; better to get back to work, out onto the steel, and put the accident, however awful, behind. Unfortunately, that was not an option right now at Columbus Circle, because the work had slowed to an excruciating pace. The reason was lack of steel. The recent building boom had created so much demand for steel that fabrication mills were having a difficult time keeping up. ADF Group Inc., the fast-growing Canadian fabricator that supplied steel to the Time Warner Center, was overextended: a convention center in Pittsburgh, an airport in Toronto, a stadium in Detroit, not to mention several lesser steel jobs in New York. The company simply could not produce enough fabricated steel to satisfy the demand of all these jobs at once. So instead of the usual nine or ten trucks arriving at

Columbus Circle every day, the ironworkers were getting three or four. This was not enough steel to keep four tower cranes busy. It was hardly enough for two.

"Every day, it's the same story," said Joe Kennedy, the ironworkers' superintendent, as he sat in his trailer, surrounded by shop drawings, sounding weary and besieged. "They tell me they got more steel coming just around the corner. But then it never comes. It kills the men. They walk around with their heads down. You're an ironworker, you want to put up some iron and look back over your shoulder at the end of the day and see what you did—this is what they take away from us when we don't have enough steel to set. It's extremely frustrating."

It was particularly frustrating to the raising gangs, who thrived on action and competition. Some days, Bunny and Jerry found themselves moving port-a-pottys and Dumpsters around on the crane, tedious and unsatisfying work. Weeks passed without noticeable upward progress. The idleness gnawed at Bunny and made him irritable. "To tell you the truth, it sucks," he said one evening after work. "Everybody's pissed off, nobody's got anything to do, everybody's bitching and moaning. It's no fun coming to work when it's like this."

One afternoon, Chett Barker, the 55-year-old signalman in Bunny and Jerry's gang, announced that he'd decided to take some time off. The pain in his ankles was nearly constant. Simply walking across the derrick floor was difficult. A few days earlier, one of his ankles had given way. Chett had stumbled and fallen, and now his back bothered him, too. When he left for home that afternoon, he told the men to give him a few weeks for the pain to go away, then he'd be back, good as new. In fact, the pain would not go away and he was gone for good, effectively retired after 37 years in the trade, but he didn't know that yet.

The gang shifted to accommodate his absence. George asked Bunny to take over as signalman temporarily. This gave Matt Kugler the opportunity to move into position as the gang's second connector.

Nothing could have thrilled him more. "They can send the rest of them boys away," he announced one afternoon at the Coliseum. "I'll set the whole thing myself. What ya say, Jerry? You and me."

Jerry grinned. "The whole building? I don't know. It's a pretty big building."

By 5:47 on the morning of June 28th, the temperature on the digital screen on the south side of Columbus Circle had reached 78 degrees. "Mostly Sunny," read the forecast on the screen. "Hot and Humid." Already the air felt soupy as the sun rose over the corner of Central Park. You could see how hot the day was going to be in the faces of the early-bird joggers returning from the park, flushed and gasping. Just after six, the first ironworkers began to arrive, rising out of the subways at the end of their long journeys from home. The men got coffee and papers then clustered around the front of the building. The gate opened around 6:30. Some went in, though most lingered out front. At 6:55, Ky Horn, a quiet young connector who worked with Chad Snow, walked out to the paved island in the middle of Broadway and sat on a bench, glancing at the big digital clock. When it turned to 6:59, he stood up and walked back to the gate.

A few hours later, around 11 A.M., as the mercury shot up past 90, the phone rang in Joe Kennedy's air-conditioned trailer. On the other end was a woman's voice. She needed Bunny to call her, she told Joe; it was urgent. Joe radioed George, the foreman, who relayed the message to Bunny on the derrick floor. Bunny dropped his headset and strode quickly across the floor, his heart pounding—had something happened to one of his daughters? his wife?—then ran up the metal stairs to the trailer.

"What's up, Joe?"

"I don't know. Your wife wants you to call home right away. It's important."

Bunny dialed his number. His wife picked up. "Keith, it's Weedy."

Weedy was the nickname of Bunny's cousin, Kenny McComber, a

young ironworker, just 22 years old. He'd been working night shifts near home, retrofitting a bridge over the St. Lawrence River.

"What about him? What happened?"

"There was an accident. One of the outriggers on the crane broke. The rig fell over and pulled him into the water. They can't find him."

"All right, listen," said Bunny. "I'm coming home."

By early afternoon, he was on the New York State Thruway, racing north to Kahnawake.

# PART II
# The Bridge

# SIX

# Kahnawake

Interstate 87 changes a few miles north of Albany. The four-lane road has been flat and straight but now it starts to bend and pitch in the foothills of the Adirondacks. The air cools, the traffic thins, and oaks and maples give way to dark pine lit by flashes of white birch. For the Mohawk ironworker returning home, the change is more than superficial. He is just half way to Kahnawake but he has crossed into ancestral land now, the land that Mohawks claimed for hundreds of years and which many Mohawks still believe is theirs, if not in law then at least in spirit. *Kanienkeh*—the Land of Flint, as the Mohawks called their dominion—covered more than 15,000 square miles. It extended west from the Hudson River Valley and Lake Champlain over the mountains toward the Great Lakes. The southern border of the territory was the valley of the Mohawk River, where Interstate 90 now runs between Boston and Buffalo. The northern border was the St. Lawrence River in southern Quebec. For the next several hours, everything to the left, through the driver's-side window, once belonged to the Mohawks.

The drive from Manhattan to Kahnawake takes over six hours,

though it can be done—God and the New York State Troopers willing—in five and a half. Before the Northway opened in the 1960s, the journey home took 11 or 12 hours on Route 9, the beautiful and treacherous two-lane road that once served as the main artery between New York and Montreal. The men drank more in those days, often starting with a few beers at a tavern, then sipping all the way home, and the 400-mile drive could be as lethal as the work. These days many of the men make the drive home in one fell swoop. A handful, though, still pull off at Exit 36, about an hour past Albany, for refreshment at the Black Bear.

The Black Bear is a ramshackle but cheery tavern nestled into a hollow where old Route 9 curves into the town of Pottersville. Mohawk ironworkers have been stopping off here since the early 1950s, when an Indian's car broke down one night near the tavern. The owners brought him in, fed him, and gave him a place to sleep. The Indian returned the favor by showing up a week later with fifty homebound ironworkers, and Mohawks have been coming ever since. Fewer men stop at the Black Bear nowadays, but on any given Friday evening a couple dozen ironworkers still pull into the parking lot under the high wall of pines, step out into the mountain air, and walk into the haze of smoke and ethanol fumes and good fellowship. A painting of a Mohawk brave hangs behind the bar. A stuffed bear lunges from a corner of the room. On cold nights, a wood fire crackles in the cast-iron stove at the far end of the bar. A couple of drinks, a few stories, a bite to eat from the restaurant, then the ironworker is back in his car, racing home with renewed urgency over the path that Mohawk ironworkers have been taking for generations—and that Mohawks walked four hundred years earlier on their way to Kahnawake.

Long, long ago, the earth was covered with water and the ancestors lived in the sky. They were the Sky Dwellers. One day, according to the creation myth of the Iroquois, the Great Leader pushed his pregnant daughter through a hole in the sky. As Sky Woman fell, the water animals below prepared to cushion her landing. Water Fowl flew up and took hold of her and lowered her gently onto the back of the Great Sea Turtle. Sky Woman was the first human to live on earth.

The terrestrial Mohawks lived mainly in the area around what is now Albany. Like all Iroquois, they dwelt in longhouses, rectangular bark-covered cabins shared by several families. The women farmed the fertile banks of the Mohawk River for corn and beans and squash, while the men disappeared into the mountain forests for long stretches to hunt for deer and bear and to fish for trout and perch. Occasionally, the Mohawks joined the other nations of Iroquois Confederacy to wage war. They were notoriously fierce warriors. Before going into battle, they took oaths to the sun, praying for victory and promising to eat their victims in sacrifice. They tended to keep that promise. The name "Mohawk" is not itself a Mohawk word. It was given to them by their anxious enemies, the Algonquin. It means "man-eaters."

Of the five (later six) nations of the Iroquois Confederacy, the Mohawks lived farthest to the east, which brought them into early contact with Europeans. First, the Europeans spread their diseases to the Indians, in the form of smallpox, which killed about 5,000—well over half the Mohawks' total population—in a matter of months. Then they imposed their religion, as Jesuit missionaries arrived near Albany in the mid-seventeenth century and began to convert the "*sauvages*" to Catholicism. In 1676, a large group of converted Mohawks and other Iroquois were persuaded by the missionaries— and perhaps more convincingly by antagonistic non-Christian Mohawks—to travel north and settle on the banks of the St. Lawrence River. The first settlement was at the Lachine Rapids, just east of Montreal. The Indians named it *Kahnawake*—"By-the-Rapids." The settlement moved upriver several times over the next half century, but held onto its original name. Kahnawake moved one last time, in 1716, to its final, and current, location on the southern banks of the St. Lawrence, eight miles upriver from Montreal.

Life was different on the great river. Along with traditional long-houses, the Mohawks now built sturdy stone houses and a stone church and rectory for the pursuit of their new religion. But it was commerce, not Christianity, that made the biggest impact on Mohawk culture. The St. Lawrence, reaching from the Atlantic Ocean to the Great Lakes, was fast becoming a superhighway into the interior for European speculators, and the men of Kahnawake worked as river guides, or "voyagers," transporting fur pelts east from the Rockies or south from Hudson Bay. When the fur trade began to dry up in the 1820s, the Mohawks turned to timber rafting, negotiating the goods of white men through the turbulent Lachine Rapids that ran just downriver from the reservation.

Living on the banks of the St. Lawrence placed the Mohawks in proximity to another of the white man's enterprises: the construction of the iron and steel bridges that began to span the river in the middle of the nineteenth century. The first of these was the Victoria Bridge, an iron tubular bridge erected seven miles downstream from Kahnawake in the 1860s. The Canadian Trunk Railroad purchased stone for the bridge piers from a quarry on the reservation, then hired Mohawk boatmen to transport the stone to the bridge site. It's not clear whether the Mohawks climbed up into the superstructure of this bridge, but certainly the Victoria gave them a taste of iron construction. Apparently they liked it. When the Canadian Pacific Railroad undertook a new bridge over the river 20 years later, the Mohawks were determined to participate more directly.

This time the bridge was closer to home. In fact, one end of it was to be set on land at the northeast corner of the reservation. As part of the contract to obtain land rights, the bridge company agreed to hire Indians to work on the project. Originally, the Indians were meant simply to assist the bridgemen as day laborers, but they were not content with this supporting role. They began to climb up on the trestles at every opportunity.

"It was quite impossible to keep them off," an official of the Dominion Bridge Company later told the writer Joseph Mitchell. "As the work progressed, it became apparent to all concerned that these Indians were very odd in that they did not have any fear of heights. If not watched they would climb up into the spans and walk around up there as cool and collected as the toughest of our riveters. . . . We decided it would be mutually advantageous to see what these Indians could do, so we picked out some and gave them a little training." Dominion Bridge trained three riveting gangs. The men of these gangs, in turn, trained other Indians. "It turned out," said the man from Dominion Bridge, "that putting riveting tools in their hands was like putting ham with eggs."

A hundred and sixteen years later, an ironworker returning home from New York who enters the reservation from the east will pass through an old stone tunnel that runs under the railroad tracks. If he glances over his right shoulder as he exits the tunnel, he will see the old bridge, two dark humps against the sky. People here call it the Black Bridge. It's a rebuilt double-tracked version of that first bridge, the original bridge where it all began: all the wealth and pride and death and grief.

## THE RIVER

The night Bunny's cousin died was hot and windy. Kenneth "Weedy" McComber was working the graveyard shift on the deck of the Champlain Bridge, just a few miles downriver from the reservation. Around 3:15 A.M., he was walking between the crane and the low concrete barrier that ran along the edge of the bridge when one of the outriggers supporting the crane snapped. The crane heaved over the side of the bridge, plunging about a hundred feet into the river.

Vea Kateri Cemetery, Kahnawake.
Many of the graves of fallen ironworkers are marked by steel crosses.
*(Photo by the author)*

The crane operator managed to scramble out of the cabin moments after it hit the water. The current was so strong he was halfway to the Victoria Bridge by the time the rescue boat got to him.

There was no sign of Kenneth McComber.

Through dawn and into morning, the Sûreté du Quebec—the provincial police, known as the SQ—searched the 20-foot-deep water with boats and divers, then later with a helicopter. At 10:15 A.M. they called off the search. For many people at Kahnawake, this was evidence of the SQ's contempt for the Indians; had the boy been white, some suggested, the search would have gone on far longer. "The SQ performs searches like this during the winter, even under the ice, for days," an angry Kahnawake woman complained to the local newspaper. "Here it isn't even twelve hours and now it's over. That's unforgivable."

Bunny, his father, and several cousins arrived at Kahnawake that evening, after driving straight home from New York. The men briefly stopped off to pay their respects to the young ironworker's family, then went directly out onto the water in boats that a few of the men kept at the marina. All night, by flashlight, they searched the river downstream of the bridge, looking for signs of Kenneth. Shortly after dawn, another shift of men arrived to take over the search, and Bunny went home to get some sleep. He was back on the water that afternoon. Several boatloads of relatives and friends had joined in the search, including divers from the reservation's scuba club. One of the divers found a key and a shoe belonging to Kenneth. Both were about 250 feet downriver of the bridge. This seemed to confirm the working assumption that the fast current had swept Kenneth downstream, meaning his body could be just about anywhere between Montreal and Quebec.

On Friday evening, Bunny visited a medicine man on the reservation. The medicine man burned Indian tobacco, a means of communicating with the Creator, and afterward told Bunny to look for the number 3—this was the number he'd seen in his vision during the tobacco ceremony. The following day, Saturday, Bunny and the other men returned to the water to continue the search. That morning, the divers discovered a white barrel on the riverbed under the bridge. On the side of the barrel was a number: 3.

"I looked and I said, 'Holy shit, it's gotta be around this area somewhere,'" Bunny recalled later. "Of all the millions of digits, how can anybody come up with that? The hair stood up behind my neck."

But there were no other finds that day, and by the end of Saturday, the search party was frustrated and the family of the young ironworker was despondent. That evening, Bunny went to visit a different medicine man, an ex-ironworker he'd known for years. The second medicine man gave Bunny a new set of clues. "He told me a concrete pillar with some of the concrete broken, I guess by the current. You could see some of the rebar, it was rusty. And he said—he's there. That's where you'll find him."

The broken pillars sounded like the reinforced concrete piers of the bridge. If the medicine man was right, it meant Kenneth's body had not been swept downstream after all, but remained near the spot where he fell. The news excited Bunny. "That night, after that information, I went to everybody's house that was searching. I got in touch with a couple of the divers. I told them what my friend had seen. We had to get everybody out there—everybody together one last time. We had to try one more time."

At six o'clock the next morning, the search party reconvened. The men narrowed their search to the area under the bridge, around the submerged crane. They found nothing. At noon, Bunny came off the water and paid another visit to his friend. The medicine man was fairly confident that Kenneth McComber's body had remained near the bridge but allowed that it might have drifted overnight. "The water is so strong," he told Bunny. "It does what it wants. If you don't find him, go look in the bay. Look for uprooted trees lying in water. Look for a stone fence that was built by humans in the background. If he's not under the bridge, he'd be in that bay, floating. If you go in with a boat, and you get close enough, you can see him. He's facing up."

Bunny returned to the river in the afternoon. Before turning downstream to search the bay, the party continued to look under the crane. "I was hoping he'd still be there," said Bunny, "hoping we didn't have to go downriver. We searched the whole area. We searched on the side of the rig, underneath the platform. But he wasn't there. The divers decided, let's check around the crane one more time. They snagged a rope on the crane, then pulled themselves down toward the crane. They both searched. They looked at each other." Nothing.

One of the divers emerged on the surface and climbed into the boat next to Bunny. The other diver emerged from the water a moment later. "Let me check one more time," he told the men in the boats.

"So he went down," said Bunny. "He went underneath the crane, and he went around a little further than he'd gone before. And then he saw him. He was sitting right there, right by the crane. The diver got hold of his hair and pulled him up. . . . I was more relieved than grieving. That the body had been found. And proving the SQ wrong." Bunny shook his head. "What a hell of an experience. Something I don't want to do again. But eventually, it's gonna happen."

Indeed, as Bunny knew, it had happened before, many times. The river had given the Mohawks a great deal in the way of opportunity and prosperity, but it had exacted, in return, a terrible price.


## THE GREATEST BRIDGE

In the spring of 1907, about 40 Kahnawake bridgemen traveled 140 miles down the St. Lawrence to a deep narrow channel 6 miles west of Quebec City. The Indians had been in the bridge-building business for 20 years. They had worked on bridges along the length of the St. Lawrence, and had recently returned from work on an enormous bridge at Cornwall, Ontario, where they probably shared their knowledge of high-steel riveting with another band of Mohawk Indians, the Akwesasnes, who lived on a reservation near Cornwall. Now the men of Kahnawake came east to build an even greater bridge. It was going to be, in fact, the greatest bridge in the world.

The Quebec Bridge had been under construction for seven years by the summer of 1907. When complete, it would extend 3,220 feet, end to end. It was not its full length, however, that was going to make this bridge great. Virtually any competent engineer can design a long bridge, provided he has the means to support it from below at regular intervals. What makes a bridge truly great is the length of its center span, or *clear* span. This is the part of the bridge that stretches between supports; the unearthly part that stays aloft in defiance of gravity and common sense.

The Quebec Bridge was to be erected over a deep, fast-moving channel, so the supports that held it up would have to be very far apart, at least 1,600 feet. To make matters more challenging, this bridge, like many great bridges before it, would rise over an important commercial waterway. Even if the depth and current of the river had allowed for falsework, river traffic ruled it out. So the 1,600-foot center span would have to be built in the air, without temporary support from below. And to make matters somewhat *more* challenging, the bridge would have to be built on a tight budget, as the Quebec Bridge Company, its underwriter, was perpetually and notoriously short of cash. Such a bridge would require an engineer of untold ingenuity and experience. An engineer, that is, like Theodore Cooper.

Theodore Cooper was one of the most widely respected structural engineers in the United States in 1900. Early in his career, he had earned a reputation not only for engineering acumen but also for physical courage. He'd served valorously in the navy during the Civil War, then gone to work as a bridge inspector on the Eads Bridge in St. Louis, the first indisputably great American bridge. Cooper did not hesitate to crawl out on the girders with the bridgemen and inspect the metal close-up. One December day, he stumbled and fell 90 feet into the murky water of the Mississippi, plunging all the way to the river bottom. Still grasping his drafting pencil, he swam to shore, changed his clothes, and promptly reported back to work.

In 1884, Cooper published *General Specifications for Iron Railroad Bridges and Viaducts*, a book, later expanded to include steel specifications, that became a sort of bible for engineers trying to gauge the stress tolerances of metal. Nobody in America, perhaps in the world, understood the capacities and tolerances of structural metal better than Theodore Cooper. Certainly Cooper himself believed this to be true. "There is nobody," he once told a colleague, "competent to criticize us."

For all his knowledge, Cooper lacked the singular achievement that would put him in the ranks of his old boss, James Eads, or his fellow alumnus of Rensselaer Polytechnic Institute, Washington Roebling. Now advancing in age and failing in health, Cooper looked to the Quebec Bridge as the capstone of his career, the job that would place him squarely in the pantheon. This ambition might explain his willingness to work for extremely low pay, a total of $32,225 for eight years of work for Phoenix Bridge, the company contracted to fabricate and erect the bridge. As consulting engineer, Cooper would not draw the designs for the bridge—that task fell to Peter Szlapka, an in-house engineer at Phoenix Bridge—nor would he have on-site responsibility for the details of erection. But every important question of design and erection would be referred to him. He would be the ultimate authority. The Quebec Bridge was to be Cooper's bridge.

The first major decision confronting Cooper was the type of bridge it would be. The length of the span put a normal truss bridge out of contention. One option was a suspension bridge like Roebling's Brooklyn Bridge. But there were problems with suspension bridges for rail lines. They tended to move a lot and were deemed untrustworthy under very heavy loads. Cooper favored, instead, a cantilevered truss bridge, or "flying" cantilever. Cantilever bridges had been built sporadically for many years—the Eads Bridge was a form of cantilever—but had recently gained in popularity among bridge engineers after the erection (1879–1900) of an enormous cantilever over the Firth of Forth in Scotland. That bridge, 5,666 feet long with two 1,700-foot clear spans—the longest clear spans in the world—was the undisputed King of Bridges.

A cantilever is a structure or object that projects into space, supported at one end, unsupported at the other. Applied to bridges, the advantage of a cantilever is that it allows engineers to build inward over the river from each shore, meeting in the middle to form the span, and to do this without any support from below. Generally, each cantilever is centered on a pier that has been set in the riverbed near the shore. The cantilever is anchored and balanced by a truss on the shore side of the pier, then extended, panel by panel, over the water. Obviously, a cantilever requires enormous material strength simply to hold itself up. One reason cantilevers had become so popular at the turn of the century is that steel's enormous bearing capacity made them possible. Steel could support loads inconceivable just 20 years earlier.

The Firth of Forth bridge was commonly acknowledged to be massively overbuilt and exorbitantly expensive. Theodore Cooper had strong feelings about overbuilt bridges; he considered them sins of engineering. In an essay published in 1898, two years before signing on to the Quebec Bridge job, Cooper approvingly quoted another engineer, named Unwin, on the subject of overbuilding: "If an engineer builds a structure which breaks, that is mischief, but one of a limited and isolated kind, and the accident itself forces him to avoid a repetition of the blunder. But an engineer who from deficiency of scientific knowledge builds structures which don't break down, but which stand, and in which material is clumsily wasted, commits blunders of a most insidious kind." These words would come back to haunt Cooper and everyone involved with the Quebec Bridge. In the meantime, the engineer's prejudice against wasted material suited his financially squeezed employers just fine. Where the Scottish bridge was massive and thick, the Canadian bridge would be slender and lacy, almost delicate in appearance. It would be an extraordinary demonstration of engineering prowess and steel capacity dominating gravity.

And there was one other thing: in May of 1900, Cooper recommended increasing the length of the center span from 1,600 feet—which already qualified it as one of the longest spans in the world—to 1,800 feet. Cooper determined that building the piers closer to shore, in shallower water, would shave a year off construction. Coincidentally, it also would make the center span of the Quebec Bridge 100 feet longer than the Firth of Forth's. It would now become the longest clear span in the world.

The bridge was still half a bridge in the summer of 1907. On the north shore, erection of the anchor arm of the truss was just getting underway. On the south shore, it was nearly complete. The tapered arm of the cantilever reached hundreds of feet over the St. Lawrence. Each complete cantilever would eventually reach out 562½ feet and would support a central 675-foot "suspended span" between them.

About 120 men worked on the bridge that summer, 80 or 90 of them stationed on the south arm. A few of the bridgemen were French Canadians who lived nearby, but most came from elsewhere. They came from New York City and Buffalo, from Columbus, Ohio, and from Fall River, Massachusetts, and Wheeling, West Virginia. The greatest number came from Kahnawake, 140 miles upriver. Since entering the trade two decades earlier, the Mohawks had flourished as bridgemen. Seventy of the 600 adult males on the reservation worked in high steel in 1907. That summer, over half of these men were employed on the Quebec Bridge, mainly as riveters.

The bridgemen, Americans and Indians alike, boarded at rooming houses in New Liverpool or St. Romuald, small towns near the bridge site. They seemed to find the accommodations hospitable. Indeed, several American floaters were so taken with the surroundings they'd remained in Canada after work shut down the previous winter, ostensibly to hunt deer. "But we think there were other reasons," the secretary of the local union speculated in *The Bridgemen's Magazine* in June of 1907, "judging by the rapid progress some of these pretty French Canadian girls have made in learning to speak English." At least two weddings between bridgemen and local girls were celebrated that July.

As for those American floaters already married, several had

brought their wives and families. One of the wives wrote a letter to *The Bridgemen's Magazine* that summer expressing her delight with the surroundings. "We have quite a nice place on the banks of the St. Lawrence river, and the job is quite good, so we manage to get along well. . . . I must say for a positive fact, we never met such a crowd of gentlemanly bridgemen—some of the best men anybody could find."

They worked six days a week, 11 hours a day. Sundays were for sport. The Americans played baseball, the "North Shore Nine" dominating the "South Shore Nine." The Mohawks preferred lacrosse. One Sunday in mid-August, the Caughnawaga Lacrosse Team, with its roster of Indian riveters, scrimmaged on a field near the river. Afterward, the men posed for a photograph in the grass. They wore uniforms of black turtlenecks and white shorts and cradled their hand-made sticks. They were perhaps still a little breathless from the practice, but as they peered into the camera, they appeared relaxed and fit and understandably proud, for the lacrosse players of Caughnawaga (the common spelling of the reservation's name until the 1980s) were the finest and most famous in the world. It was they, after all, who introduced lacrosse to white Frenchmen in the middle of the nineteenth century, and who later traveled to England to demonstrate the sport to the Queen.

In 1907, the fame of Caughnawaga Indians still derived largely from their prowess on a lacrosse field. That was about to change. In the distance, looming over the trees behind the lacrosse players like a fin, was the slightly blurred outline of the bridge where 8 of the 13 men, among many others, would die before the month was out.

The bridge had progressed without incident through most of the summer, but with August came trouble. Early in the month, the bridgemen went on strike to protest Phoenix Bridge Company's practice of docking pay for traveling expenses whenever a man quit the job. The strike only lasted three days, but a number of rankled

Caughnawaga Lacrosse Team, August 1907.
*(Courtesy of Kanien'kehaka Raotitiohkwa Cultural Center)*

floaters never returned to work, leaving the bridge shorthanded. The bridge lost another man on the morning of August 20th, when a popular American, Joseph Ward, lost his balance at the extreme end of the cantilever and vanished beneath the water 180 feet below. His was the first death on the bridge.

Strikes and occasional deaths were to be expected on a bridge. More uncommon and disturbing was the condition of the structure itself. The first indication of a problem had arisen as far back as June, when a few of the chord pieces on the anchor arm failed to line up as they were meant to. This had not alarmed anyone much—even now, it's a rare bridge or building in which all the pieces fit perfectly—and the problem was fixed and work continued. But now, in August, it was becoming clear that the problems on the bridge went well beyond the usual fabrication errors. The bridgemen and on-site engineers began to notice ominous bends in the metal, particularly in two sections of the bottom chords of the anchor arm—the steel pieces that were meant to transfer most of the bridge's compressive weight to the stone pier. The bends were severe enough to require jacks to straighten them out before the steel could be riveted. When field engineers reported these bends to Cooper in New York, he was more quizzical than alarmed. "It is a mystery to me," Cooper wrote to Phoenix Bridge on August 9, "how both of these webs happened to be bent at one point and why it was not discovered sooner." A few days later, inspectors on the bridge discovered more bending, and the mystery deepened. Still, no one seemed unduly concerned.

The obvious explanation to the men in charge, including Cooper and John Deans, chief engineer of Phoenix Bridge, was that the steel had received some sort of blow. Deans thought it must have been damaged at the bridge shop or dropped in the steelyard. Cooper wondered if it had been hit by another piece of steel during erection. He asked his inspector, a young Princeton graduate named John McClure, to investigate.

Only McClure, performing more or less the same function on the Quebec Bridge that Cooper had performed years earlier on the Eads Bridge, seemed clear-eyed enough to recognize what was happening, even if he didn't quite grasp its significance. On August 12, he wrote to Cooper: "One thing I am reasonably sure of, and that is that the bend has occurred since the chord has been under stress, and was not present when the chords were placed." To accept McClure's premise was to accept the inconceivable: that the great bridge was buckling before their eyes; that seven years of work and millions of dollars had gone into building a bridge that could not hold itself up; that Theodore Cooper himself had overseen and approved a design that was profoundly flawed; and that this bridge, which was meant to be the greatest in the world, was doomed.

Part of the grim fascination that comes in reading the letters and telegrams sent between the principals in these last days of August is in watching otherwise intelligent and accomplished people try to explain away the obvious. The chief engineer of the Phoenix Bridge Company, John Deans, continued to insist that the bends had occurred before the steel was erected, and maintained this position even as McClure's measurement on the bridge proved conclusively the steel was bending *after* erection.

The Sunday before the collapse, a cold front moved into Quebec, pushing the hot summer air away and pulling in rain and wind and cool autumnal temperatures behind it. Monday and Tuesday the rain continued and only a few men worked on the bridge. McClure visited the bridge Tuesday and discovered alarming new evidence that steel in the bridge was failing: a piece in the anchor arm had bent an inch and a half since his last measurement less than a week earlier. McClure and several other engineers huddled over the chord and discussed what to do about it. The 38-year-old erection foreman, Ben Yenser, was sufficiently concerned to announce his intention to call his men off the bridge.

On Wednesday, August 28, the wind continued to blow but the sun came out and the men reported for work as usual. Mysteriously, Yenser had changed his mind overnight and decided to keep the men on the bridge after all. It was an odd decision, given Yenser's reputation for caution, and because of it Yenser is often given the rap for putting his men at risk. But Yenser was no engineer. He certainly would not have resumed work without tacit approval, if not outright pressure, from his own bosses. In fact, such pressure seems to have been applied by E. A. Hoare, chief engineer of the Quebec Bridge Company, who admitted as much in a letter he sent to Cooper that same afternoon. "I requested him to continue," wrote Hoare, "as the moral effect of holding up the work would be very bad on all concerned and might also stop the work for this season on account of losing men." The bridge was already undermanned. Hoare and others worried that halting work now, and thereby admitting concerns about the bridge, would send more men packing. With cold weather approaching, and the rush to complete the south arm before winter, this was a costly prospect. In a second letter, sent immediately after the disaster, Hoare would revise his account, suggesting that Yenser had made the decision to continue work entirely on his own. Blaming Yenser would be convenient, since the foreman would no longer be alive to defend himself.

In the end, whether it was Yenser or Hoare or anybody else who made the decision, the only person whose opinion really mattered was Theodore Cooper's, and he was 440 miles away in New York City. "It was clear that on that day," an inquiry into the bridge collapse later concluded, "the greatest bridge in the world was being built without there being a single man within reach who by experience, knowledge and ability was competent to deal with the crisis."

On Wednesday afternoon, 29 hours before the fall, McClure boarded a train from Quebec City to New York to consult with Cooper in person. By now, every man on the bridge knew that something was wrong. That evening after work, a number of the bridgemen paid a visit to the lower chord. The group included a Detroit native named D. B. Haley who was serving as president of the local bridgemen's union in Quebec. Haley was no engineer, either, but it was obvious to him, and to every other bridgeman gathered around, what was happening. "The inside web was bending toward Montreal and the outside was bending toward Quebec," he told investigators later, "showing that there was too much compression put on and it would not stand the strain and it was giving."

That night half a dozen of the Indians talked about the bridge at the house where they boarded. A white bridgeman named John Splicer was present and later recalled the conversation. "They said there was a place in that chord, I do not know whereabouts, where it was bent, and they were trying to jack it together, and they could not jack the plates together and riveted up the way it was. . . ." Splicer was so shaken by the conversation he decided not to report to work the following morning.

Thursday, August 29, was a blustery day, fair skies, in the mid-60s. Before work began, a few men gathered again around the bent chord to have another look. They were thoroughly apprehensive by now. "By God," Delphis Lajeunesse told himself, "I am going home before some accident." But he stayed, as did most of the men. Apparently, for all their fears, they still trusted the bridge, and the engineers, with their lives.

A bridgeman named Theodore Lachapelle decided to quit for the day around nine that morning, just two hours after starting time. He quit not for reasons of apprehension or prophecy, but simply because, as he later explained, "a man feels like work one day, and he does not another day." At 2 P.M., a 26-year-old riveter named Dominick McComber, one of the Mohawk lacrosse players, got into an argument with his foreman and stalked off the bridge.

John McClure, in the meantime, had reached New York. He was there to greet Theodore Cooper as the engineer arrived at his office on lower Broadway that morning. McClure's report caused Cooper concern, though apparently not enough for him to demand an immediate cessation of work. Instead, Cooper sent a telegram to John Deans at Phoenix Bridge Company in Phoenixville, Pennsylvania. "Add no more load to bridge until due consideration of facts." Later, Cooper and the press would make much of this telegram, as if its prompt delivery to the bridge might have prevented the tragedy. Cooper told the *New York Times* that the telegram ordered "the man in charge of the work there to get off the bridge at once and stay off it until it could be examined." In fact, the telegram said nothing of the sort.

After leaving Cooper, McClure boarded a train and followed the telegram to Phoenixville, where the bridge company had its headquarters. He went to consult in person with Deans and Peter Szlapka, the chief design engineer. Back in Quebec, around the same time that McClure was arriving at the Phoenixville depot, a Mohawk riveting foreman named Alex Beauvais noticed that rivets were starting to shear on the lower chord. Ingwall Hall, working atop the traveler, noticed that the cantilever had become "springy," bouncing slightly whenever a load of steel landed on it. "It would jar enough so you would notice it good and plain and you would feel afraid."

McClure reached Deans' office at Phoenix Bridge Company around 5:15. Deans had gotten Cooper's telegram but had not acted on it, apparently considering it less than urgent. McClure sat down with Deans and Szlapka and they briefly discussed the situation. At 5:30, they decided the best course of action was to await new information from the bridge site and resume their discussion in the morning. As they were standing to leave the meeting—at 5:31 P.M., just half an hour before quitting time in Quebec—the bridge, 500 miles to the north, finally did what it had been threatening to do for weeks.

Eighty-six men were on the south arm when a loud "grinding sound" shot out from the bridge. The 19,000 tons of structural steel toppled slowly at first, then the cantilever tower kicked out from the stone pier and it fell fast. A few of the men near shore had enough time to make a mad dash and save themselves. Men farther out over the river had no such option. Eugene Lajeunesse, who always worked side by side with his brother, Delphis, was standing on the south arm above the pier, waiting for his brother to lower a bucket of bolts, when the collapse began. "I made a jump and I went down and I do not know anything about it. . . . I said, 'I am finished'; that is all. I did not see anything."

Ingwall Hall, another survivor, rode the big traveler crane 300 feet to the water. "Well, I could feel it start to go down and it was going down so fast you got tears in your eyes and you could hardly realize anything beside you."

"It left me, sir," Oscar Lebarge later testified. "I was in space, in the air. It traveled a great deal quicker than I did."

D. B. Haley, the local union president, had a similar experience: "I was at the extreme end of it and the first I knew I caught myself going through the air. I realized that the iron fell very much faster than I did and left me falling through the air. The next thing I remember I was in deep water."

The bridge hit the river with a "clap of thunder," as one witness put it. The *New York Times* described the sound as "a terrible crash which was plainly heard in Quebec, and which shook the whole countryside so that the inhabitants rushed out of their houses, thinking that an earthquake had occurred." When D. B. Haley and Ingwall Hall came back up to the surface, injured but alive, the water was turbulent and filled with debris. "Everything was out of sight except timbers," said Hall, "and I do not know how many voices were hollering for help."

Most of the men had been dragged deep into the river by the steel and killed outright. Nearer the shore, where the water was shallow, men were trapped but still alive. They remained so as night began to fall. "Their groans can be heard by the anxious crowds waiting at the water's edge, but nothing so far can be done to rescue them or relieve their sufferings," reported the *New York Times.* "There are no searchlights available, and by the feeble light of lanterns it is impossible to even locate some of the sufferers." A village priest lowered himself by rope down the face of the cliff on the south shore, then waded into the shallows to administer last rites to the trapped men. Then, as the horrified spectators watched and listened, the tide came in and washed over the men, and their voices went silent. Of 86 men who had been working on the south arm of the bridge that afternoon, 75 were dead.

The collapse reverberated around the world. Its shudders were felt with particular keenness south of the border. The bridge was in many ways more of an American enterprise than a Canadian one, built by

The southern arm of the Quebec Bridge, August 28, 1907,
one day before the collapse.
*(Courtesy of National Archives of Canada, PA-029229)*

an American bridge company and by American methods, and overseen by an esteemed American engineer. Many saw its collapse as an
American failure. "The fall of the great Quebec cantilever bridge is
the most disastrous calamity that could possibly have overtaken the
profession of bridge engineering in this country," lamented *Scientific
American* two weeks after the collapse. "The tremendous significance
of this disaster lies in the suspicion, which to-day is staring every
engineer coldly in the face, that there is something wrong with our
theories of bridge design, at least as applied to a structure of the size
of the Quebec Bridge." It was almost too disturbing to contemplate. If

Theodore Cooper had been wrong, how confident could other bridge builders be that they weren't wrong, too?

The press treated Cooper kindly in the days after the collapse, as if he were the victim of bad luck rather than bad design; or as if the very practice of bridge engineering were to blame, rather than Cooper himself. But an inquiry launched by the Canadian government in the aftermath of the disaster quickly determined otherwise. The Royal Commission found Cooper to have committed several blunders that were attributable not to a failure of engineers *as a body*, but to his own poor judgment.

After the collapse.
*(Courtesy of National Archives of Canada, C-009766)*

The gravest error concerned the weight of the bridge. While the bridge was still in its design stage, Szlapka, with Cooper's blessing, had estimated a total weight for the bridge of 31,400 tons. Later, when it became clear that the weight of the bridge would be significantly higher, more like 38,000 tons, Cooper did nothing to change the specifications of the steel. He decided the new loadings fell within the margins of error figured into the bridge's design and pronounced them safe. By doing this, he was allowing a *unit stress* on the steel—that is, the pounds per square inch the steel would be expected to bear—that was 20 percent higher than the standard practice of his day. Cutting so close to the bone might have been warranted in a smaller, more typical bridge, but in a bridge of this magnitude, where there was little precedent to rely on, it was foolhardy and arrogant. Cooper trusted the steel too well. And others trusted him too well.

In Cooper's defense, he was underpaid and overworked. Lack of money tied his hands. He could not conduct tests that might have proved informative; he could hardly afford a secretary to help him with paperwork. The report took these facts into consideration and spread blame around. But most of the blame it placed squarely on the shoulders of Cooper and Peter Szlapka, the Phoenix Bridge engineer who drew the design. The language in the report by the Royal Commission was plain but devastating: "The failure cannot be attributed directly to any cause other than errors in judgement on the part of these two engineers. . . . The ability of the two engineers was tried in one of the most difficult professional problems of the day and proved to be insufficient to the task."

The words were a wakeup call to engineers around the world, who checked and rechecked their calculations. To Cooper, they were as good as an epitaph. Though he would not in fact die for another 12 years, his career as an engineer was over, his reputation destroyed. For all his accomplishments, only one fact really mattered about Theodore Cooper now: he was the man who built the Quebec Bridge.

Beyond its significance as a monumental engineering debacle, the fall of the Quebec Bridge was, of course, a human tragedy. The tragedy was especially staggering at Kahnawake. Of the 75 men who died, 33 were Mohawks. Many families on the small rustic reservation of 2,000 people had lost a relative. In the days after the collapse, the bereaved clustered in front of the post office, an old stone structure that possessed the single phone in the village. They waited for news and tallied the loss. Twenty-four women were widowed. Fifty-six children were fatherless. One family, the D'Aillebouts, lost four brothers, as well as an uncle and a cousin. Joseph D'Aillebout left 11 children behind.

A delegation from the reservation traveled downriver to gather the dead, but there were few bodies to bring home. Most were pinned underwater by the failed steel, where they remain today. A funeral for the eight men whose bodies were recovered took place the Monday after the collapse. The village was almost entirely Catholic in those days, and the ceremony was held in the St. Francis-Xavier Mission, a stone church near the river. Eight simple coffins lay on a platform in front of the altar. A local choir sang liturgical chants in Mohawk. The Archbishop of Montreal said mass to the overflowing church. "I am here to pray and share your grief," the Archbishop told the mourners, as a priest translated his sermon into Mohawk. "A father is above all in sympathy with his children in trial. Yours is a severe one. The remains of eight victims now lie before us; but how many more have found a watery grave, perhaps never to be recovered? Like Rachel's, your sorrow is one that will not be allayed."

## BOOMING OUT

The sorrow had a peculiar effect on the Mohawks. Rather than end or diminish their enthusiasm for high steel work, it seems to have done precisely the opposite. In 1915, just 8 years after the disaster, an investigator for the American Board of Indian Commissioners visited Kahnawake and reported that 587 out of 651 adult males belonged to the structural steel union, up from less than 100 in 1907. Even if this figure is inflated—it's difficult to believe it's not—there does seem to have been a real surge in interest. Apparently, the danger of the work only added to its appeal. "It made high steel much more interesting to them," a retired Mohawk riveter told Joseph Mitchell in 1949. "It made them take pride in themselves that they could do such dangerous work."

According to reservation lore, the women of Kahnawake imposed a condition on the men: they would no longer travel to jobs in large groups. Rather, they would spread out in smaller groups, minimizing the chances for wholesale slaughter of the sort that had occurred on the Quebec Bridge. It was thus, according to the lore, that men began "booming-out," traveling in smaller groups to faraway places like Buffalo and Detroit and New York City.

Mohawk ironworkers had been working as far south as New York well before the Quebec Bridge disaster—as early as 1901, in fact—but over the decade that followed they came in greater numbers. By the early 1920s, Mohawks were regularly crossing the border to work on bridges and buildings up and down the Eastern Seaboard, traveling together in tight four-man gangs, communicating on the steel in Mohawk, boarding together wherever they could find inexpensive housing. The practice was nearly halted in 1925 when an ironworker named Paul Diabo (a common surname at Kahnawake) was arrested for illegal immigration while working on the Delaware River Bridge at Philadelphia. Diabo's case resulted in a landmark decision by a federal court in 1927. Citing the 150-year-old Jay Treaty, the judge ruled that Mohawks, whose land had once overlapped parts of both countries, were entitled to pass freely over the border from Canada into the United States.

The ruling removed legal hurdles for the Mohawk itinerants but it didn't make the commute any shorter. The drive between Kah-nawake and New York still took nearly 12 hours, making frequent visits home impractical. In lieu of returning home to their families, many of the men moved their families down from the reservation to live with them near the job site. Communities of Mohawk ironworkers quickly grew up in sections of Philadelphia, Detroit, Boston, and, most significantly, in Brooklyn.

The Brooklyn families lived close to each other in the neighbor-hood of North Gowanus (now Boerum Hill), around the intersec-tion of Fourth Avenue and Atlantic Avenue. Over the next several decades, the Mohawks' presence there grew into a full-fledged ethnic enclave. By 1950, at least 400 Mohawks lived in Brooklyn; as many as 800 were there by the end of the decade. Apartment buildings filled up with Mohawk families. Bernie's Grocery on Atlantic Avenue sold a special cornmeal called "o-nen-sto" that the Indian housewives needed to make their boiled cornbread. The tiny Nevins Bar and Grill became known as "the Wigwam," the center of the community where men could meet, learn of jobs, and keep in touch with home. Drawings of Iroquois warriors and photos of the Native American athlete Jim Thorpe decorated the walls, and the hard hats of Indian ironworkers who had died on the job were displayed as memorials. "The Greatest Iron Workers in the World Pass Thru These Doors," read a sign posted at the entrance.

The children attended the local public school or one of several parochial schools in the neighborhood. Most Mohawks still prac-ticed Catholicism, but there were enough Protestant converts among them to inspire the local Presbyterian minister, Reverend David Cory, to learn Mohawk and offer a service every week to the Indians in their language. Cory's church, the Cuyler Presbyterian on Pacific Street, became a gathering place for Presbyterians and Catholics alike.

Ironically, even as Reverend Cory was learning Mohawk, the Indi-ans were forgetting it. Their children were growing up on English—

*Brooklyn* English, no less—and American television. Many of the young ironworkers married non-natives, Italian and Jewish and Puerto Rican women who lived in the neighborhood. Some even moved from Brooklyn to the suburbs of Long Island and New Jersey. They were partaking of that all-American rite of passage: assimilation.

The Mohawks lived quietly in Brooklyn for a decade or two without much remark from others. They simply formed one of the many ethnic enclaves in the demographic stew that was New York. But in the middle of the century, white people—white journalists, more precisely—began to take notice. The city-dwelling "redmen" who performed death-defying stunts on steel proved irresistibly exotic.

Joseph Mitchell deserves much of the credit, and blame, for sparking interest in the subject. His 1949 article for the The New Yorker, "Mohawks in High Steel," described the settlement in Brooklyn and included a history of the itinerant Mohawks from Kahnawake, "the most footloose Indians in North America," as Mitchell referred to them. While Mitchell's article was clear-eyed and well grounded, it contained the seeds of a misconception that many white people, and some Indians, have held about Mohawk ironworkers ever since: that in addition to being footloose, they are preternaturally sure-footed; that they are innately endowed for life in high places and immune to fear of falling. It was Mitchell who first quoted a Dominion Bridge official's opinion that the Indians were "agile as goats" and gladly would "walk a narrow beam high in the air with nothing below them but the river . . . and it wouldn't mean any more to them than walking on the ground."

Several years after Mitchell's article, *National Geographic* ran a profile of the Brooklyn Mohawks that gave this notion greater credence and wider circulation. "Why did the Caughnawaga Mohawks take so eagerly to this spine-chilling high-iron work?" the magazine wondered rhetorically. "The answer seems to lie in a puzzling characteristic found in many North American Indian tribes, and outstandingly in the Iroquois: they are almost completely lacking in fear of heights." The magazine quoted an early eighteenth-century English surveyor named John Lawson, who wrote of the Tuscaroras, another Iroquois nation: "They will walk over deep Brooks and Creeks, on the smallest Poles, and that without any Fear or Concern. Nay, an Indian will walk on the Ridge of a Barn or House and look down the Gable-end and spit upon the Ground, as unconcerned as if he was walking on Terra firma." Scientists, according to *National Geographic*, could not explain this peculiar behavior.

In his *Apologies to the Iroquois*, published in 1959 (in a volume that included Mitchell's article), the writer Edmund Wilson suggested that the Mohawks' fearlessness derived from their earlier life in the forest, from scaling mountain peaks and canoeing in rapids. He also noted their habit of walking by "putting one foot in front of the other, instead of straddling as, when they see our tracks, we seem to them to do." Presumably, this peculiar stride (which sounds more like that of a fashion model on a catwalk than an ironworker on steel) equipped them for traversing narrow surfaces.

The claim for Mohawk fearlessness and sure-footedness has been repeated, with greater or lesser degrees of credulity, in countless newspaper and magazine articles. Alongside it has grown another popular idea: that *only* Indians have the capacity to walk high steel. "Virtually all of New York City's skyline has been built by American Indians; Mohawk Indians," began a brief article in *Parade* in 1982. The first misconception—that Mohawks are genetically equipped for life in high places—naturally gives rise to the second.

In fact, Mohawks have never made up more than 15 percent of the ironworking force of the city. As for fear and agility, they exhibit no more or less of these than any of the other 85 percent of the men who walk steel for a living. Nor do they get injured or die less frequently than their Caucasian counterparts.

Around the same time that journalists were discovering Mohawk ironworkers, a young Columbia University–trained anthropologist named Morris Frielich undertook a more scholarly study of the subject. He began hanging out as unobtrusively as possible at the Wigwam (he feared getting beaten up, he admitted), observing the behavior of the Mohawks. He published his findings in 1958.

The Mohawks' affinity for ironwork, both for its itinerancy and its danger, was best explained not by genetics, thought Frielich, but by cultural atavism. For hundreds of years, the role of the male in Iroquois society had been to leave his family for long periods of time to hunt and wage war. Working on high steel, a Mohawk man reprised his warrior role, traveling to perform acts of daring and either getting killed or returning home with booty (U.S. dollars, in this case). "Here in the world of men, one could fight, boast, talk men's talk and be a warrior," wrote Frielich. "Colloquially speaking the warrior returned to the tune of 'Home the Conquering Hero Comes,' and to hear it again and again, he necessarily had to keep leaving for war." In short, "that the formula *'to be a man = to be a warrior'* changed in a relatively short time period to *'to be a man = to be a steel worker'* was due to similarities in the essence of the two ways of life."

Frielich's cultural explanation, while intriguing, is in some ways as problematic as the genetic explanation. The very existence of the place where he did much of his research—the Mohawk community in Brooklyn—seems to contradict his premise that Mohawk ironworkers were intent on getting *away* from their wives and families. Wouldn't their role as warriors have played more convincingly if they'd kept the wife and kids up on the reservation while they whooped and plundered afar? Apparently, they felt the tug of other roles Frielich doesn't consider: father and husband.

What, then, does explain the persistence of Mohawks in high steel ironwork for 120 years? If you ask a Mohawk ironworker this question, he is likely to shrug and blame it on luck. "I'm just glad we didn't go into plumbing," is how a young ironworker named J. R. Phillips put it. "Nobody would be interested in us if we were plumbers."

Ironwork happened to become available to the Mohawks at a time when few occupations were open to them, and they were happy for it. They stuck with it because it paid well and they'd learned it well; it offered a lucrative, if perilous, niche. Were they good at it? Yes. Was it exciting work? Yes. Did it provide its practitioners with pride? Certainly. But in all likelihood, these were secondary considerations, and fortuity, not genetic or cultural destiny, best explains the Mohawks' predilection for high steel; and practicality, not anthropology, best explains their footloose ways. In the end, the most remarkable aspect of the Mohawks' itinerancy is not how far they went away from home but how much effort they always made to come back.

In 1949, Joseph Mitchell wrote that the Mohawks showed signs of "permanence" in Brooklyn. Ten years later, their population there peaked at around 800. Ten years after that, they were all but gone. The Mohawks' exit from Brooklyn was triggered, in part, by the soaring crime rates that hit New York City in the 1960s. At the same time, many native communities in the United States and Canada were undergoing cultural retrenchment, embracing their Indian heritage and rejecting assimilation into mainstream white culture. At Kahnawake, this new sentiment found expression in the growing popularity of the Longhouse religion, a traditionalist faith based on the teachings of an eighteenth-century Iroquois prophet named Handsome Lake. It found expression, as well, in the determination of many Mohawks to return and live on the reservation, on the land of their ancestors.

The simplest explanation for why the Mohawks left Brooklyn, though, was neither crime nor culture. It was a highway. In the 1960s, Interstate 87 was extended north beyond Albany to the Canadian border. The new road, the Adirondack Northway, halved the driving time to Kahnawake, making weekly commutes plausible if not quite pleasurable. Now the ironworkers could board in Brooklyn during the week and return home to their families on the weekends. Which is what they have been doing, in greater or lesser numbers, ever since.

## HOME

On a steamy Sunday afternoon in late July, Bunny drove to the outskirts of the reservation to visit his cousin's grave. Kenneth McComber had been laid to rest in the wide yard between the Longhouse and the quiet two-lane highway leading out to the golf courses. A knee-high mound of dead flowers and bright ribbons marked the grave. Clumps of upturned dirt lay scattered in the grass. A holly bush and wildflowers grew nearby. Bunny stood at the grave for a few minutes, his hands tucked into the pockets of his cut-offs, then turned and walked across the yard to the Longhouse. His flip-flops skimmed through the grass.

The front door of the Longhouse was unlocked. Bunny pulled it open and stepped inside. The air was cool and smelled of cut pine. Everything was wood—floor, ceiling, walls, benches—except the iron stoves at each end and the light fixtures hanging from the ceiling. Afternoon sun slanted through the windows. A month earlier, the Longhouse had been filled with the grief and tears of mourners. Now it was empty and tranquil. According to Handsome Lake, the Iroquois founder of the Longhouse religion, the spirits of the dead rise into the sky and travel the Sky Road (the Milky Way) to heaven. That is where Kenneth McComber had gone now. The light in heaven was forever dazzling, promised Handsome Lake, and the air was fragrant with the sweetness of wild raspberries that grew there in abundance.

Back outside, Bunny ducked into his car. He turned out of the parking lot onto Route 207. The windows were open and the radio was set to K103, Kahnawake's local radio station. Bunny smoked and piloted the big sedan toward the center of the reservation. He was subdued, maybe pensive after the visit to his cousin's grave or maybe just listening to the music. It was a Sunday afternoon. Earlier in the day he'd taken one of his daughters into Montreal to go shopping. Soon he'd go home and eat dinner with his family, then lie down for an hour or two before setting out for New York.

Bunny cruised down Old Malone's Highway, a sort of main street for the reservation, lined with gas stations and shops and restaurants. He waved to a guy passing the other way in a pickup, then turned off Old Malone's into the welter of side streets.

It is one of the oddities of modern Kahnawake that most of its streets still follow the maze of the dirt trails scuffed out by ancestors who lived on the reservation hundreds of years ago. As a result, it is entirely possible for an outsider to believe he is driving east for ten minutes and end up, somehow, west of where he started. To make navigating somewhat more challenging to the outsider—and this must be partly the point—none of the streets off Old Malone's Highway are named. Street names are unnecessary in a community where everybody already knows where everybody else lives.

Other than the streets, which have always been loopy and nameless, life has changed considerably on the reservation over the last century. No longer does Kahnawake resemble the small rustic village with outlying farms that it was at the time of the Quebec Bridge disaster. The population has quadrupled to 8,000. The Catholic Church now shares its formerly exclusive metaphysical turf with Pentecostals and Presbyterians and the followers of the Longhouse. The town's infrastructure is thoroughly modern. Plumbing did not arrive here until the late 1950s, but you'd never know it from the countless swimming pools shimmering in backyards.

Altogether, Kahnawake is a prosperous, even idyllic place where you can feel, at moments, as if you've stepped back in time—not to

1907 but to 1957, to a suburban tableau of kids in bathing suits sprinting across lawns from house to house, pool to pool, and young moms calling to each other over back fences, while friendly local police officers (they're called Peacekeepers here) glide by in cherry tops, waving through open windows. Crime is low. Families usually live in close proximity to each other, brother by brother, adult children near elderly parents. On summer weekends, the reservation gives itself over to recreation, to the bustling community pool and the canoe club, to speedboating on the river, and, most of all, to golf. No less than four golf courses accommodate the residents of the reservation. This is one of the other oddities of Kahnawake: there must be as many acres of links per capita here as anywhere in the world.

Bunny drove by the canoe club and the community pool, then turned at the old stone church, the Mission of St. Francis Xavier. Beyond the church, the St. Lawrence glinted and boats plied the Seaway. Farther along the river, children played lacrosse on the wide green lawn next to the Cultural Center. An odd dark structure rose from the grass there: two steel columns, about 10 yards apart, joined at the top by a steel crossbeam. It looked like the sort of modern sculpture you might expect to find on the campus of a well-endowed liberal arts college, but in fact its purpose was sport, not art. The steel had been erected some years ago for field day competitions. Ironworkers would take turns racing up and down the columns (sometimes greased to make the sport a little more interesting). Bunny remembered the competition from his childhood as a thrilling event, but it had been stopped years ago. "Too many guys were getting their pride hurt, I think is what happened."

As Bunny continued along the river, he passed a tall steel cross erected in 1907 to commemorate the dead of the Quebec Bridge—a reminder that the pleasures of life at Kahnawake have not come cheaply—then drove through a tunnel under the railroad tracks. He turned sharply into a small gravel lot and parked. He got out and walked to the steps that rose to the bluff where the tracks ran. A uniformed sentry came out of a small shack near the tracks. "Where are you going?" she asked Bunny.

"Out onto the bridge. Any trains coming?"

She gave him a once-over, enough to satisfy herself that he was a Kahnawake Mohawk and therefore entitled to trespass. "You've got some time," she responded casually, then stepped back into the shack.

On the sentry's vague assurance—*some time,* whatever that meant—Bunny climbed the stairs to the railroad tracks, then started walking across the short drawbridge that spanned the Seaway. He continued out onto the dark steel of the Canadian Pacific Railroad bridge.

This latter bridge is the rebuilt version of the Canadian Pacific Railroad span where Mohawk ironworkers got their start in 1886: the same Black Bridge where Bunny, and so many other young Mohawks, first pitted their skill and courage against high steel. A great many stories regarding the Black Bridge circulate around Kahnawake. Some of these stories involve daredevil stunts, like the one about the boys who rode their bikes over the bridge—not on the rail bed, which would have been challenging enough, but on the 16-inch-wide top chord of the bridge. One ironworker dismissed this account as extremely unlikely—*The top chord? Ridiculous!*—then proceeded to tell a story of a fire-breathing white horse that haunted the bridge, which he swore was *absolutely* true.

Bunny had his own story about the bridge. A few years back, a German journalist had come to town to write an article on Mohawk ironworkers. He asked Bunny to take him to the bridge. They walked out, as Bunny was now doing, to where the top chord curved sharply up from the track bed. When they got to the chord, the German started to climb it, as so many boys had done over the years. He apparently felt a need to experience the Mohawk gestalt.

He was almost near the top when he suddenly froze. He could not go up, he could not come down. He was locked in a full-blown attack of acrophobia. Bunny spoke to him quietly for a while, then climbed behind him and walked him down, step by step. The German promised to send the article when it was done, but Bunny never heard from him after that.

Looking down now beyond the wooden ties, Bunny could see one of the endless barges pushing down the Seaway toward Quebec. He could see the river, too, of course—the river in which so many Indians had drowned and died, the river of wealth and grief. Still wearing flip-flops, Bunny walked over to the edge of the ties and leaped up onto a box girder running along the edge of the bridge. He stood there for a few moments, looking across the river toward Lachine and down toward Montreal. Then he stepped down onto the track bed and strolled back to land. It was time to go home and get ready for the week ahead.

## MEMORY

A few days later, a retired ironworker named Alec McComber sat in the air-conditioned bar of Kahnawake's Knights of Columbus Hall, sipping Bud Light from a bottle. The bar was nearly empty, just Alec and few younger men who had some time to kill on a Tuesday. Bunny and the other ironworkers were gone, off to New York and elsewhere, and the reservation was quiet. Outside, in the heat of the late afternoon, kids were doing bike tricks on the melting parking lot. Alec's dog, an old black mongrel named Jimbo, snoozed in the shade of a pickup truck.

Alec McComber was 84 years old, which made him one of the oldest ex-ironworkers alive in Kahnawake. Neither the work nor the itinerant lifestyle—the heavy drinking, the fatty diet, the all-night travel—were conducive to longevity, but he had managed to defeat the risk factors. He appeared fit and in robust health.

Alec believed he might be related to Bunny, and to Kenneth McComber, the boy who'd recently died, but he wasn't sure precisely how. Like Diabos and Beauvais and Kirbys and Skyes and Horns and Snows and Deers, McCombers were plentiful at Kahnawake and hard to sort. A great many of these McCombers were, like Alec, ironworkers.

Alec had been in the trade for 50 years. Thirty-four of those years he was a foreman, mainly for Bethlehem Steel. He'd worked all over America, Alaska to Florida to New York. He'd had a reputation as a hard-driving, demanding pusher. He was known by his men as "One-More-Piece Alec," because there was always time to set one more piece before quitting. It was difficult to see the hard boss now beneath the bleary green eyes and the sweet, nearly toothless smile, but some of the old authority was still there. When Alec spoke about the old days, the younger men at the bar listened attentively, occasionally helping him out with a detail or two.

Not that Alec needed much help. His memory was uncannily sharp. He recalled the gauge of chokers and the precise weight of girders he'd handled half a century ago. He remembered how toggle bents were used to hold up the cantilevered arms of the Rainbow Bridge over Niagara Falls while it was under construction in 1940, and he remembered the weight of the heaviest sections of steel on that bridge (75 tons) and the size of the gap between the two arms of the cantilever when they were complete (18 inches). He remembered details of tricking up columns for the Chase Manhattan Building in New York (54 tons each, using a 75-ton derrick supported by one-and-a-half-inch guy wires). He remembered the name of the boat that ferried him and three other men from Sydney, Nova Scotia, to Port Au Basque, Newfoundland, on their way to Gander to help build an airplane hangar for the Royal Canadian Air Force in 1940 (the SS *Caribou*), and he remembered the name of the policeman they met in St. John's after riding a narrow-gauge train 600 miles across Newfoundland—and overshooting their stop by a couple hundred miles (Sergeant Mahoney).

"This was wartime, understand? So he looks at us Indians and he wants to know who the hell are we. Well, we explained the situation, and he made a call to Montreal and got it all straightened out. 'You boys, you're all right,' he said. 'Sleep here overnight. And in the morning, get back on the train. You only passed your job about two hundred miles back.'"

Alec cackled merrily at the 60-year-old memory, and the young men in the Knights of Columbus bar smiled. One of the men asked Alec if it was true his father worked on the Quebec Bridge in 1907. "Yes, he did. He didn't like the way things were going so he walked off right before it went down." And what was his name? "Dominic," said Alec. "Dominic McComber."

Dominic McComber: The young lacrosse player who got into a fight with his boss and quit the job three and a half hours before the collapse.

Alec took a last sip of beer and stood. It was time to go home. He waved farewell to the others and shuffled slowly to the door, his legs bowed and stiff. Outside in the heat, his dog rose, panting with joy, and Alec leaned over and patted him on the head. Then he straddled an old black three-speed bike that had been leaning against the side of the building and pedaled off, slowly but steadily, as Jimbo trotted along beside him. Fifty years on steel had ruined Alec's legs, but his ironworker's balance remained intact.

The following afternoon, Alec sat at the table in the dining room of his rambling white house, paging through an old book of photographs. He'd golfed that morning, and his face, already deeply tanned, was flushed by a fresh dose of sun. The windows of the house were open. The white lace curtains billowed in a strong breeze and wind chimes jangled on the porch. Alec's wife, an ironworker's daughter he'd met in Brooklyn 67 years earlier, was in Montreal at a baseball game with the grandkids. Alec had brought the book out to show to a guest.

"This," said Alec. "This is it."

The book lay on the table, along with several other books and folders containing yellowed newspaper clippings. Bound in worn red cloth, it had been bequeathed to Alec by his father years ago. It was a record of the construction of the Quebec Bridge—not the first Quebec Bridge, but the *second* Quebec Bridge, begun in 1914 to replace Theodore Cooper's fallen 1907 structure. Dominic McComber had returned to the site to work on the second bridge, which must have been disconcerting given how close he came to death on the first. More disconcerting, the second bridge fell, too, in September of 1916, and Dominic nearly lost his life all over again. This time, the collapse occurred as the ironworkers were raising a 640-foot-long center span that was to stretch between the two cantilevers. Thousands of spectators had turned out to witness the event and crowded the cliffs on both sides of the river. A steel casting that held the span on the south side suddenly ruptured. The span plunged into the river, another 5,000 tons of steel lost, another 13 bridgemen dead. The span was quickly re-fabricated and the luckless bridge was finally completed a year later, September 20, 1917, when Alec was three months old.

Closing the book, Alec turned to the small stack of photographs and clippings. The guest asked Alec if he'd ever gotten hurt on a job. He shook his head. "I was always pretty lucky." Did he know many men who had gotten killed? Alec shook his head again. "Naw. Not too many."

A few minutes later, he studied a photograph of three men posing on a bridge in New Haven. One of them was Alec, still a young man in his 20s. Another had been Alec's best man at his wedding. The third had been an usher. Alec's guest asked where these men were now.

"This fellow," said Alec, pointing at the best man, "died on the bridge a few months later." The other man died a few years after that, on a bridge in Passaic, New Jersey.

"A minute ago you said you didn't know many men who died."

"Well, that, yeah," said Alec. "I just happened to remember."

A drop of liquid appeared in the corner of his eye. Maybe it was grief or maybe just the natural wateriness of an old man's eyes. He flipped through the old photographs. For a moment, he was quiet. Then he came to a photograph of the Chase Manhattan Building under construction in 1960. He lifted the photograph and studied it, and his eyes sparkled. "That job was sixty-four floors," he said. "The turnbuckles on the derrick could hold fifty ton. Oh, that was some job."

# SEVEN

# Cowboys of the Skies

Rough pioneers are these men of the steel, pushing each year their frontier line up toward the clouds. Wanderers, living for their jobs alone. Reckless, generous, cool-headed, brave, shaken only by that grim power of Fate, living their lives fast and free—the cowboys of the skies.

—ERNEST POOLE, 1908

High steel ironworkers lived and died on an operatic scale in the first few decades of the twentieth century. They were dashing and tragic figures who walked on air like supermen and dropped from the sky like stricken birds. They were daring and restless and possibly insane. And they were also—this fact was becoming ever more inescapable—extremely violent. By the end of the first decade of the century, the ironworkers and their small union of several thousand would be the most infamous labor organization in the country and villains in one of the most gripping dramas of the time. Poor Sam Parks. The war with capital he craved he finally got, only he wasn't around to enjoy it.

---

The months immediately following Parks' death marked a moment of relative peace in relations between New York ironworkers and their employers. This ended abruptly in the fall of 1905, when the International Association of Bridge and Structural Ironworkers declared a nationwide strike on American Bridge to punish the company for using non-union subcontractors. However justified the strike may have been, it was a rash and potentially suicidal gesture by a union that seemed to specialize in such gestures. American Bridge was the largest steel fabricator in the country, owned by U.S. Steel, the largest corporation in the world. The ironworkers were a small inchoate union with exactly $1,013.64 in their coffers.

To complicate matters, local New York ironworkers voted to expand the strike to most of the large steel erectors in the city, demanding a wage increase from $4.50 per day to $5. Most of the erectors refused the increase outright, though several, including George A. Fuller Company, did negotiate a deal to hire union men at $4.80 a day. Fuller had recently contracted to build the Plaza Hotel on the corner of Fifth Avenue and 59th Street. To complete the job on schedule, the company decided it had no choice but to go ahead with union men.

Fuller's willingness to deal with the ironworkers soon backfired. The trouble began in the spring of 1906, after the company hired a non-unionized subcontractor to do some of the ornamental (non-structural) ironwork at the Plaza. The affronted union bridgemen, strategically positioned a few stories above the non-union men, contrived to drive them off the job by "accidentally" dropping tools and hot rivets onto them. This went on for a few days before Fuller thought to put a stop to it. The company hired three armed watchmen to patrol the derrick floor and keep an eye on the 30 bridgemen. These measures only provoked the structural men further. "Beat it!" an ironworker told one of the watchmen. "If you know your business you'll skidoo." The watchman, armed with a revolver, stood his ground.

On the afternoon of July 11, just after lunch, the ironworkers made good on their threat. "Events showed that the whole attack had been outlined to a nicety," reported the *Times*, "and the dispatch with which the job was executed demonstrated that each man knew just where he was expected to be when the signal should be given." First, the ironworkers cut off escape routes. Then they pounced, 10 ironworkers per watchman, beating them mercilessly with wrenches and mauls. One gang dropped watchman Michael Butler through the middle of the building from the eighth floor to the fifth. Another gang dragged watchman John Cullen to the eastern edge of the building overlooking Grand Army Plaza. "Four men had him in hand and were swinging his body to and fro and about to toss it into space to drop to the asphalt pavement in the Plaza below," reported the *Times*. Realizing that a body flying off the side of a building in the middle of the afternoon might draw unwanted attention, they instead left Cullen in a lump on the derrick floor, along with the bloodied body of the third watchman, William O'Toole, and returned to work as if nothing had happened. Cullen and O'Toole were severely injured. Michael Butler was dead.

The "Midair Murder," as the outraged press dubbed it, provided more evidence of what most steel companies, if not most New Yorkers, already believed by the summer of 1906: that unionized ironworkers were vicious and irredeemable thugs; and that the only sensible way to deal with such a union was to join arms and destroy it. This is precisely what the National Erectors' Association proposed to do.

The National Erectors' Association (NEA) was a coalition of steel fabricators and erectors that had formed in the spring of 1903, amidst the turmoil of the Sam Parks reign. American Bridge Company was by far the largest participant in the NEA and, in many ways, its guiding light, representing the interests not only of itself but also of its corporate parent, U.S. Steel. Other members included such formidable entities as McClintock-Marshall, Post & McCord, and Phoenix Bridge Company. The NEA first convened as a loose and ineffectual assemblage of competing firms, but by 1906 it had coalesced into a strong body joined in a common cause. This cause was articulated in the deceptively mild language of the NEA's constitution: "The object of this Association shall be the institution and maintenance of the open shop principle in the employment of labor in the erection of steel and iron bridges and buildings and other structural steel and iron work."

Theoretically, an "open shop" industry was one in which any man was entitled to work, whether he belonged to a union or not. More to the point, open-shop employers were entitled to hire whomever they pleased. Open shops did not explicitly prohibit union employees, but they disarmed the union of the only real weapon it had, the threat of a strike. Open-shop employers tended, in any case, to be not merely non-union but aggressively *anti*-union. They discouraged unionism by firing pro-labor agitators or signing men under "yellow dog" non-union contracts. U.S. Steel, mother company of both American Bridge and Illinois Steel (another NEA member), had maintained a strict open-shop policy since the Homestead strike of 1892.

The NEA claimed the open-shop system to be more "moral," more patriotic, than closed shop, because it gave workers the freedom to work where they pleased. But Luke Grant, who later studied the conflict between ironworkers and the NEA on behalf of the U.S. Commission on Industrial Relations, thought this righteous-sounding argument amounted to nothing more than "meaningless twaddle." The true reason employers favored the open shop was that non-union labor was cheaper than union labor. "No matter how many high-sounding phrases may be used in discussing the subject," wrote Grant, "in the last analysis it is a common, ordinary question of dollars and cents."

The "twaddle" not only obscured the real cause of the conflict, it also obscured its intensity. This was a fight to the death. The members of the NEA had only two options, declared William Post of Post

& McCord: "breaking the union or breaking themselves." The NEA instantly became, as one labor historian put it, "one of the most determined and brutal open-shop employers' organizations in the United States."

The NEA's efforts to break the ironworkers union were well planned and highly effective. By the start of 1907, only half of the union men in New York were employed. Nationally, nearly all of the American Bridge jobs were completed on schedule with non-union labor. The ironworkers were "demoralized," bragged Walter Drew, commissioner of the NEA. His claim seemed to be confirmed in an emotional debate on the floor of the 1908 ironworkers' convention. "We have come to the conclusion that this is not a winning fight," announced a delegate from Brooklyn, while another asked, "How can you expect to beat the Steel Trust?" The bridgemen had fought valiantly, the New York delegates argued, but the time had come to either throw in the towel or up the ante. Given its history of rashness, perhaps it's no surprise which course the union chose.

## DYNAMITE

In June of 1907, a Detroit ironworker named Ortie McManigal was approached by the business agent of his local union, Harry Hockin. McManigal, a short, florid-faced man of 34, had recently arrived in Detroit to help construct the new Ford Motor building. As a younger man, he'd labored in stone quarries in his native Ohio, where he'd learned a good deal about the use of dynamite. Somehow, the business agent had gotten hold of this fact.

"I am told you know how to handle dynamite," said Hockin. "I want you to use the dynamite which I am going to procure as I direct you to use it." According to a confessional account McManigal was to publish several years later, Hockin then ordered McManigal to blow up several non-union jobs in the Detroit area. "I'm going to show these fellows just what a union is," declared Hockin.

McManigal later claimed that he felt like "a cornered rat." He wanted nothing to do with Hockin's scheme, he insisted, but the business agent warned him that he would be blacklisted by the union if he refused. "I could only see my wife and children hungry," wrote McManigal, "and myself tramping about the country vainly hunting for work, or, finding it, holding it only for a day or so, to be kicked out as a denigrated thug with the instincts of a tiger." He agreed, instead, to go dynamiting. The pangs this inflicted on his conscience were somewhat assuaged by the $200 he would be paid per assignment, almost 10 times what he could make in a full week as an ironworker.

What followed, as related in McManigal's breast-beating apologia, was his gradual descent into pyrotechnical perdition. Under Hockin's direction, he blew up a non-union construction site in Detroit, then went on to perform other demolition jobs on behalf of the union, including a bridge in Clinton, Iowa, and another in Buffalo, New York. McManigal traveled the country by train, staying in hotels under aliases, slipping onto construction sites in the dead of night, then scurrying away as the 50-foot fuse burned toward its resolution under a steel girder.

At first McManigal's orders came from Hockin, but he soon came to understand that the man calling the shots stood higher in the union's chain of command: it was John McNamara, the handsome and popular secretary-treasurer of the International Association of Bridge and Structural Ironworkers. Still in his twenties at the time, John McNamara was an intelligent, charismatic, and extremely industrious young man. While carrying out his duties as secretary-treasurer, he managed to study law and gain admittance to the Indiana bar and to edit *The Bridgemen's Magazine*, in which he combined helpful tips for ironworkers' wives ("If a piece of lard about the size of a walnut be dropped into the cabbage pot it will not boil over") with union business and anti-scab polemics. Between these other obligations, he also found time to oversee one of the most extensive industrial sabotage campaigns in the country's history.

The ironworkers were not the first group of disenchanted laborers to avail themselves of dynamite to settle a grievance. Indeed, the beady-eyed, bomb-throwing anarchist was already a stock caricature by the turn of the century. No one, though, had ever used dynamite with such deliberation and abandon as the ironworkers now proceeded to do. Between 1907 and 1911, the union would dynamite at least seventy structural steel jobs, including steel mills, factories, bridges, and buildings.

In early December, at a hotel in Muncie, Indiana, Harry Hockin introduced Ortie McManigal to another of the union's professional dynamiters, a tall and reedy man named J. B. Brice. McManigal thought Brice looked familiar; he bore an anemic likeness to John McNamara, the secretary-treasurer of the union. There was a good reason for this. J. B. Brice was the alias of James McNamara, John's older brother. The elder McNamara was an alcoholic who had turned to dynamiting after losing his job as a printer. He had never succeeded at much of anything until he found his calling in blowing things up. He'd recently invented (or at least appropriated and improved) a new incendiary device called an "infernal machine." Instead of a fuse, which gave the dynamiter about half an hour to escape, the infernal machine was triggered by a fulminating cap wired to an alarm clock. The dynamiters could set the explosion for a precise time and be hundreds of miles away when it went off.

The day after they met, McManigal and McNamara drove into the country near Muncie to purchase some nitroglycerine from a well shooter. A far more powerful and dangerous explosive than dynamite, nitroglycerine—"the soup," as the men called it—now became the ironworkers' explosive of choice. One of the benefits of nitroglycerine was that it detonated with such force it left no evidence behind, not so much as a clock spring. The downside of nitro-glycerine was its extreme volatility. Traveling the country by rail with their suitcases of "soup" beside them, the men were always one big bump or lurch away from vaporizing themselves and anyone who happened to be nearby.

McManigal and McNamara crisscrossed the country for much of 1910, occasionally teaming up for big jobs. In mid-July, they parted ways. McNamara left for the West Coast on an important though secretive mission. McManigal continued to travel at a furious pace, setting off bombs in Omaha, then Duluth, then Kansas City. In late August, he arrived in Peoria, Illinois, and on a rainy evening in early September he planted four infernal machines, two under a crane at an iron foundry, two others in a railroad yard under some bridge girders stored there by the McClintock-Marshall steel erection com-pany. Later that evening, three of the four bombs exploded. The fourth failed to detonate. This is the bomb that fell into the hands of William Burns.

Detective William J. Burns was already moderately famous by the summer of 1910, having carved out a reputation as a brilliant U.S. Agent in several high-profile cases. Now he'd left government service for the more lucrative private sector. Burns counted Sir Arthur Conan Doyle and Teddy Roosevelt among his friends. Conan Doyle called him "America's Sherlock Holmes," a description that must have pleased Burns greatly. He'd badly wanted to pursue acting as a young man and still had a flair for self-dramatizing affectations, like the sword cane he frequently carried. With his jowly face and small prissy mouth, Burns did not look quite the part of dashing hero, but he was lucky to live in an age when newspapers still favored litho-graphic depictions over photographs. Artists of the time gave him a lean, flinty countenance that fit agreeably with his image as Amer-ica's No. 1 Crime Stopper.

Burns signed a contract with McClintock-Marshall, a company

that had been harder hit than most by the dynamiting and had a special interest in hunting down the perpetrators. Burns suspected ironworkers from the start—no great deductive leap there—but had little hard evidence until Peoria. Ortie McManigal's unexploded bomb led Burns and his detectives to a nitroglycerine wholesaler in Portland, Indiana. Clerks there recalled a customer named "J. W. McGraw," a short, florid-faced man who wore a cap. It was a pretty good description of Ortie McManigal.

At the end of September, Burns boarded a westbound train to attend a convention of his largest client, the American Bank Association. As fate would have it, the Great Detective was racing to Los Angeles at the very moment a massive explosion lit the skies over the dark city.

## OTISTOWN EXPLODES

Trade unionists didn't call the booming new city on the coast Los Angeles. They called it Otistown or, more completely, Otistown of the Open Shop. General Harrison Gray Otis, publisher of the *Los Angeles Times*, held no political office but he effectively ruled the city with his money and influence. He was an odd and cantankerous old man who had served in the Civil War and the Spanish-American War, and who continued to live in a perpetual state of combat readiness, dressing for work in uniform and mounting a small cannon on the hood of his car. He designed the headquarters of his newspaper to look like a medieval castle and named it "the Fortress," while his new mansion on Wilshire Boulevard was "Bivouac" and his staff of reporters and editors were "the Phalanx." General Otis occasionally drilled the Phalanx in the use of the fifty or so rifles he kept on hand in case of attack. Attack by whom? Why, his archenemy, of course: Organized Labor.

Otis had almost singlehandedly made Los Angeles the least

unionized city in the country. He despised unions. Since he knew the feeling was mutual, he fully expected union anarchists to target him and his empire. He became increasingly obsessed with self-defense over the summer of 1910, when laborites from San Francisco descended upon Los Angeles to make one last push to unionize the city. Otis may have been an eccentric but he was no paranoid. He had a good handle on how much some people wanted him dead.

Early in the morning of October 1, 1910, just a few minutes past 1 A.M., as the night staff prepared the next day's edition, an enormous blast rocked the *Los Angeles Times* headquarters. It tore through the south wall of the Fortress and blew out supports for the second floor, which collapsed under the burden of the linotype machines, which then fell through to the gas mains in the basement and severed them. Several more explosions occurred. The Fortress burned furiously. By the time the fire was extinguished the next morning, 21 people were dead and news of the explosion had raced around the country.

Otis was in Mexico at the time of the explosion, but he immediately returned to Los Angeles. He managed to put out an abbreviated paper the same day, using printing presses in his auxiliary plant. "UNIONIST BOMBS WRECK THE TIMES," exclaimed the paper's headline. There was as yet no evidence to implicate anyone, but Otis didn't hold back from shaking his fists and pointing his fingers. "O you anarchic scum, you cowardly murderers," he wrote, "you leeches upon honest labor, you midnight assassins, you whose hands are dripping with the innocent blood of your victims. . . ." Otis immediately headlined the explosion "The Crime of the Century."

Detective Burns was still aboard his westbound train when a porter woke him in his sleeping berth to hand him a telegram from the mayor of Los Angeles. The mayor informed Burns of the explosion and asked him to investigate on behalf of the city. Arriving in Los Angeles later the same morning, Burns immediately went to work. He caught a lucky break that first day when police discovered two unexploded bombs, one outside a window at Otis's home, another at the home of a local anti-labor business leader. The police accidentally detonated the Otis bomb, but they successfully disarmed and examined the other. The explosive agent on this device was dynamite rather than nitroglycerine, but otherwise the contraption bore a marked similarity to the infernal machine that Burns had recovered and examined in Peoria a month earlier. The detective wasted no time in announcing the perpetrators of this national outrage. It was, he was sure, the ironworkers.

Ortie McManigal was in Indianapolis at the time of the Los Angeles bombing. He first learned of it from a newspaper the following morning, or so he claimed. He paid a visit to union headquarters that same morning, where he found John McNamara "cheerfully" reading the news. The secretary-treasurer admitted that his older brother might have had something to do with the explosion. He then told McManigal that he wanted to follow up the blast in the west with "an immediate echo in the east." He instructed McManigal to take eight quarts of nitroglycerin and board a train to Worcester, Massachusetts, to blow up a depot under construction by the Phoenix Bridge Company. McManigal promptly set out to do as told.

As for James McNamara, McManigal did not see him again until early November. James had returned from the West Coast and was traveling under a new alias. He needed to lie low for a while, and McManigal, back from Worcester, wanted a vacation. The two men set off for a month-long hunting trip in the woods of northern Wisconsin. McNamara had gone a little "queer" since his Los Angeles venture. He was drinking heavily and looking even more anemic and ghoulish than usual. He told McManigal the story of his trip to Los Angeles: how he'd lent out his dynamiting services to a group of San Francisco radicals; that he never meant to kill so many people and was now terrified of getting caught; that he was haunted, certain that he was being watched wherever he went.

He had good reason to feel haunted. William Burns and company had been shadowing Ortie McManigal for weeks, ever since the Peoria bombing. Indeed, at the very moment that James was spilling his guts to Ortie, two detectives from the Burns Agency were camped nearby in the woods, posing as friendly fellow hunters. One Sunday afternoon near the end of the trip, McNamara made the mistake of posing for a photograph with these men. That photograph would soon become a key tool in Burns' investigation. Operatives would spread out across Los Angeles showing it to hotel and store clerks, asking questions and establishing McNamara's presence in the city before the explosion.

In the meantime, incredibly, both McManigal and McNamara returned to dynamiting. McManigal even carried out a Christmas Eve bombing in Los Angeles at the Llewellyn Iron Works. Burns detectives were hot on their trails the whole time but allowed the explosions to occur for the sake of evidence each crime generated. Finally, the detectives moved in.

On April 12, 1911, McManigal and McNamara arrived together in Detroit and registered at the Oxford Hotel under assumed names. The hotel lobby was packed with a theater troupe and no rooms were immediately available, so the men checked their suitcases—each loaded with explosives and guns—and started out for the street, planning to return a few hours later to retrieve their luggage and claim their room. They were suddenly surrounded by several Burns detectives. The detectives, who had no warrants, no jurisdiction, and no right of extradition, hustled them to a train station and whisked them out of town, effectively kidnapping them in the name of the law. Ortie McManigal, whose flair for confession was as advanced as his knack for dynamiting, cracked the moment Burns' men began to interrogate him.

Detective Burns had everything he needed now. With McManigal's confession in hand, he traveled to Indianapolis. There, on the evening of April 22, accompanied by local police and over a dozen of his own men, he burst in on a meeting of the executive board of the International Association of Bridge and Structural Ironworkers and arrested John McNamara. While several of Burns's men spirited the secretary-treasurer away, Burns and local police searched union headquarters through the night. They discovered, among other items, 100 pounds of dynamite in the basement. At a nearby barn rented by McNamara, they found a piano box packed with 17 sticks of dynamite and a couple of quarts of nitroglycerine.

Meanwhile, Burns's operatives drove McNamara by automobile to Terre Haute, Indiana, where they boarded a westbound Pennsylvania Flyer. In Dodge City, Kansas, the group changed trains to the California Limited. Already aboard that train, in another Pullman car, were McNamara's brother, James, and Ortie McManigal. Prevented from reading newspapers or talking to fellow passengers, John was probably the only person in the country who didn't know his brother was on the train with him. The arrest of all three men had been made public by now and their cross-country trip was causing a huge stir in the press, the *New York Times* calling it "one of the most remarkable trips ever made by officers with prisoners." By the time the three men arrived at the Los Angeles County jail in separate automobiles on the afternoon of April 26, 1911, an enormous crowd had gathered to glimpse them. Nothing as extraordinary or as exciting as this had ever happened in Los Angeles.

A few weeks after the McNamaras' arrest, a tall, stooped, unkempt figure walked into their prison cells and introduced himself. The man did not look much like a beacon of salvation, but to the McNamaras he must have seemed exactly that, for he was none other than the "Great Defender" himself, Clarence Darrow. Today, Darrow is best remembered for defending the science of evolution in the landmark Scopes Trial of 1925, but in 1911 he was America's favorite protector of the underdog and friend of the underclass. When union officials first approached him, Darrow was reluctant to take on the

McNamara case; perhaps he had an inkling of the grief it would bring him. Samuel Gompers, president of the American Federation of Labor (of which the ironworkers union was a member), implored him to reconsider, and he eventually did. He would have many opportunities to regret the decision.

Gompers and virtually every high official in the labor movement treated the McNamaras' arrest as a frame-up. They noted that the Fortress had been having problems with its gas system for weeks before October 1 and suggested this as the probable cause of the explosion. Some even hinted darkly that Otis himself planted a bomb as a ruse to defame unionists. Otis was a monster, Burns was a stooge, McManigal was a stool pigeon, the McNamaras were martyrs—this was the party line, and it wasn't just unionists who bought it. The McNamaras' arrest occurred at a moment when progressive ideas were taking root in an American public fed up with enormous cor-porations that treated workers like chattel, and the arrest of "the boys" struck a chord among many in the middle class. Progressives throughout the country rallied to the cause, holding fund-raisers and purchasing McNamara buttons and McNamara stamps. The highlight of many of these fund-raisers was a feature film about the McNamaras, in which two handsome young actors played the brothers. (Their bereaved mother and several union officials appeared as themselves.) In Los Angeles, marchers took to the streets by the tens of thousands. A Socialist, Job Harriman, ran for mayor and looked like a winner, thanks largely to pro-McNamara/anti-Otis fervor. A socialist mayor of Otistown? It must have seemed like a cruel joke—no, a demonic hallucination—to the General.

And then, just as the trial was about to get under way, the pro-McNamara machine came to a crashing halt. Clarence Darrow had come to realize, thanks largely to information provided by his spies on the prosecution team, that the evidence against the McNamaras was overwhelming. The brothers' only hope, he believed, was to make a deal with prosecutors and save themselves from the death penalty. On the afternoon of December 1, James pled guilty to the *Times* bombing. As for John, there was little evidence to connect him directly to the *Times* explosion, but there was plenty to prove he'd ordered McManigal's Christmas Eve dynamiting of the Llewellyn Iron Works. John pled guilty to this lesser charge.

"Please say to the papers that I am guilty, but I did what I did for principle, and that I did not intend to murder a man," James told reporters from his cell in the county jail that night. "When I set that bomb, I only meant to scare those fellows who owned the *Times*."

For the millions of Americans who had supported the McNamaras and contributed to their defense, the guilty plea was a kick in the stomach—a knife in the back. A reporter found Samuel Gompers looking "depressed and haggard" in a New York hotel lobby the day after the plea. Some conservatives suspected that Gompers had known of the McNamaras' guilt from the start—may even have had a hand in it—but Gompers insisted he was as shocked as the rest of the true believers. "We, who were willing to give our encouragement, our pennies, our faith, why were we not told all from the beginning? We had a right to know." In Los Angeles, Job Harriman, the Socialist candidate for mayor who had seemed such a sure bet only weeks earlier, was easily defeated by the incumbent. The labor movement in Otistown was finished.

James McNamara died in San Quentin prison in 1941 at the age of 59. John McNamara, released 20 years earlier, died two months later while attending a mine workers' rally in Montana. He was 57.

The McNamara trial nearly ruined Clarence Darrow. Conservatives despised him for representing the McNamaras, while liberals questioned his decision to let the brothers plead guilty. In January of 1912, Los Angeles prosecutors indicted Darrow for attempting to bribe one of the McNamara jurors. Only his famous eloquence saved him from jail. "Will it be the gray dim walls of San Quentin?" he woefully addressed the jury. "Oh, you wild insane members of the steel trust. . . . Oh, you bloodhounds of detectives who do your masters' evil bidding. Oh, you district attorneys. You know not what you do!" The jury acquitted him after 11 minutes, but it took him years to regain his reputation.

The ironworkers union still had an ordeal to face, too. Fifty-four high-ranking union members were indicted for their participation in the so-called "Dynamite Conspiracy" of the previous six years. Thirty-eight of these men were eventually found guilty, largely, again, due to testimony from Ortie McManigal. Herbert Hockin was given a six-year sentence. The union's president, John Ryan, got seven years.

The public, meanwhile, was left to wonder what exactly possessed the ironworkers. What had driven them to commit such wanton destruction? It's a question that would puzzle labor historians for years to come. For Louis Adamic, who wrote about the ironworkers in his 1934 study of industrial violence, *Dynamite*, the ironworkers' propensity to violence was best explained by their peculiar personalities. "Only men of great physical strength and courage became skyscraper men," wrote Adamic. "Putting their lives in daily danger as they did, they developed a psychology of recklessness and violence that people in less hazardous occupations may find difficulty in understanding." Ironworkers were naturally half-cocked, in other words. Compounding this tendency was their belief that they were in a fight for their union's survival. They were cornered rats— to mix Ortie McManigal's metaphors—with the instincts of a tiger.

Some members of the press, including the celebrated muckraker Lincoln Steffens, excused the ironworkers on the grounds that they were incited to dynamiting by the intractable steel erectors. This view was echoed in Luke Grant's 1915 study for the U.S. Commission on Industrial Relations: "They found themselves overmatched and, believing the existence of their organization was at stake, they hit below the belt in trying to turn the tide in their favor. If the union resorted to unfair and unlawful methods . . . the erectors were in a degree responsible." This is no doubt true. But whatever drove the ironworkers to use lethal force, absolution was, and remains, a tough sell. After all, the ends-justifies-the-means logic that made sense to the dynamiters of 1910 is the same logic that led terrorists to blow up the World Trade Center in 2001.

The McNamara case produced neither heroes nor martyrs, but it did mint a few winners. General Otis, of course, came off looking more like a sage than a crank. William Burns, the detective, was elevated to national fame. He wrote many articles about the case, published a book, saw himself portrayed in a Broadway play, and was later appointed by President Harding to run the country's Bureau of Investigation, precursor to the FBI. (As his assistant director, he named an ambitious 26-year-old agent named J. Edgar Hoover.) Ortie McManigal, the Great Confessor, didn't fare too badly, either. He'd been granted immunity for his testimony and was given a large sum of money by the NEA for his help in convicting the ironworkers. Afterward, he became a watchman in Los Angeles. He spent the last years of his life guarding the Los Angeles Bureau of Records, a building he'd once tried, and failed, to blow up.

## INTO THE ETHER

*Oh, a pioneer*
*Is the riveteer*
*Till his pinnacle scrapes the dome.*
*He swings away where the planets play.*
*The ether is his home.*
— THE BRIDGEMEN'S MAGAZINE, September 1909

At the end of September of 1911, as the McNamaras were preparing to go on trial, an ironworker named Morgan Richards, of 101 West 130th Street, entered the East 22nd Street station house in New York.

He was a large man, over six feet tall with a husky build. He approached the desk and asked the policeman there to call his wife for him. "What fer?" the cop asked. "Telephone to her yourself."

"No, you do it for me," pleaded Richards. "It'll be easier all around." He'd been mugged by a gang of seven men, he explained, and they'd stolen his week's wages. "It ain't the money, honest. What's worrying me is how the Missus will take it. Now, be a good fellow and call her up."

"GIANT FEARS HIS WIFE" read the headline in the next day's paper. The short article that followed was hardly newsworthy, but what editor could pass up such a delicious man-bites-dog twist? An iron-worker—a man who presumably feared nothing—terrified of his *wife*!

By the end of the first decade, the Ironworker had become a type. He was fearless, careless, defiant. He was the "Industrial Daredevil," as *Scientific American* tagged him in 1912, "a peculiar type of human being." He was "daring to a degree which is almost criminal," according to the *Literary Digest*. He was an outlaw, a wander-luster, a renegade from a class of men "as reckless with their money as they are with their lives." He was also, of course, a fighter. He was, for example, Arthur McGlade of East 178th Street, who appeared true to type in the *Times* in January of 1912. Like the hapless Richards before him, McGlade had run into a gang of thieves. They picked his pocket then attacked him on the platform of the Third Avenue El, unleashing the righteous fury of The Ironworker.

> "Take my $28, will you?" exclaimed the ironworker, as he dealt blows right and left.
>
> Other men passengers watched and women scurried from the platform to avoid the fight, but McGlade kept right on. With five blows he knocked down the five men, and as the first one rose to his feet the ironworker was ready for him again. Each time his huge fist whistled through the air there was a thud as it struck one of the five,

and a second thud as the young man who was struck hit the platform flooring. Presently two of the men lay on the platform where McGlade had knocked them, afraid to get up.

One of the others rose and tried to run away. McGlade caught him and threw him down the stairs after the first man. He seemed to like this idea, for before they could move he caught two of the others and tossed them down also. The two remaining jumped to their feet and took the steps at a couple bounds to escape the enraged ironworker.

McGlade stormed, shouting, about the platform, looking for more foes.

Now *that* was an ironworker. So was Joseph Eick, a foreman accidentally buried under 4,000 pounds of steel beams in 1915. As men scrambled to remove the beams from their presumably dead boss's body, they heard his voice calling from beneath the steel. "Easy, there! Easy, there. Now—one two three!" Eick directed the rest of the rescue operation from beneath the steel, and when the last beam was off, he stood up and brushed himself off. "I'm all right," he coolly announced. "It takes more than that to hurt an ironworker."

Between the tragedy of the Quebec Bridge and the infamy of the dynamiting campaign, ironworkers had been in the news a good deal lately. The great majority of the men, though, carried on in peaceful anonymity, building bridges and skyscrapers in ever tinier silhouette against the sky. Strikes continued in New York, but employers and ironworkers found ways around them. The big jobs were officially open shop, but union men worked alongside non-union men. They needed the job, and the erectors were happy to have them as long as they didn't make an issue of their affiliation. Many charges could be leveled against union ironworkers, but no one, with the exception of a few folks in the NEA, ever claimed they weren't capable and hard workers. The wage in 1911, about $4.80 an hour, wasn't much better than the union men had been making 10 years earlier, but it was still high by the standards of other blue-collar workers, most of whom still earned less than two dollars a day.

The ironworker was compensated, in part, for the risks he took, still considerable at the start of the century's second decade. In the fiscal year 1911–12, the international union paid out 124 death claims for a membership of about 11,000—over one percent of the members. Between 1910 and 1914, according to the Bureau of Labor Statistics, structural ironworkers suffered 12 deaths and 353.2 accidents per thousand workers—well over a third of the workforce killed or injured within four years. "The erection of structural steel," concluded the study's authors, "must be recognized as one of the most, if not the most, hazardous industrial operations" in the country.

The passage of New York State's workers' compensation law in 1914 was the single most important event in the work lives of ironworkers before the Second World War. Workers' compensation laws required employers to contribute to an insurance policy that would pay out automatically to an injured worker. The new law not only provided a financial cushion for injured ironworkers and their families, it also gave an incentive to employers to find ways to prevent accidents and keep insurance premiums low.

Meanwhile, the frenzy of steel construction in New York that had begun at the end of the previous century occasionally paused for economic readjustments like the Panic of 1907, but otherwise continued unabated. By 1910, four of the longest bridges in the world reached across the East River into Brooklyn and Queens. The tallest building in the world, the 47-story Singer Tower, was completed in New York in 1908—a huge leap skyward. Even for ironworkers acclimated to height, the "Singerhorn," as the building was popularly known, offered a new thrill, and at every chance they shinnied up the steel flagpole atop the tower. The foreman would return, wrote journalist Earnest Poole, to find "some delighted man-monkey high up on the big brass ball, taking a look out to sea."

The Singer Tower held the title as World's Tallest for less than a year. The Metropolitan Life Tower vaulted over it in 1909, rising to 50 stories, or 700 feet. Earnest Poole went up to visit the man-monkeys atop this building, too. Although these skyscrapers were built by huge corporations, the view that Poole described from above was graphically democratic:

> [L]ooking straight down through the brisk little puffs of smoke and steam, the whole mighty tangle of Manhattan Island drew close in one vivid picture: Fifth Avenue crowded with carriages, motors, and cabs, was apparently only a few yards away from tenement roofs, which were dotted with clothes out to dry. Police courts, churches, schools, sober old convents hedged close round with strips of green, the Tenderloin district, the Wall Street region, the Ghetto, the teeming Italian hive, lay all in a merry squeeze below: a flat bewildering mass, streets blackened with human ants, elevated trains rushing through with a muffled roar.

In the interest of mollifying a public still timid about skyscrapers, the new tall buildings were extremely well built, even overbuilt. Theodore Cooper had pushed the edge of the envelope with his Quebec Bridge, then fallen off it; the engineers of these buildings would take no such chances. They solidified the superstructures with ample diagonal bracing, making them very much like the triangulated trusses of a bridge. Any doubts about the strength of either the Singer or the Metropolitan towers were dispelled by a freak storm in 1912 that produced exactly the kind of winds that give engineers night sweats, with speeds sustaining 96 miles per hour. Both buildings survived perfectly intact.

Every bit as remarkable as the new heights were the newly achieved speeds of construction. The steel frames of tall buildings like the Singer and Metropolitan Life were erected in a matter of months. This was the era of "Taylorism," so called after Frederick

Taylor, the same efficiency expert who'd prescribed ox-like laborers for steel companies twenty years earlier. Taylor had recently published his best-selling book, *The Principles of Scientific Management*, and his ideas were very much in vogue. To do a thing efficiently, to not waste a step or a moment—this was the new American ideal in steel plants, in factories, in offices, even in homes, where housewives strove to Taylorize their domestic chores. "In the past the man was first," Taylor had written; "in the future the system must be first."

Taylor's vision of progress was blatantly dehumanizing, but to a writer from *Harper's Weekly* who visited a job site in 1910, the ironworkers did not seem to resent the push toward speed; rather, they seemed exhilarated by it. They took a "savage joy" in it, as gangs tried to outdo each other with feats of prowess. "They wait for nothing and obey no precedents in the building of the express skyscraper," wrote the man from *Harper's*. "The skyscraper is altogether an American institution. Its express speed of construction is also exclusively American, an expression of American enterprise, American inventiveness, American impatience and daredeviltry, American workmen."

One ironworker did complain mildly: "This going up at a story a day interferes with me social life. On that Thirteenth Street building there was a hotel within arm's-reach, and one day I got to talking with a pretty maid—through a window. Next day I had to talk down to her, and the next day I had to yell to her, and in two days more I had to say good-by. 'Good-by,' says she, 'Sorry to see you go; but I'll introduce you to my friend Katie who works on the tenth floor.' "

The future of the skyscraper, *Harper's* concluded in 1910, was not greater height, but greater speed: "The limit of height has been reached." But this was not quite so. Three years later, the Woolworth Building topped out at 792 feet, almost 100 feet higher than the Metropolitan Life Tower.

For Frank Woolworth, founder of the chain of five-and-ten-cent stores that bore his name, it wasn't enough for his building to be tall.

At the top of the Woolworth Building, 1914.
*(Brown Brothers)*

It had to be the *tallest*; the most extraordinary building ever constructed. To design it, Woolworth chose Cass Gilbert, one of the country's leading architects. Gilbert clad the towering steel frame in terra cotta and decorated it like a cathedral, complete with gargoyles and a Gothic portal. His building was to be the "Cathedral of Commerce," as the Reverend S. Parkes Cadman christened it in his foreword to a 1913 publicity brochure. "Just as religion monopolized art and architecture during the medieval epoch," wrote Cadman, "so commerce has engrossed the United States since 1865." This new building—or "Building," as publicity writers usually wrote it, with divine uppercase B—would be "the chosen habitation of that spirit in man which, through means of change and barter, binds alien people into unity and peace. . . ."

Fifteen years earlier, the sheer height of the Woolworth Building would have terrified most New Yorkers, but they were accustomed to skyscrapers now. They were assured, furthermore, that the Woolworth Building was the safest building ever made. It was fireproof, its elevators were accident proof. Its steel was stronger, too, for Bethlehem Steel had recently developed a technique of rolling wide-flanged shapes that could handle more stress than earlier shapes. As the brochure informed its readers, "it may be safely stated that a hurricane, blowing at 200 miles per hour, would not damage the framework of this Building in any way. Winds of such velocity are, of course, unknown."

Not even God Himself, in other words, could blow this thing down.

## THE GOLDEN AGE

Near the end of 1923, a Philadelphia trade magazine, *The Building Age,* sent a questionnaire to several hundred American men between the ages of 20 and 26. The goal of the survey was to gauge the young men's enthusiasm for the building trades. Its results distressed the editors. Only a third of respondents professed any interest in entering the trades, despite the fact that construction paid relatively well. Of the 70 or so who thought they might be willing to give construction a chance, 25 percent preferred bricklaying and 20 percent preferred carpentry. How many wanted to be ironworkers? Exactly 3 percent.

The real wonder, after 20 years of bad press, wasn't why so few young men wanted to be ironworkers, but rather: who were those 3 percent? What sort of man wanted to risk his life in a job infamous for killing and maiming its practitioners or to join a union infamous for thuggery?

As it turned out, those who took their chances were in for a wonderful ride.

There had been economic booms before, but never one quite like the one that took hold of America in 1923 and lasted seven strange and fabulous years. In the 1920s, America would produce roughly 45 percent of the manufactured goods in the world, the economy would grow an average of 6 percent a year, average incomes would rise over 40 percent, the number of automobiles in the country would approximately quadruple, and the stock market would grow by leaps and bounds.

To those who were living through it, nothing symbolized the economic exuberance of the age more perfectly than the buildings that began to rise from all the loose money and speculative real estate. Skyscrapers climbed up from the ground almost as fast as Model T's rolled off Henry Ford's assembly lines. And what Detroit was to the automobile, New York was to the skyscraper. By the end of the decade, half of the country's 377 skyscrapers—defined as buildings 20 stories or taller—would be in New York City, and nearly half the structural steel in the country would be shipping to New York.

To live in New York in the 1920s was to inhabit a world under feverish overhaul. A constant caravan of trucks carried steel from river barges to construction sites. Plumes of dust released by round-the-clock foundation digging wafted down the avenues, accompanied by the *rat-a-tat-a-tat* of pneumatic rivet guns, "commonly complained of more than any other source of noise," according to the *Times* in 1928. A promising solution, already in the works, was the "noiseless construction" of electric arc welding pioneered by Westinghouse. For the moment, though, the din of riveting was inescapable.

Equally inescapable was the fact that the Woolworth Building's reign as the world's tallest would not survive the boom. The only questions were when it would be surpassed and how high its successors would rise.

Economics was, as always, the ostensible reason to build high: as real estate prices rose, it only made sense for builders to add vertical square footage. That said, it wasn't always clear whether real estate prices were driving skyscrapers upwards or skyscrapers were driving real estate prices upwards. Because the capacity to build high on a plot of land automatically increased its value, builders *had* to build high to recoup real estate costs. "If laws were passed restricting the height of buildings here as height is restricted in London," wrote architect Harvey Wilson Corbett in 1929, "the price of our most valuable parcels of land would drop at least sixty percent."

Economics did not adequately justify very tall buildings in Manhattan in any case, for at a certain point the price of the structure canceled out any possible income to be derived from it. And economics did not explain why tall buildings continued to rise, ever more urgently, through the late '20s, even though the real estate market was already glutted with office space by 1927. Clearly, the bottom line wasn't driving the skyline.

The truth is, tall buildings told more about American swagger and one-upmanship than about the rational application of greed. This truth was demonstrated in the spring of 1929, when two buildings—or, more accurately, the egos of the men who financed and designed them—competed to vault past the Woolworth Building and claim the title as supreme master of the skies. One of these men, Walter Chrysler, founder and president of Chrysler Motors, had hired the architect William Van Alen to design an appropriate object of grandeur as his headquarters. No sooner had Van Alen finished his plans for an 808-foot tower than an architect named H. Craig Severance announced that his Bank of Manhattan building at 40 Wall Street would be 840 feet tall, or 32 feet higher than the Chrysler. As it happened, Severance and Van Alen were ex-partners who despised each other, so the competition to build the highest building in the world became intensely personal. Through the summer, the buildings rose, four miles apart. The architects fiddled with their plans and jockeyed for position. By autumn, the Bank of Manhattan appeared the winner at 927 feet. But Van Alen had a final trick up—or rather down—his sleeve: a stainless-steel pole, 185 feet long, that ironworkers secretly assembled inside a shaft in the center of the building's peak. On October 16, the ironworkers hoisted the pole out through the top of the roof. The Chrysler was now 1,046 feet tall, over a hundred feet taller than the Bank of Manhattan.

The press called the competition the "Race Into the Sky," but it hadn't been a race, exactly, for victory went to the highest, not the fastest. (In fact, the Bank of Manhattan had gone up much faster than the Chrysler.) What this competition really resembled was two boys standing back to back on their tippy-tippy toes, then brushing their hair up into a ducks' bill to gain a few inches on each other. There was nothing intrinsically significant about the outcome. The Chrysler Building "won" with a steel pole—an uninhabitable, decorative, eminently useless *pole*. How odd that skyscrapers, born 45 years earlier of practicality and common sense, had come to this.

But somehow this "race," and all that useless height, mattered. It captured the exuberance of the 1920s and seemed to suggest deeper truths about America, land of the skyscraper. Skyscrapers had graduated from mere real estate and become symbols—the primary symbol—of everything that was extraordinary about this country, including its ingenuity and its ambition, but also of what was a little scary and silly about it: the grown men up on their tippy-tippy toes, doing whatever it took to win.

A writer named Edmund Littell visited the Chrysler Building and the Bank of Manhattan while they were going up. For him, the most compelling participants in the "race" weren't the architects or the financiers, but the men who were out there on the steel. "Yes, here it is that real battles . . . are being waged, and here is where the romance of the skyscrapers is being worked out. Up there in his habitation of height and steel the ironworker heaves himself from one beam to another, upward, always upward—his shoulders bulging, his knees tense, but his face as placid as the blue sky only an arm's reach beyond him."

Never had there been a finer time to be an ironworker than in the late 1920s. Putting aside labor disputes for a moment, and ignoring the fact that most of the ironworkers were employed under open-shop conditions the union had been fighting against for years, the work was abundant and the money was good—$14 a day in New York by 1926, $15 a couple of years later. Itinerancy was a constant, but the travel had been eased considerably by automobiles, the inexpensive "flivvers" that ironworkers earned enough to own and fuel.

The work was less dangerous, too. Derrick floors were more likely to be planked, and men were less likely to engage in the perilous practice of riding loads up from the street. "Nowadays, of course it's different," commented a veteran ironworker named Bill Ritchie, who figured he'd seen about forty men fall to their deaths. "Hardly anyone gets hurt. Not what I call hurt." Ironworkers still suffered about twice as many accidents as general construction workers or coal miners, but the odds that a man would make it to old age were certainly better than they'd been when Bill Ritchie entered the trade.

The greatest difference in the now prolonged lives of ironworkers was how they were perceived by the public: with admiration and respect rather than fear and loathing. The whole city seemed suddenly enthralled by these high-steel men. Crowds gathered at every new steel frame to watch them walk beams overhead or illicitly ride loads of steel hundreds of feet over the street.

Journalistic emissaries from terra firma made frequent excursions skyward and brought back breathless reports for popular magazines like *Collier's* and *Literary Digest* and *The American Magazine*. The writers told tales of falls and near falls and related encounters with remarkably fearless men who, in the words of one writer, did "a good deal of strolling on the thin edge of nothingness." Their feats were prodigious. Even their appetites were prodigious. One iron-worker named Binzen, *Collier's* informed its readers, sat on a beam 38 stories above the ground and ate "four three-ply beef sandwiches, two bananas, two apples, a quarter of a four-story cake, a pint of black high-voltage coffee and a load of scrap eating tobacco."

In years to come, Indians and raising gangs would get star billing, but now it was Scandinavians and riveting gangs. The square-rigger days were long gone, but the squareheads still had it in their blood, or so they said, and every magazine story featured a "Swede" named Gunderson or Hagstrom or Sorenson. As for the riveting gangs, they were nothing new to Manhattan, but the higher the buildings rose, the more spectacular their feats appeared—the heater tossing his white-hot rivets in "hissing parabolas" *(Collier's)*, the catcher snatch-ing them from the air, as insouciant and consistent as Babe Ruth at Yankee Stadium. "There, in the windy reaches of the unfinished frame," wrote C. G. Poore in the *New York Times Magazine,* "they put on a show that most unfailingly delights the crowd below."

As magazines provided the public with close-up views of life on the girders, daily newspapers published stories of off-the-steel escapades that seemed to confirm the ironworkers' reputation as daredevils and lunatics. In 1925, Joseph Maloney, an ironworker from the Bronx, bet his friends a dollar that he could climb the brick façade of an apartment building. He'd almost made it to the fourth floor when police reached out and hauled him in through a window. He didn't get to keep his dollar but he got his name in the papers. The kind of man who would climb a brick wall for a dollar was a man born for exaltation in the 1920s.

Probably no ironworker expressed the spirit of the age more dra-matically, and more succinctly, than James Bennet. Bennet had been committed to the Manhattan State Hospital for the Insane on Wards Island after suffering delusions that he was a famous inventor. On an autumn morning in 1929, a few weeks before the stock market went into free fall, he escaped from the hospital and climbed up a pier of the Hell's Gate Bridge. "Stay where you are," the ironworker shouted at an attendant who tried to follow him. "I know what you are after. You want to lock me up so you can get my invention." For six hours, as a crowd of thousands watched from below, police chased Bennet through the steel superstructure of the bridge, but none of the officers could match his climbing skill. Finally, a policeman named Charles Saeger of the Marine Division snuck up on Bennet and grabbed him. The two men tussled for 10 minutes on a catwalk 135 feet over the deadly cross-currents of the East River. Several times, to the gasps of onlookers, they nearly tumbled off together, but at last Saeger managed to get the ironworker into an arm-lock and subdue him. Police tied Bennet up and lowered him from the bridge with a rope. "Gosh," said a woman spectator holding a baby, "that was better than a movie thriller."

In fact, the DeMille film company had already produced a movie about ironworkers in 1928, but it was more of a "farcical melodrama," as one reviewer put it, than a thriller. *Skyscraper* starred William Boyd as a riveter named Blondy working on a skyscraper with his best friend, Swede. They were "bang-'em and slam-'em rough neck riveters, flirting with death far above the street," according to the film's ad copy. The plot involved Blondy falling in love with a dancing girl, but the real subject of the movie was the high jinks of ironworkers. There were practical jokes and fistfights, harrowing close calls and, inevitably, death. It was not a good movie ("A wild attempt to glorify the steel riveter," is how the unimpressed *Times* dismissed it), but that hardly mattered. The age of the ironworker had arrived, not only in New York but all the way across the country in Hollywood, in the very city where ironworkers had been convicted, not so long ago, of extraordinary crimes.

## HEROES

A few weeks after the ironworker James Bennet climbed into the steel trestle of the Hell's Gate Bridge, the exuberance of the 1920s came to an abrupt end. The stock market crashed in late October and the economy tumbled wildly. In a matter of months, businesses shut their doors and thousands of workers found themselves on the street with nowhere to go and little to do but loiter on corners and watch the escapades in the air.

The ironworkers were lucky, at least initially. Many of the buildings conceived in the height of the boom were too far along to halt. Among these was the grandest and tallest of them all, the Empire State Building.

The Empire State Building was the brainchild of two immigrants' sons who rose to the height of power in New York. John Jacob Raskob was a prominent millionaire; Al Smith had been the governor of New York. The wisdom of adding 85 stories—2,158,000 square feet—of office space to a city that needed exactly none was questionable, but when it came to the construction of the building, the decisions of Raskob and Smith were generally sound. Their best decision was to hire the construction firm of Starrett Brothers & Eken.

The Starrett brothers, William and Paul, were living biographies of the skyscraper age. Born in Kansas, they moved as children to Chicago with their three other brothers (two of whom also became well-regarded builders). They were young men in Chicago as skyscrapers began to rise there. Both Paul and William eventually went to work for the George A. Fuller Company and moved to New York in time to help build the Flatiron Building. Since then, a Starrett had had a hand in nearly every important skyscraper in the city.

The Starrett brothers had a reputation for working fast; these were the contractors, after all, who managed to erect the steel of the Bank of Manhattan Building in three months. Now they resolved to outdo every record of construction they or anyone else had ever set. The average rate for setting steel in those days—it's still true today— was about two floors a week. The Starretts, with Post & McCord as their steel erector, intended to set four floors a week at the start, then five floors a week as the building rose and narrowed, and they intended to do this without resorting to costly overtime. The only way to succeed was with planning and organization, and with a force of ironworkers willing to work like hell.

Post & McCord hired two companies to fabricate the steel, American Bridge Company and McClintock-Marshall. The order for 57,000 tons of steel—almost 50 percent more steel than had been used in the Chrysler and the Bank of Manhattan *combined*—was the largest in history. U.S. Steel milled the shapes at its plants near Pittsburgh, then shipped them to the fabrication shops, where the columns and beams were cut and hole-punched to specifications. The steel was then shipped by rail to Bayonne, New Jersey, stacked and sorted, floated by barge to docks on the East River, and finally hauled by truck to 33rd Street and Fifth Avenue. Enormous derricks bowed and lifted whole loads in a single pick. As the building rose beyond 30 stories, relay derricks lifted the steel partway, then erection derricks lifted it to the top. From the moment the rolled steel came out of the mill to the moment the raising gangs slipped in the first temporary bolts, the journey took as little as 80 hours.

None of the Starretts' methods of construction were exactly revolutionary; most were techniques that had been honed since they were young men in Chicago, and since that day long ago when William Starrett hired Sam Parks to push his riveting gang. The incredible speed they achieved, as Paul Starrett acknowledged, was facilitated by the simplicity of the structure. The frame of the Empire State was made up of classic box-shaped grids, with lots of repetition from floor to floor. As a result, the builders could achieve an assembly line–like efficiency. In many ways, the Empire State was the ultimate triumph of Taylorism applied to construction. But this was a humanized version of Taylorism. The Starretts did not use men up and spit them out; indeed, they paid a good deal of attention to their employees' comfort and safety. Rumor had it that as many as 48 men died during the building's construction; in fact, just five men died, a remarkably low number for the day.

"[W]hile the theorists lament that the machine age is making robots and automatons of all men," wrote Margaret Norris after visiting the Empire State during its construction, "here is one type of workman, the steel man, the very spirit of the skyscraper, a direct product of the power age, whose personality the machine exalts." Ironworkers reconciled the two opposing ideas of a worker, one as an efficient automaton, the other as an autonomous individual of spectacular achievement. It was a combination that both capitalists and the proletariat alike could share, admire, and mythologize.

As it happened, the perfect mythmaker was on hand. He was Lewis Hine, a shy 56-year-old photographer who'd made his reputation years earlier photographing the poor and the vanquished inside coal mines, sweatshops, and overcrowded tenements. The assignment to photograph workers on the Empire State Building was an odd one for Hine, as his employers were the capitalistic builders. In lesser hands, the job might have amounted to that of corporate flak. Hine turned it into exhilarating art. He climbed out onto the steel with the ironworkers and dangled from a derrick cable hundreds of feet above the city to capture, as no one ever had before (or has since) the dizzy work of building skyscrapers. His subjects sit or stand on minuscule purchases, the street a thin gray strip below. They hang off guy wires and catch forbidden rides on the steel balls of derricks. To Hine, many of these men were "heroes," and he portrayed them in heroic poses, shirtless and musclebound, with strong jaw lines and sun-bleached hair.

One of Hine's heroes was a young connector named Victor Gosselin, known as "Frenchy." Born and raised in Montreal, Frenchy had

"Frenchy" on the Empire State by Lewis Wickes Hine.
*(Avery Architectural and Fine Arts Library,*
*Columbia University, New York)*

been an ironworker for 15 years when he got to the Empire State Building. Before that, he'd been a sailor, a lumberjack, and a deep-sea diver. He'd traveled all over the country, and to France and Persia. He'd been everywhere and tried everything. In Hine's photographs, Frenchy is shirtless and wears cut-off blue jeans that reveal scrapes and bruises on his legs. Why a connector, who slides up and down rusted steel columns all day, would wear shorts is beyond imagining, but there he is, riding the derrick ball, handsome and swashbuckling, a half grin on his face. In one shot, his cut-off shorts ride up his legs like a chorus girl's.

"It's funny about this business," Frenchy said one afternoon while chomping a huge steak sandwich on the edge of the 84th floor. "Everybody seems to think you have to be a superman or something to work on steel. Of course, it ain't no picnic, but then there's lots of jobs I'd pass up for this. I wouldn't wanna be no taxi driver, for instance. Looka them down there, dodging in and outa that traffic all day long. A guy's apt to get killed that way."

Frenchy himself had come close to getting killed in falls several times. He'd seen dozens of men die. He'd seen many men lose their nerve. And what did his wife think of his work?

"She don't think nothin' about it," shrugged Frenchy. "You don't see Lindbergh's wife telling him he can't fly around in airplanes, do you? All she ever said about it was, 'Good-by, baby; don't get hurt.'"

Sometimes titled "Lunchtime on a Beam" or simply "Men on a Beam," this famous photograph was shot in late September of 1932, 800 feet over Sixth Avenue during the construction of the RCA Building, as part of an elaborate Rockefeller Center publicity effort. It is often taken, incorrectly, for a Lewis Hine photo; the identity of its true photographer is unknown. As for the identity of the ironworkers, many Mohawks are convinced that the fourth from the left is Joe Jocks of Kahnawake, while Newfoundlanders insist that the shirtless man in the middle is Ray Costello of Conception Harbour. Captions on other photographs taken that same day identify the three men on the far left as John O'Rielly [sic], George Covan, and Joseph Eckner. The shirtless man whom Newfoundlanders believe to be Ray Costello is identified elsewhere as Howard Kilgore (though people who knew Costello swear it's he) and the next three are identified as William Birger, Joe Curtis, and John Portla. The name of the man on the far right, drinking from a flask during Prohibition, is not recorded.

*(The Rockefeller Center Archive Center)*

# EIGHT

# Fish

Joe Lewis sat in the kitchen of the small row house in Park Slope, Brooklyn, resting his meaty forearms on the Formica tabletop. As his wife, Beverly, looked on beside him, he opened and closed the fingers of his right hand, clenching a fist, then letting it go. "I'll tell you what it's like," he said. "It's like you're playing ball, right? And the ball comes in and hits you on the fingers. Your hand goes all numb, right? That's how mine is all the time. It's not so bad. Just strange, really."

Outside the air was muggy and sooty, but here in the kitchen it was cool and dim and smelled faintly of Pine Sol. Seven men usually boarded in the row house without benefit of female company. They took turns cleaning and thought they did a pretty nice job of it. Then one of their wives would drop in, Snow White–like, and discover dirt in places it had never occurred to the men to look. Since Beverly arrived a few weeks earlier to visit her injured husband, the auto magazines were neatly stacked, the curtains were laundered, the floors were mopped, the windows were washed. To Joe, it was still a revelation that windows needed washing. "Windows?" he would say to Beverly. "We don't wash *windows*."

Joe and Beverly had the row house to themselves. The other men who boarded here—this included Joe and Beverly's three grown sons, Bob, Joe Jr., and Rickey—had gone back home to Newfoundland for the summer. Beverly would be returning home soon, too. Then Joe would be here alone in the doldrums of August, filling out endless paperwork, waiting for doctors and lawyers to tell him when he could get back to work. He'd already seen practically everything the Discovery Channel, his favorite, had to offer. Once a day he went on a walk, following doctor's orders, lugging his numb appendage through the borough of Brooklyn.

Nine months earlier, Joe had been working as a signalman in the raising gang on the Ernst & Young building on Times Square with Brett Conklin. The job had been going well, and the gang had shaped up nicely. They'd started several floors behind, but by Christmas they'd caught up and passed the other gang. Then Jeff, the tagline man, got hurt; a beam hit him in the chest and his ankle twisted sharply and snapped in the corrugation of the decking. Two months later, Brett had his accident, falling from the column on that dreary February morning. Two months after that, it was Joe's turn—the third man in the five-man gang to be disabled within six months.

Joe's accident occurred on a May morning on the corner of 59th Street and Sixth Avenue, just east of Columbus Circle (and the Time Warner Center), across the street from Central Park. What remained of the old gang from the Ernst & Young building had come here to add a few floors to a luxury hotel. Joe's brother-in-law, Billy Moore, was superintendent. Joe's sons, Rickey and Joe Jr., were on the job, too. They'd all wake up in the row house in Brooklyn and travel to work together—a big happy family.

"So I'll tell you what happened," said Joe now, speaking in his thick Newfoundlander's brogue as he sat with his wife at the kitchen table in Park Slope. "We were finished up on top. We come down and we were shagging around some stairwells. We had the stairwells planked over, but this weren't that really good plank. You'd put 'em across a long span and there'd still be a give to them, right? So we put plywood on 'em to make sure we wouldn't go through. Well, I walked toward the wall, and there was a couple planks with no plywood—and soon as I stepped on 'em, I was gone. They snapped in two, and I went through the floor. As I was going down, I grabbed onto a big brace. It was just luck, I guess. I was reaching to grab something and that's where I hung up. I held there. I couldn't get back up because my arms—the strength was gone. Below was the floor, a good 15 feet, easy, that. When I look up, the guys are looking down at me. They say, "You all right?" I say, "I'm all right, man, but I can't let go. If I let go, I'll break my legs."

There wasn't much the men could do but watch. Joe managed to work his way down the diagonal of the X brace and get to the column. He slid down the column to the floor. The other men insisted that he go to the hospital, but Joe refused. He felt fine. So he went back to work.

Ten days later, something strange began to happen to his arm. It felt tingly when he woke up that morning, and as the day wore on, it became increasingly numb, and by supper he could hardly feel it at all. The nerves had apparently been damaged. Joe was not a tall man, but he was stout, nearly 230 pounds, and as he'd reached out and grabbed the diagonal section of brace to stop his fall, his right hand caught first on the higher end. That arm had taken most of Joe's falling weight. The doctors subjected the arm to a battery of high-tech tests—MRI, nerve scans, CAT scans—and one rather medieval treatment that involved Joe dipping his hand in a bucket of hot candlewax. Joe had no idea what this was supposed to accomplish, but he was fairly sure it accomplished nothing, since he still could not feel a thing.

Beverly sat next to Joe at the table and listened to his story quietly. They had known each other most of their lives, since they were children in Newfoundland. But, like many Newfoundlander couples, they had spent more of their lives apart than together, in different countries and different environments. You could see it in their complexions. Hers was pale and smooth, evidence of a life spent on an island that was moist and foggy most of the time. Joe's face was tanned and lined, his cheeks ruddy. As Joe spoke of his accident, Beverly's expression remained placid. Men getting hurt at ironwork was something she knew all too well.

"I was used to it," she said when Joe got up to leave the kitchen for a moment. "My father was at it, and my brothers. Both my grandfathers. My father broke both his legs once. The only thing that saved him was he fell onto another guy. Then my brother Terry got hurt. How many floors did Terry fall, Joe?"

"Terry didn't fall, toots," said Joe, returning. "Terry got jammed up with a column. It was wintertime. One big huge column lying on top of another, and the skids—those wood pieces between them—must have been frozen. The column slid and it happened he was close by. It almost cut his leg off."

Joe Lewis was not a man to complain. The way he saw it, most ironworkers got injured sooner or later, and he had managed 37 years in the business without so much as a—well, come to think of it, there was that one time he fell fifteen feet from a ladder. Then there was that time a beam rolled over onto his fingers and cut the tips off, but the tips had all been collected and sewn back on, good as new. Those injuries were hardly worth mentioning. Even this newest affliction, this numbness that began in his hand and crawled up his forearm, wasn't so bad, not compared to what happened to some.

Joe tried not to think too much about the worst part of it, what it meant to his music. He was a gifted musician who played nearly every stringed instrument—fiddle, banjo, guitar. He was fairly good on accordion, too, and could make his way around a piano keyboard. For much of his life he'd played in bands after work, all over Canada and America. Country, Irish, rock. Joe liked all of it. Here in Brooklyn, he and his brothers—they called themselves the Lewis

Brothers—had played regular gigs at a few pubs and clubs. That would have to end now, at least temporarily. Joe could still bow and he could strum rhythm, but he could no longer pick or finger the strings. Everything felt off, strange, like it wasn't quite him doing the playing. This was a cruel irony. Music was the thing he'd always relied on to take his mind off his troubles. Now, when he really could have used it, it was unavailable to him.

And here was another irony: For the first time in his adult life, Joe had an opportunity to be home in Newfoundland for a long stretch. He'd yearned for this for years. What better time to go back than now, since he could not work anyway? But the doctors and lawyers, the endless appointments and paperwork, stuck him here in Brooklyn in August. That was especially cruel.

## THE ROCK

Newfoundland is a place out of whack with the rest of North America. Separated from the continent by the Gulf of St. Lawrence and the Cabot Strait, the island is closer to Europe than to most of Canada or the United States. By car, Brooklyn to Newfoundland is a three-day journey, east-by-northeast along the seaboard of New England, then eastward across New Brunswick and Nova Scotia, then due east by 16-hour ferry across the North Atlantic. By the time a traveler arrives in the port of Argentia, he has covered almost 1,400 miles, is as near to Greenland as to Brooklyn, and is one and a half hours ahead of Eastern Standard Time. Newfoundland is one of a handful of places on earth where the time, relative to Greenwich Mean, runs on the half.

Guidebooks call the landscape of Newfoundland "rugged." Newfoundlanders themselves call their island the Rock, because that's essentially what it is, a raw convulsion of ocean crust punched up by the same tectonic forces that gave rise to the Appalachian Mountains to the southwest. Newfoundland is a hard, unforgiving land, the poorest province in Canada, but it is also a profoundly beautiful place. Sheer cliffs drop off into the icy green North Atlantic. Rivers tumble out of the highlands into the bays. Saltbox houses cling to rocky shores. All of this makes for dramatic and stunning vistas. Unfortunately, visitors to the Rock seldom get to enjoy these vistas. Newfoundland comes with a few catches, and one of them is fog. The fog comes in wisps, in scrims, in shrouds and blankets. Newfoundlanders have many words and phrases to describe its varieties. "Mauzy" means warm and foggy. "Capelin weather" means foggy and drizzly and cold. "RDF" means rainy-drizzly-foggy.

Newfoundland English is filled with colorful locutions, all pronounced in a brogue that is a frequent source of puzzlement and amusement to off-islanders. The vowels are thick, and whole sentences are often mashed into a single extended diphthong climaxing in a contraction. So, for instance, instead of a straightforward query like "How is he doing?," you might get something like "Owsee gettin' on, b'ys?" ("B'y" being the Newfoundland equivalent of "man" or "dude" in American slang.)

Newfoundlanders may be frequently unintelligible to off-islanders, but they have an admirable way of saying exactly what they mean. This practice is conveyed in the names their ancestors chose for the bays and coves around which they live, a geographic index of regret and resignation: Bay of Despair, Chance Cove, Cuckold's Cove, Deadman's Bay, Gin Cove, Mistaken Point, Mosquito, Stinking Cove, Useless Bay, Witless Bay.

Joe Lewis comes from the more auspiciously named Conception Bay near the northeastern tip of Newfoundland, on the Avalon Peninsula. Conception Bay is surrounded by hills of black spruce and butte-like humps of rock that Newfoundlanders call tolts (pronounced "towts"). Compared to much of Newfoundland, the topography of Conception Bay is gentle, even soothing. The bay is almost 20 miles across at its mouth, but narrows at the head to small coves that appear as enclosed and protected as mountain lakes. Six small towns cluster around the coves. The names of these towns, east to west, are Chapel Cove, Harbour Main, Holyrood, Avondale, Conception Harbour, and Colliers. Most of these six towns are furnished with a white Catholic church, a red brick post office, a tavern, and not much else. Any one of them you could careen through on the curvy two-lane coastal road, Route 60, and experience only the dimmest sense you'd passed a town at all. Avondale is the second largest of the towns. It's got a white Catholic church, a red brick post office, and a tavern, but it also boasts the only restaurant for miles around. The restaurant is a small diner in a railway car next to the old train depot. The specialty of the house is fried cod tongue.

The largest of the towns, and the most picturesque, is Conception Harbour, Joe Lewis's town. Conception Harbour is set on the western shore of a cove. The church, Our Lady of Saint Ann, marks its center. Everything north of the church is known as Up-the-Bay. This includes the old fishing hamlets of Bacon's Cove and Kitchuses and the high fields of bush and grass beyond. Standing on these hills on a rare clear summer day, you can often see schools of pilot whales—Newfoundlanders call them potheads—knitting in and out of the water below, chasing capelin fish.

South of the church—Down-the-Bay, that is—Church Street crosses Route 60, forming an intersection that locals call the Cross. This is the practical, if not the spiritual, focus of the town. Just beyond the Cross, Route 60 rises sharply up Lewis's Hill. Larrasey's general store and the small red brick post office are on the right. Higher up the hill is a funeral home, and a little beyond it, the Conception Harbour Tourist Inn, a bed-and-breakfast run by the town's mayor, Marg O'Driscoll, and her husband, Paul. Locals refer to the crest of the hill as the Pinch, probably because it rises like a fold of pinched skin. On the other side of the Pinch, at the bottom of a long steep grade, is the town of Colliers.

Across the street from Larrasey's store—heading back down toward the Cross now—is the tavern. It used to be Doyle's but is now Frank's, though pretty much everybody still calls it Doyle's. It is a cavernous, windowless hall, room enough for hundreds if there's a band playing or a dance. On most nights, though, half a dozen patrons mill around the small bar at the front. The bartender is a pretty, soft-spoken woman named Lorraine Conway, who happens to be Joe Lewis's sister. Lorraine is somewhat famous around the head of the bay for having gone to Nashville a few years back and cut a country-western album. Some evenings she gets up on the little stage near the back of Frank's and sings about found love and broken hearts in a sweet soprano. Her husband is often away in Alberta, 2,500 miles to the west. Like so many absent men from around here, he's an ironworker.

Until you step into Frank's and listen to the conversation and notice the Local 40 decals on the wall behind the bar, there are few signs around the head of the bay to tell you of the remarkable link between this place and New York City. There is little outward evidence to suggest that this tiny speck on the map, these six towns, a few square miles with a total population of several thousand, have produced a huge percentage of the men who erected the steel infrastructure of Manhattan, not to mention other American cities. Indians from Kahnawake may have gotten most of the attention from the press, but Newfoundlanders and their offspring—other ironworkers call them "Fish"—have made up the backbone of the New York local for many years.

You don't have to go into Frank's to recognize this fact. You could, alternatively, walk up to the cemetery at the top of Colliers Hill, behind the church. Much of the cemetery is overgrown with wildflowers, but if you push them aside you can see the names on the gravestones: Burke, Cole, Conway, Costello, Doyle, Kennedy, Kenny, Lewis, Moore, St. John, Wade. Stop by any steel job in Manhattan and you will hear these same names today. They belong now to the grandsons and great-grandsons of the earlier Newfoundlander ironworkers. Most of these younger men have never seen Conception Bay, having been born and raised in Park Slope or Bay Ridge or in the suburbs around New York. Once their fathers and grandfathers left Newfoundland, they never really came back. This was just another of Newfoundland's catches. The island was a kind of paradise. But the only way to live here was to go away.

Conception Harbour, Newfoundland.
*(Photo by the author)*

## JIGGING AND SWILING

John Cabot, the Spanish-born English explorer, was among the first Europeans to see the rocky fogbound island when he sailed across the Atlantic in 1497. He was hoping to find a western route to Asia. What he discovered instead, and promptly claimed for England, was this "newe founde lande." Though the island looked austere and desolate from his ship, he immediately noted the attraction that would draw people here for the next several centuries. "The sea is swarming with fish," Cabot reportedly claimed on his return, "which can be taken not only with the net, but in baskets let down with a stone." The fish were cod, and by the middle of sixteenth century fleets from France, Portugal, and Britain were making frequent summer trips to the Grand Banks near Newfoundland to scoop them up. While the shoals off Newfoundland became the world's premiere fishery, the island itself served mainly as a convenient place to dry the fish. Nobody seemed to seriously entertain the idea of living there.

The first true immigrants to Newfoundland came from the British Isles near the end of the eighteenth century. Some of them came from rural England, but the great majority came from the southeastern counties of Ireland. They were a seafaring people who probably arrived as crewmen on English fishing vessels, then remained out of some brave and foolish notion they could scrape a living out of these rocky harbors and exquisitely cold waters. They settled the outlying coves around St. John's, the "outports," as they are still called, on the Avalon Peninsula. Among these early outports was Cat's Cove, probably named after a cougar who lived in the area. In 1870, the people of Cat's Cove changed the name of their small outport to Conception Harbour.

It's an indication of the hardship these people must have come from that this—this *rock*—seemed to offer something more promising. Farming wasn't really an option in Newfoundland. The land was too rocky, the soil too shallow, and the growing season too brief to cultivate anything more elaborate than a vegetable garden. The only way to earn a living here was by fishing.

The cod fishery was summer and autumn work, from June to October. The men would sail out to the Grand Banks in schooners, then lower themselves to the water in small dories, two men per boat, and "jig" for fish with a small lead ball and hook. They would jig until the dory was filled with as much fish as it could hold. Then it was a matter of gingerly making the trip back through the swells to the schooner without sinking—assuming the fishermen could find the schooner. Getting lost in a squall was easy. Fog, too, was a constant danger. Every time a man went out to the Grand Banks, he stood a good chance of never coming home.

Early spring was the seal fishery. Sealing, or "swiling," as Newfoundlanders call it, was an even more treacherous business than cod fishing. The men would sign on for a berth on a schooner out of Conception Bay or St. John's and sail "down to the Labrador"—actually, hundreds of miles to the north. Starting out in early March, the schooners battered their way into the loose ice pack flowing south out of the Baffin Islands. For a short season, no more than a few weeks, mother seals gave birth to their young on the moving pans of ice. The baby seals, called whitecoats, were the prey of the hunt.

Once the schooners were lodged in the ice pack, the men went over the side and hiked for miles on a rough landscape of pressure ridges and slushy troughs, jumping from ice pan to ice pan, often venturing beyond sight of the ship. Finally, they would spy the seals, thousands of whelping pups grouped together in herds—"whelping ice," it was called. Killing the whitecoats was a matter of walking up to them and whacking them on the head with a gaff. That was the easy part. Afterward, the men gutted the carcasses with sculping knives, then hauled the hides back to the boat as the sun fell and the sky turned dark, with the prospect of sleeping on a ship oozing seal blood and grease. The ship would have tens of thousands of pelts stowed aboard before the trip was done, as many as 50,000 in a bumper season.

The seal hunt was a gory and brutal business, and it did little to enrich the men who partook in it, since most of the profit went to the ship owners and the captains. Sealing was also, on the face of it, ludicrously risky. Ships routinely got locked in the ice. When this happened, the crew would try to tow the ship by rope and hand to freedom, exploding dynamite to loosen the surrounding ice. This failing, they might abandon the ship and try to walk to land, many miles over drifting ice. Sometimes they made it, sometimes not.

Men died on the seal hunt even barring these larger calamities. A storm might come up and they would lose their way back to the ship and freeze to death out on the ice field. Or they might find themselves on a pan of ice that had broken free from the pack, surrounded by dead seals, floating out to oblivion. Altogether, it was a hard, dangerous, ruthless business. It was also excellent training for an ironworker.

## THE HIGH LIFE

No one knows exactly when the first Newfoundlander left the water and took to ironwork, but the turn of the last century is a good bet. A ship from Conception Harbour or St. John's probably sailed down the New England seaboard, to the "Boston states" with a catch of fish to sell. Aboard that ship was a restless young man from the head of Conception Bay. When his ship docked in Boston, or perhaps it was New York or Philadelphia, he jumped off during shore leave, took a stroll around the city, and marveled at the tall buildings and sweeping bridges. He found his way to a skyscraper under construction, watched the men work, inquired how much they earned, and liked the sound of it. He let the ship sail home without him.

The Newfoundlander would have been a natural for the work.

Like the Scandinavians who were already common in the trade by 1900, he would have possessed the sea legs and the rigging skills that were so important to the job. He also would have been accustomed to working hard under risky circumstances and not fretting too much about it. Compared to hauling seal carcasses across a shifting ice field in the Labrador, or climbing a ship's mast on a stormy sea, the feat of balancing on a steel beam several hundred feet above the streets of New York was a cakewalk.

The lore around the head of Conception Bay has it that the original Fish ironworker was Frank "Red" Treahy (pronounced Treddy) from Conception Harbour. Those who later worked with Treahy say he was a tireless and prodigious ironworker, the kind of man who would show up an hour early at a job site and leave an hour late; the kind of man, in other words, employers love. According to lore, Treahy sent word back home of this new lucrative trade, and other men followed him to the States. When he vouched for a fellow Newfoundlander, contractors took his word.

Whether on Treahy's invitation or their own initiative, other Newfoundlanders were working steel in the States by the turn of the century. Evidence of this hangs on a living room wall in Bayside, Queens, at the home of a retired ironworker named Jack Costello and his wife, Kitty. Like Joe Lewis, Jack Costello was born and raised in Conception Harbour. Unlike Joe, he moved to New York as a young man and has lived there as an American citizen ever since.

When a guest visits, Jack and Kitty steer him to a wall on which hang three framed photographs. Jack points to an old black-and-white print of two serious-looking young men posed formally in a photographer's studio. They sport thick moustaches and identical uniforms, probably in anticipation of a Labor Day parade. Badges on their lapels read "International Association of Bridge and Structural Ironworkers." The men appear to be in their late 20s.

"His name was Tim Costello," says Jack. "He was my grandfather."

"And the taller man on the right was Charles Newbury," says Kitty. "He was my grandfather."

"My grandfather," continues Jack, "was born in Conception Harbour in 1869. He can't be older than thirty there." Meaning the photograph must have been taken around 1900.

"Your grandfathers knew each other?"

"Oh, they were good friends," says Kitty, clearly relishing her guest's astonishment.

"Now look at this," says Jack, pointing to another studio photograph. Two different young men, some years later. "This was taken in the twenties, we think in New York. These are our fathers."

"So your fathers were friends, too?"

"*Best* friends," says Kitty, grinning.

Finally, hanging between these two old black-and-white photographs, is a color photograph from the mid-1990s. This one shows Jack and Kitty's three sons, two of whom are currently ironworkers. A concise history of Newfoundland ironworkers—four generations, including Jack himself—is contained in that living room in Bayside.

Jack Costello's grandfather, Tim Costello, deserves as much credit as anyone for stocking the trade of ironwork with Newfoundlanders. Even as he worked steel in New York, he returned home often enough to sire nine children. Seven of the nine were boys, and every one of them grew up to be an ironworker. Each of these seven sons then had a large family, and all of *their* sons—Jack and his many first cousins—became ironworkers in the 1940s and 1950s. By the time Jack and Kitty married in 1960 and started raising little ironworkers of their own, the name Costello was ubiquitous among ironworkers in New York.

This same pattern of proliferation occurred in other large Catholic families from the head of Conception Bay. They sent five or six boys at a time to Boston or Philadelphia or New York to become ironworkers. Whichever city the men settled in, they tended to lodge near each other. In Brooklyn, young men who had grown up a mile or two apart at the head of the bay pressed into rooming houses around Ninth Street and Fifth Avenue. Many of the married men had left their families back home, but others brought their wives and children along, and together they made a Little Newfoundland neighborhood in Park Slope: the bars where the men gathered after work, the living rooms and kitchens where they socialized on weekends, St. Thomas Aquinas church on Sundays. One of the peculiarities of the arrangement was that men who left their families back in Newfoundland came to know their fellow Brooklyn Newfoundlanders better than they knew their own wives and children. So while young Kitty Newbury, born and raised in Brooklyn, saw her future father-in-law nearly every weekend—she called him Uncle Willie—Jack Costello, growing up in a house on the Pinch, saw his own father but once a year.

The married men must have experienced occasional carnal temptations, 1,400 miles from home and wives 11 months of the year, but the presence of other Newfoundlander families, and the ties to home they represented, tended to keep the men on even moral keels. As for the wives back home, there was little chance of their straying from the bonds of matrimony. Their workloads, as they singlehandedly raised large broods in small houses without benefit of electricity, running water, oil heat, or refrigeration—while also tending vegetable gardens, caring for livestock, and making nearly every financial and parenting decision alone—would have made the very idea laughable. In any case, there were few men around other than the priest, who must have been pleased knowing that when sex did occur, it was demonstrably procreational. You could plot a man's visits home by his children's birthdays.

At mid-century, as post-war America marched steadily toward its modern destiny of steel and automobiles and electronics, the people of Conception Harbour continued to live a kind of rural existence most Americans had left behind in the nineteenth century. Cars were rare and roads were dirt. Fires and kerosene lamps provided indoor light, and the only radio in town was a battery-operated device owned by Master Keating, the school headmaster. Electricity was ten years off. So was plumbing. Medical care was rudimentary. Doctor O'Keefe from Avondale, the only physician for miles around, doubled as the dentist, pulling teeth without novocaine. Babies were delivered at home by Agnes Walsh, the midwife.

It was Agnes Walsh who delivered Joe Lewis on July 4, 1945, in an upstairs bedroom of a small white saltbox, just down the street from the house where Joe's mother lives today. At the time of Joe's birth, his mother, Bride, was a pretty young woman, barely 20. His father, Moses, was a 28-year-old ironworker.

Joe began his education in a one-room schoolhouse on the Pinch. Older boys attended Master Keating's Academy near the church, while older girls attended the convent school. Discipline was strict and harsh, the slightest infraction met by a sound strapping. Greater infractions were handled by the priest, Father Casey, the voice of patriarchal certitude in a place where adult men were scarce.

For all the punishment and privation, life was hardly dour. On the contrary, people who grew up in Conception Harbour remember it as an idyllic place. Children were free to wander as they pleased, to fish and swim and climb trees in search of robins' eggs. In August, the annual garden party drew people from all over the head of the bay to the church lawn. Winters were magnificently cold and snowy and brought different excitements. There was skating on Healy's Pond and sledding down Lewis's hill or over the other side of the Pinch into Colliers. At Christmas, gifts were rare but fathers came home and pigs were slaughtered, so for once there was meat instead of tiresome fish.

Joe Lewis, like most of the children in town, did not see much of his father. Even when Moses Lewis was home from ironworking he spent most of his time cutting firewood for the long winter. Two hundred years of human habitation had stripped the shore clean of trees, so Moses and the other men woke before dawn and rode horseback inland for several hours to the forest. By the time they cut the wood and hauled it back home, the December sky was well past dark.

But the moments Joe spent with his father he would not forget, for Moses Lewis—Mose, everybody called him—was one to leave an indelible impression. He was a high-spirited, fun-loving man, "always jolly and laughing, steady-go," as Joe recalls. "And everybody that knew him, they'd say, 'Oh, your father, he was something else, he was some fellow to be around.' "

One of Mose's friends had a car, among the first in town, and Joe remembers how as a small boy he'd squeeze into the rumble seat in back with his father and they'd drive out to Bacon's Cove, where his father was born, speeding along the church road on the high bluff above the sea, laughing and singing. There was always singing when Mose Lewis was around. He loved to sing, and was much admired for his voice. One ballad Joe recalls his father singing, called "Babe in the Woods," told the story of a mother searching for her lost children. It was 46 verses long and took over half an hour to complete. His father knew every word.

Both of Joe's parents were gifted musicians, so it was no surprise that their children proved to be quick studies. Moses taught Joe, the eldest of the ten children, how to play the fiddle. He started him on a simple jig, "Maple Sugar." Joe picked it up effortlessly and he, in turn, helped the younger ones learn. On Saturday evenings, Mose would chug up the hill to Doyle's tavern and return home with a dozen friends, men and women, and they would gather in the kitchen around a pot of soup and sing. Much of the singing was a cappella, but when the adults wanted instrumental accompaniment, they turned to Joe and his siblings. The children would take turns playing fiddle or accordion, and afterward one of the men would say, "Come here, little fellow, 'tills I give ya some money," and hand Joe or one of the others a coin. Joe loved music, and he liked the idea of making money from music. He thought that instead of becoming an ironworker, like his father, perhaps he'd be a musician when he grew up.

On a summer day in 1958, Joe and two friends walked out to the great blueberry patch at the Cat Hill Gullies, about seven miles inland from the sea. Joe, now 13, had recently become interested in girls, and he and his friends had taken to hanging out in the shadows of the big stone tolt that jutted up along the road between Avondale and Conception Harbour. Teenagers would congregate and stroll along the lane under the tolt, flirting and teasing. Joe and his friends had set their sights on a few pretty Avondale girls they'd met under the tolt. When the boys caught wind of the girls' plan to go blueberry picking in the Cat Hill Gullies, a cluster of ponds and thickets, they conspired to try a little blueberry picking themselves.

"Oh, jeez, they had big buckets already full with a few gallons by the time we got there," recalls Joe 43 years later. "We only had little cans, little bean cans, probably not even a pint. We were just going to chase 'em, that's all. We started chatting and following them around in the berries. Well, I guess they knew what we were about, and told us to go on back home. 'Go on and get a bucket,' they said, 'never mind your bean cans.' Before we goes, though, I spoke to her. I don't remember what I said. Probably something foolish." The girl to whom he uttered his foolish words had auburn hair and freckles, and her name was Beverly Moore.

Joe wasn't sure he was in love—he was just a kid, after all—but he would never regret that walk to the blueberry patch at Cat Hill Gullies. He had his sweetheart, he had his music, and for the next two years, he was as contented as a boy could be.

Joe was visiting his friend Frankie Mahoney's house on a June afternoon in 1961, sitting on the couch and watching the Mahoneys' new television, one of the first in town, when the front door opened and the priest walked in. Not Father Casey, who was on vacation, but his stand-in, young Father Hearn. "Joe, I got bad news for you, son," blurted out the nervous priest. "Your father has died." Joe did not hear any more. He got to his feet and ran out through the Mahoneys' front door onto the street. He ran all the way home, tears streaming from his face, then ran up the stairs into his room—the room he shared with three of his brothers—and cried without pause for two days.

Joe's father had been working up north in Labrador on a steel-enforced dam near Churchill Falls. A poorly moored derrick toppled and fell onto him, killing him instantly. He was 43 years old. His widow, Bride, was 35. The 10 children ranged from a baby girl of 8 months to Joe, at 15.

"Oh, man, it was something. I think music is what kept us together through that," Joe recalls. "There's something about music, when you're playing it, your mind thinks of nothin' else. It just goes into the music. We all got together in the kitchen, and we played and played, until my mother begged us to stop."

There wasn't much time for grieving. Joe, as eldest, was the man of the family now. Money would come later from the union and from a settlement with the steel company, but even then it would be hard going for a family of 11. So a few months after his father died, Joe boarded a plane and flew to Labrador City to find a job at the iron ore mines. A man who knew Joe's father hired him to clean the miner's bunkhouse. Joe did that for a few months, got lonely and went home, then returned to Labrador. The spring he was sixteen he signed on for the seal hunt—still active in the 1960s—but found he had no heart for the brutal work. "I let 'em go," says Joe. "I didn't want to kill 'em. They were too cute to kill, like little puppy dogs."

While Joe was shuttling back and forth to Labrador, Beverly Moore had moved to New York, where her father was an iron-worker. There was nothing in Conception Harbour for Joe now. It was time to make a move and earn real money. So he got on a bus and traveled 1,300 miles west to Toronto. He kicked around at a few jobs there, none of which paid well or gave much satisfaction. All along Joe knew what he wanted to do. It was the last thing on earth he should have wanted to do, but he wanted to do it anyway. One evening he sat down and wrote a letter to his mother telling her that he'd made up his mind: he was going into ironwork. She wrote back at once. You will do no such thing, she instructed him. Your father was an ironworker. Don't you know he got killed? Don't you know the danger? You'll probably end up the same way he did.

Joe read the letter through a few times, and then wrote his response. It was already decided, he told his mother. The money was good, and they needed it. He would be all right. He would take good care of himself.

He neglected to tell her how afraid he was. He knew very well the dangers of the job, and was none too fond of heights, either. Yet there was something about it that drew him, something other than the money. "I don't know how to explain it. It's a rush is what it is. It's like driving fast. You know there's danger there, but you push yourself to see if you can do it. People say you're crazy, and maybe you are in a way."

He was lonely one evening in Toronto and picked up the phone, but instead of calling home to his family, he dialed a number he'd been holding onto for a while. It was a Brooklyn number. Beverly Moore picked up the phone. Joe hadn't seen her for a couple of years and he didn't know what made him call her now, but they spoke for a long while, and by the time they hung up, she'd promised to come up to Toronto to see him. A few months later, in the fall of 1965, they were married in a small church downtown. Joe was 21 years old. Beverly was 20.

Joe still remembers the first time he drove into New York. It was the late 1960s and there was a strike on in Toronto, and Joe and a friend named Patrick Grace boomed south in Patrick Grace's brand new bright yellow Plymouth Road Runner. They drove straight into Manhattan. Patrick Grace was afraid for his car, that it would get scratched or dented or stolen in the mayhem of the city. Joe, as he looked up at the buildings, had other concerns on his mind. "Holy shit, man, I hope we don't get on one of *those* jobs, way up in the sky," he thought to himself. They drove down to the Local 40 shape hall. Patrick Grace told the business agent he wanted to go connecting. "Well, I ain't goin' connecting on *them*," announced Joe. So Patrick went connecting, and Joe went out on tagline with a gang of Indians. A few weeks later, Patrick Grace got caught in the drift of a column and seriously injured his leg. He returned to Toronto to recuperate, dropped out of ironwork, and Joe never saw him again.

Joe soon got over his initial trepidation. He started connecting and found he loved it. Beverly came down to join him in New York, and they moved into an apartment next to her parents' home in Park Slope, over an ironworkers' bar called the High Spot. Newfoundlanders were all over Brooklyn in those days, at Snitty's and Tyson's, at the shortlived Newfoundlanders Club on 69th Street in Bay Ridge, at church on Sundays. Most of the Newfoundlanders came from the head of Conception Bay, but ironwork had spread to other pockets on the Avalon Peninsula. The Hartley brothers, for instance, came from Placentia Bay, on the southern shore of the peninsula. They settled in a small Newfie outport in Lindenhurst, Long Island. (The director Hal Hartley, son of a Newfoundlander ironworker, later used this neighborhood as a backdrop in several films.) Newfoundlanders were well represented in the union, too, constituting about a quarter of Local 40's membership and holding much of its political power. They ran the union as they had been running it since 1937, when Jim Cole, a Colliers man, was voted in as president. Jim Cole was succeeded by Ray Corbett, whose family came from Harbor Main, and Ray Corbett would soon be succeeded by Ray Mullet of Conception Harbour, who would eventually be succeeded, in the 1990s, by Jack Doyle of Avondale.

One afternoon, on a skyscraper job on State Street, Joe saw an ironworker die for the first time. The victim was a fellow Newfoundlander named Bobby Burke. Joe glimpsed him plummeting off the edge of the 44th floor. "It looked to me like a bag of garbage. That's what I thought it was. I said, 'Someone's thrown a bag of garbage off the side of the building, they shouldn't have done that.' When we went down, they called out the name of everyone there, 'cause they didn't know who it was. There was nothing there, just—I don't know what it was. Just his boots. Some clothes. And a little soap stone that must have fallen out of his pocket, a little white spot." It was difficult to go back after something like that; you'd feel sick to your stomach for a few days. But then the sickness would pass and work, and life, would resume.

Most of Joe's memories from back then are good ones. It was wonderful to be young and strong and building skyscrapers in the grandest city on earth. The days were exciting and interesting, and there was always beer or something stronger around to lend a festive atmosphere to the proceedings. All the drinking was foolish, in retrospect, but at the time it made you feel invulnerable, like you could dance over the steel—hell, you were a hot shit Newfoundlander ironworker—and no one, not even a hot-wrench Indian, could touch you.

Ironworkers still had a foot in their antic past in those days. Riding the load was by now strictly forbidden, a firing offense, but men still did it when they thought they could get away with it. Joe remembers going to a bar for lunch one afternoon with a fellow ironworker who was already so drunk the bartender refused to serve him. The ironworker threw a fit, then tossed a glass into the mirror behind the bar, shattering both the glass and the mirror. As the bartender called the police, the ironworker dashed out of the bar and jumped onto a load of steel that happened, at that very moment, to be rising off the back of a truck across the street. He ducked down and rode the steel up to the top floor, where he hid until the police had come and gone.

New York was a town of extraordinary events. There was that morning on the East Side, for instance, when a 7-ton derrick lifting a 10-ton load of steel broke loose from the guy wires holding it atop a building and all 17 tons of steel plunged 18 stories onto the street in the middle of rush hour. The falling steel demolished the flatbed truck below and turnbuckles smashed through a restaurant window across the street, but, miraculously, nobody was seriously injured. And then, moments later, another miracle: a geyser of water burst from a broken water main under the street and shot a 100-foot spout into the sky. As Joe remembers the story—he was not there himself to confirm it—hundreds of tiny fish came raining out of the geyser and landed flopping on the streets of New York. Real live fish.

No event was more extraordinary than the building of the World Trade Center. Joe went there in 1968 and stayed two full years, working in a gang on Tower One. Few jobs were as swarming with Fish as that one. The Moores were all there, and Willie Quinlan and Jack Doyle, and Jack's brothers, and Joe's brothers, Ron and Jerry, and dozens of others. There were times, standing a thousand feet above the city, with a watery view of the harbor and a fog sweeping in from the east, when you could look around the derrick floor and everyone you saw came from a small patch of rock at the head of Conception Bay.

But New York was not home, and in 1975 Joe and Beverly, realizing that it never would be, moved the family back to Conception Bay. They wanted to raise their three sons—and later, a daughter—in Newfoundland. "Growing up in the place, I just loved it that much. I figured, why let them miss what I had growing up at eight, nine, ten years old? The fishing and the woods and the water. There's no place like it on earth. And it's what I wanted for them." The old Newfoundland catch, of course, was that Joe had to leave his family at once and go back out into the world to make a living. Like his father and many other fathers before him, he would be gone months at a time, returning home at Christmas and summers, his children grown a few inches taller every time he saw them.

The separation was probably harder on Beverly than on Joe. She raised the four children mostly on her own. Then Joe came home on holidays, barging into the order she had arranged, and they were like strangers who hardly knew each other. In retrospect, this wasn't all bad. "There's a special thing to it, even it being hard," says Joe. "You get that special time when you come home. It's like you met her for the first time in your life. When you're living with a person day after day after day, maybe it's good. But I don't think it's the same."

Joe missed home terribly when he was away. "You go out to the bars on the weekends, meet up with the guys, have a few beers. You go home half-drunk, then get on the phone for an hour talking to your wife—you'd want to be home—and the next day you gotta break your back to work again. The only time you wouldn't think about home was when you're working, 'cause your mind was on the job, to watch so you didn't get hurt." Mose Lewis' death had put an end to any aspirations Joe once harbored of being a full-time professional musician, but music remained central in his life. He played with his brothers in bands all over New York, and when he boomed out to California and Tennessee, he always brought along his guitar or fiddle. Music was a consolation for a man far from home.

The part that made it all worthwhile—the flip side of the catch—was the return. The pre-Christmas drive through Maine and Nova Scotia, the endless quiet highway. The hours of anticipation on the ferry, standing on the deck, the bow breaking through the North Atlantic, and somewhere in the foggy distance your family waiting for you. No place on earth was better than the head of Conception Bay, and a man could put up with a lot of hardship for the pleasure of going home. "It was," says Joe, "like going back to heaven."

Joe did not see much of his sons while they were young, but when they grew up they followed him into ironwork, and now he spent most of his free time with them. They were more like brothers than sons, solid and capable young men to whom he could speak of anything. Like Joe, they traveled between Brooklyn and Conception Bay. All three of them had bought houses in Conception Harbour, and it was there they planned to raise their own families. "I say, son, you're going to do the same thing I did, all over again. Maybe that's the way it's got to be. I say if you're happy with it, then go for it. They're like me. They work in the city, but all they want is to be back home."

By the summer of 2001, Joe Lewis and his three sons were among the last of the true migrating Fish. Most of the old timers had made their lives around New York. Their children and grandchildren were born and raised in the suburbs, spread out over Westchester County or Connecticut or Long Island. Many of the younger generation earned their livings as ironworkers, but they were not Fish anymore, not really. They were Americans.

A great many men from Conception Harbour still practiced the trade of ironwork, but most did it in Canada now, going out to build oil rigs in the North Atlantic or traveling a few thousand miles west to Alberta. Newfoundland had come a long way since Joe was born. The cod were gone and Greenpeace had put an end to swiling, but oil and mining were strong. Tourism was on the rise, too. Many of the tourists who visited Newfoundland in the summer were American-born sons and daughters and grandchildren of ironworkers come back to see the Rock. They'd show up at Frank's, which everybody still called Doyle's, and drink and talk with the Newfoundlanders who shared their last names and some of their blood. The Yanks and the Fish sometimes had difficulty understanding each other after a few beers or a shot of screech (a rum-based drink so called because it makes you *screech* when you drink it), when the most frequently uttered word in a conversation between a Yank and a Newfoundlander was likely to be "What?" Or, as the Newfoundlander would put it, "Wha'?"

Joe Lewis would finally get the O.K. from the doctors and the lawyers to go home. It would be late fall by then, many weeks after the terrorist attacks of September 11, and the world would be a very different place than on the August day Joe sat at the kitchen of the row house in Brooklyn and spoke of the bad luck that had afflicted his old raising gang. Newfoundland had never seemed as utterly peaceful and distant from Manhattan as it would in the autumn of that *annus horribilis*. Joe would celebrate Christmas in the old house near the bay, where he grew up and where his mother still lived, just across the street from his own well-tended white clapboard house.

The numbness in Joe's hand would improve, but only slightly. Joe would never pick the strings of a guitar or handle a fiddle with his old finesse. On New Year's Eve, Joe and his brothers would take the stage of the Oasis, the tavern he and Beverly owned in Colliers, just over the Pinch from Conception Harbour. Joe would look out into the crowd and know every one of the two hundred or so faces looking back at him, and the Lewis brothers would begin to play. During the instrumental sections, Joe would mostly pretend to strum the guitar while his brothers covered for him. But when it came time to sing, Joe would not have to fake anything. He'd still have his voice. He'd sing a country song, then a few rock ballads, and then, for the old-timers, some of the jigs and reels he used to play in the kitchen when he was a boy. He'd sing "The Star of Logy Bay." He'd sing "Kelegre's Swarree." And then, of course, he'd sing the song that every true Newfoundlander knows by heart, "I's the B'y":

> *I's the b'y that builds the boat*
> *I's the b'y that sails her*
> *I's the b'y that catches the fish*
> *And brings them home to Lizer.*
> *Cods and rinds to cover your flake*
> *Cake and tea for supper*

*Cod fish in the spring of the year*
*Fried in maggoty butter.*

Everybody in the Oasis would be stomping their feet and singing along, and a few of the old-timers would stand and begin to dance, the large tavern vibrating and warming with moving bodies. Then the front door would open and someone would enter, and as a blast of cold air rushed into the Oasis, a scrap of music would slip out into the night and go skipping up over the spruce trees to the cemetery on top of Colliers Hill, where Mose Lewis and the other dead lay buried. A clear cold sky would be glittering overhead, and the black bay heaving in the distance, and if you were lying on top of the hill on this frosty night, you might hear the faint strand of music from below and you might remember, for a moment, what it was to be alive.

# PART III
# The Fall

# NINE

# The Old School

**B**unny Eyes quit one hot afternoon at the start of August. Or was fired. Or was fired and then quit—the details depended on who was offering them and nobody was offering much. This part was certain: Bunny and George, the gang's foreman, got into some kind of dispute about the heat, which had soared into the high nineties several days earlier and been parked there every day since. Heat waves brutalize ironworkers. All other trades on a skyscraper job work under the derrick floor, in shade, but there is no shade for the ironworkers on top. The sun beats down on them mercilessly, and it radiates back up at them from the stainless steel decking and the beams and columns.

On the fourth day of the heat wave, Bunny announced that he favored cutting out early. George wanted to keep working. The argument quickly escalated, and before it was over, George told Bunny he no longer wanted him in the gang and he could now consider himself a bolter-up. No one expected Bunny to accept this—"Bunny's a raising gang man," said Matt, "no way was he gonna bolt up"—and Bunny promptly quit. It had been a long time coming. As Matt said later, "Bunny was never happy in this job."

The real reason Bunny quit, or got himself fired, or whatever happened exactly, wasn't that he held anything against George or the gang, and it wasn't that he couldn't take the heat—Bunny *liked* it hot. It was, simply, that he hated the job. He had come to loathe it. "That job was just a horror," he would say later. What made it such a horror? "Just the job itself," he would vaguely elaborate. "Christ, just everything."

The job had turned out to be nothing like what he, or any of the men, expected. The great competition he'd looked forward to, those four kangaroos bobbing and swinging, the four raising gangs clambering over the frame, pushing themselves to excel—none of this had come to pass. Instead, the Time Warner Center had crept upwards at an excruciating pace. Six months had elapsed since that morning in February when Bunny and the rest of the raising gang arrived, five months since the ironworkers began setting steel. And the building was only on the fifth floor. A floor a month. Given the acreage and the size of some of the steel members, this represented a good tonnage of steel, but still—five floors in five months? No ironworker at Columbus Circle could remember a job that had advanced at such a slow grind.

The problem was the same one that had plagued the job since May: lack of steel. The ADF plants in Quebec were pumping out fabricated shapes at full throttle, but this was not fast enough to feed the hunger of the Time Warner Center. To make matters worse, when the steel finally did arrive, the ironworkers complained that it was poorly fabricated. It didn't fit as it was meant to. The bolt holes did not align properly. Or the piece came a few centimeters too long and had to be trimmed to size with an acetylene torch. Often, the only way to get the steel to match was by hitting it again and again with beaters, or by slamming the ball of the crane into it, or by straddling it and bucking up and down on it or, all else failing, kicking the shit out of it. The goal of all this activity was to get the holes of the facing pieces close enough together that you could stick the tapered end of your drift pin through both—getting a "bite," this was called—then pound the pin in with a beater, pulling those two holes, and all the others on the facing pieces, into alignment. Only then could you fit your bolts and move on.

It was arduous and joyless work. Connections that should have been made in three or four minutes routinely took an hour. Instead of setting 40 or 50 pieces a day, as they should have been doing, the gangs were lucky to set 10 or 15. Joe Kennedy, the superintendent, had recently brought in Tommy Emerson's raising gang from the Random House job to take over the northeast crane but he hardly had enough steel to keep two cranes busy, much less three.

The last anyone saw of Bunny around Columbus Circle, he was sitting at the bar of the Coliseum on a Thursday afternoon. The place was sparsely populated and deliciously cold. A few men slumped listlessly over the bar, and a few other men slumped over tables against the wall. Nobody was saying much, certainly not with any animation, except for Chad Snow, the connector in Chappie's gang. Chad sat on a bar stool near Bunny telling stories about close encounters he'd had with death, each story slightly more harrowing than the last. "When I landed," Chad was saying, "I hit right on my sternum. They wanted to take me down in a scale box but the last guy I'd seen go down in a scale box died, so I said no way, and I walked down the stairs. All I knew," said Chad, "is there was no way I was going in that box."

Chad had suffered many accidents in his 36 years. Even before he'd learned to walk he'd almost killed himself by crawling into his older sister's walker, pulling himself up to his feet, then shuffling over to the stairs and tumbling down them. Since becoming an ironworker, he'd fallen badly three times and had many close calls. Chad was short but quick and solidly built, with wide bow legs and large thighs, and he had proven himself to be fairly indestructible. He was in the middle of telling a new story about the time a piece of steel flew out of control and nearly knocked him off the edge of a building when Bunny, who had been quiet and remote, looked up from his beer and turned his liquid blue eyes on Chad. "Christ, Chad, didn't anything good ever happen to you?" Chad paused for a moment, then went on telling his story. Bunny took a last sip of beer, stood up, and walked out without a word.

Quitting was a right ironworkers took as God-given. An ironworker owed his loyalties to his union and his trade, not to any specific job. Indeed, an ironworker was expected to quit if he was unhappy in a job. "You can shove this job up your ass," a New York ironworker told his foreman one day, according to a well-traveled bar story. Off the man went to find a new job, booming down south, all the way west, up north, but no luck, there were no jobs to be found. Finally, he returns east, just where he began. "If that job's not too far up your ass," he says to his old foreman, "I'd like it back now." The real punchline is that he got it back, no hard feelings.

In a boom, a new job was pretty much guaranteed to a good raising gang man like Bunny. The local would send him right back out for a fresh start. A construction slowdown might change the equation—a man was more likely to stick it out when there were few other jobs to go to—but the standing rule was that an ironworker worked at his own discretion. He earned that right by the risks he took. Every decision, even one ill advised or lightly made, could turn out to be the decision that saved his life. In 1907, Dominic McComber walked off the Quebec Bridge three and a half hours before it fell because he'd gotten into an argument with his foreman. No matter why he made it, that decision, that single autonomous act, turned out to be the most important of his life.

In the spring of 2001, the American Psychological Association published the results of a study on human happiness. According to the study, happiness is nourished not by popularity or affluence or the pursuit of pleasure. Rather, it derives from a recipe of four ingredients: autonomy, competence, self-esteem, and relatedness. Autonomy tops the list.

Ironwork provided all four. It was difficult work that gave men a chance to apply their physical strength and skill to the problem of handling and connecting steel. It was work most other people found inconceivably dangerous and which set apart its practitioners as men of courage. As a result, most ironworkers were fairly bursting with pride. The work also provided "relatedness." Once an apprentice survived the ribbing and hazing that was part of his initiation into ironwork, he belonged to a tight fraternity, a "family," as many ironworkers described it. For many of the members, of course, the relatedness was literal. They were cousins and brothers and fathers and sons.

But it was autonomy, in the end, that set ironwork apart from most blue-collar jobs. Autonomy is what blue-collar jobs are generally supposed to lack. Lack of autonomy, in fact, is one of the defining characteristics of working-class occupations. "Class is about the power some people have over the lives of others, and the powerlessness most people experience as a result," writes the labor historian Michael Zweig. "For all their differences, working class people share a common place in production where they have relatively little control over the pace or content of their work, and aren't anybody's boss."

Ironworkers were indisputably members of the working class, but throughout most of their history they'd exerted a good deal of control over the pace and content of their work. Gangs of ironworkers operated as self-determined units. As long as they completed the work in a timely fashion, they were free to carry it out more or less as they pleased. Within the gang, the foreman was the leader, but in most gangs, especially in raising gangs, his rank was only marginally higher than that of the others. They were all members of the same union, and the foreman earned just a dollar more per hour. Nor was his rank permanent; it lasted as long as the job. On the next job, he might find himself back in the gang; he might very well find himself working for one of the men he was now pushing. He did well not to lord his power over the others.

A journeyman ironworker went where the union sent him and carried out the tasks that his foreman or super assigned him. Beyond this, he was given a wide berth. If he didn't want to come to work one day, well, all right. If he felt like coming to work drunk, nobody would say anything against him, just so long as he could hold his liquor and didn't slow down the gang. If he was inspired to slide down a column upside-down or do cartwheels on a six-inch beam, he was probably a fool, but foolishness was his prerogative. Within the quasi-socialistic brotherhood of unionism, ironwork was a libertarian's paradise.

Or rather, always had been. In the summer of 2001, it was a paradise quickly vanishing, much to the dismay of the men who lived in it.

## SAFE NEW WORLD

Joe Kennedy, the white-bearded superintendent of the ironworkers, just a few jobs shy of retirement and peace, stood near the front gate on Columbus Circle, in the three-sided court that would eventually become the magnificent portal of the Time Warner Center. The budding towers rose on either side, casting afternoon shadows over the court. Above Joe, to the south, George's gang, minus Bunny, was "jumping" its kangaroo crane, an astonishing process whereby the crane lifted itself on hydraulic pistons while the raising gang slipped a new 13-foot tower section into the gap. Matt Kugler and Jerry Soberanes stood on the tower section, hanging by the crane's hook. John White and Danny Donohue were whacking away at the tower, pulling out pins to make room. To a man looking for signs of progress, and Joe was such a man, this was a good one.

On the other side of the court, a crane lifted a stack of stainless-steel decking. As the decking rose and yawed slightly, several hundred gallons of brown water poured out of its corrugated hollows and cascaded down onto the concrete floor. Joe lifted his two-way radio from his belt.

"Jesus Christ, Tommy, you guys break a water main up there?"

"No, Joe," came the response. "That's me taking a piss."

"That's lovely, Tommy, thank you for that information."

"Any time, Joe."

Joe Kennedy passed most of his days inside a small trailer propped on the scaffold bridge over the sidewalk of Columbus Circle. The trailer was furnished with a few phones and drafting tables and reams and reams of shop drawings. From this vantage, Joe attended to the hundreds of logistical problems that beset the assembly of a steel building in the middle of Manhattan, from arranging deliveries of materials to coordinating with other trades to dealing with catastrophes. These days he spent a lot of time placating the general contractor, Bovis Lend-Lease, about the all too evident lack of steel. "There's absolutely nothing I can do," said Joe. "I can make phone calls and holler and scream and stamp my feet as loud as they do, but I get the same result." The project manager from ADF kept assuring Joe that more steel was around the corner, that the bottleneck was about to bust open. "Every week he tells me it's great, it's gonna be fine, and I say, 'Listen, you tell me that every week for the last month. You better change your system or do something different, cause it ain't changing any.' From our end, all we want is to be able to order the steel, have it delivered, erect it, bolt it up, plumb it up, whatever we have to do. But it isn't happening."

Superintendent is a powerful but thankless position, the intermediary between impatient contractors above and unruly ironworkers below. Nobody loves a superintendent except his own family, and Joe couldn't even count on *them* since several of his brothers and sons worked for him. "When you're super, you're the boss, which makes you the enemy," said Joe. "The pay is better, but there's everything else that goes along with it. To be honest, it's not much fun."

There were moments of pleasure, however, and this was one of them. In the afternoons, when things quieted down, Joe stepped out of the trailer and took a tour of the building. He walked slowly, with the measured authority of a bishop admiring his cathedral. Even now, after all these years, Joe got a charge out of the sight of iron rising and cranes jumping. These were accomplishments you could measure and appreciate with your eyes.

"Joe, why aren't they tied off?"

Joe's reverie was abruptly terminated by the approach of a large bearded man named Mike. The site safety manager for Bovis, Mike looked ponderous and grim, as he often looked when approaching Joe. He pointed up to a wide girder running along the edge of the courtyard. Several plumber-uppers stood on the girder, drawing a tape measure between two columns, unaware they were under observation.

"They aren't tied off."

"They aren't tied off," responded Joe, "because they aren't thirty feet over the floor."

"Looks like thirty feet to me."

"Well, it isn't. It's twenty-nine feet, ten and a half inches."

"You measured it?"

"Yeah, we measured it. It's an inch and a half in compliance. You want to measure yourself, be my guest."

Mike squinted up at the beam skeptically. He was a heavyset man and no ironworker. He scratched his beard like he was thinking about it.

"Twenty-nine feet, ten and a half inches. All right, then."

"Every day the safety thing is a headache," said Joe after Mike had departed. "Everything is changing. The men don't like it, but that's the way it is, and they gotta get with it or go."

The "safety thing" was a new set of revised OSHA regulations known officially as the Subpart R Steel Erection Standard. Subpart R dictated how ironworkers were to rig steel, how they were to land it on the derrick floor, how they were to connect it in the air. Most significantly, as far as the ironworkers were concerned, Subpart R mandated that ironworkers use fall protection whenever they worked a considerable distance above the ground or the floor below. That is, they had to "tie off" by wearing a harness attached by cable to a nearby beam. Most ironworkers would have to tie off when working more than 15 feet above the derrick floor or the ground. Connectors would have to tie off at 30 feet.

Tying off was not a new practice, but contractors had always been pretty lax about enforcing it. That was about to change. Insurance companies would not carry contractors with high accident rates. Even contractors with good safety records would suffer premium boosts if a single employee got injured on one of their jobs. "I tell the guys, don't think for one second they're worried about your health," said Joe Kennedy. "It's all about dollars and cents."

The majority of the ironworkers loathed the practice of tying off. This was one of those mysteries that the good people of OSHA simply did not understand. OSHA had probably saved hundreds of ironworkers' lives and prevented many more injuries since President Nixon signed the agency into law in 1970. Now, with Subpart R, they had crafted and honed a package that would, by their analysis, reduce fatalities from an average of 35 or 40 a year to about 5 a year, while cutting the number of injuries in half. The regulations had been conceived to save ironworkers. But rather than applaud them, what did the ironworkers do? *They got angry.* "It is odd," Richard Mendelson, area director for OSHA, conceded. "The ironworkers are one of the few trades that argue *against* compliance."

Obviously, nobody wanted to get hurt or killed, and the majority of the OSHA regulations made good sense to the ironworkers. The phase-in of slip-resistant steel surfaces and the removal of lugs and other tripping hazards from steel beams were examples of measures the ironworkers backed. They likewise supported laws that forced contractors to hang safety nets under bridges and along the sides of buildings. But tying off was different. Many ironworkers considered the practice an imposition, at best, and very likely counterproductive. Connectors, most audibly, tended to believe it made their work *more* dangerous by restricting movement. Nearly every connector had been in a situation where a quick duck or leap had saved him from a wild piece of steel. Yes, the safety harness might protect them if they were knocked off, but they preferred to avoid getting hit in the first place. "I'll wear the harness if they make me," said Jerry Soberanes. "But there's no way I'm tying it to anything."

In the end, whether the new rules saved lives or cost lives wasn't the whole issue to the ironworkers. Every work site would be staffed—it was already happening—with several full-time safety inspectors like Mike, whose entire job was to watch them, *spy* on them, and reprimand them for infractions. For men who were used to doing things their way, autonomously, this was galling. "Fuck the insurance companies," said a middle-aged veteran plumber-up one afternoon as he sat in his usual lunch spot on the sidewalk. "We'll get up a few floors, and then we'll do whatever we want."

## KEITH AND MARVIN

"Yo, get in the truck and back it up, ya bonehead!"

The truck driver, a small bald French Canadian who had driven four hundred miles to deliver a load of steel and get abused by Keith Brown, grinned sheepishly and stepped up into the cab of his truck. On 60th Street, Keith took a last drag of his French Canadian cigarette—a cigarette from a pack, as it happened, provided to him several minutes earlier by the truck driver in the futile hope of placating

Tying off.
*(Photo by Michael Doolittle)*

Keith—and threw it to the ground, as if the cigarette suddenly disgusted him, as if the ground itself rubbed him the wrong way.

"Hey, moron," he called to a young apprentice loitering near the back of the truck. "Quit scratching yourself like a retard and stop traffic so this shit-for-brains can back his rig out." The apprentice ran out into the street, nearly getting clipped by a taxi.

"Now look at this idiot," muttered Keith. "He's gonna get himself killed down here on the fuckin' *street?*" He pulled another cigarette out of his pack. He stuck it in his mouth and struck a match.

If there was anyone to light a fire under a slow job it was Keith Brown, the walking boss, recently arrived at Columbus Circle in the August heat, bringing with him his impatience, his shouting and cursing, his disgust for the lazy and the incompetent, for no-good apprentices and French Canadian truck drivers. He split his time between overseeing the raising gangs up top and coordinating the delivery of steel down on the street, stalking back and forth with a cigarette in his mouth and a scowl on his face. Folded lengthwise in his back pocket was a schedule of truck arrivals. Now and then Keith would pull the schedule out, glance at it, and shove it back into his pocket. The secret of the schedule was that it was meaningless. Trucks routinely showed up a day early or a day late. A truck due tomorrow would arrive today and two trucks due today would not arrive at all. It was enough to make a relaxed man crazy, and Keith Brown was far from a relaxed man. He was, as he himself admitted, wired for movement, for combustion. When he removed his hard hat to air his scalp, as he often did, he revealed a small fuzzy bald spot on the crown of his head. It did not look so much like the hair had fallen out. It looked as if it had been singed.

If Keith Brown was a first class ball-buster, he was also, as apprentices and even some truck drivers came to realize, a decent guy—a "real ironworker," as the journeymen said of him, which is about the highest compliment one ironworker can pay another. None of these tributes made Keith exactly cuddly. And as soon as you dismissed his ranting as humorous—it *was* humorous—he reminded you that, like most humor, his rose out of deep convictions. He really did hate these kids sometimes. "Don't you fuckin' ruin my business, you and the rest of you lousy apprentice shits," he liked to shout at them. "You're not gonna ruin this business if I can stop it." In his quieter moments, Keith conceded that it was probably already too late. "Oh, God, I used to love this business. Now, it's just a job. I'm just glad I'm on my way out."

Keith Brown was a Mohawk by blood, a New Yorker by birth and attitude. He spent his early childhood in an apartment on State Street in the old Mohawk neighborhood in Brooklyn, while his father worked on the Verrazano-Narrows Bridge. The family moved from Brooklyn to the suburbs of New Jersey as soon as the bridge was finished.

As a boy, Keith had only the vaguest sense of what ironworkers did. Sometimes his father came home with broken bones and sometimes he came home drunk—this was the sum total of Keith's knowledge of his father's occupation, and neither part held much appeal. "Don't worry about me drinking," he assured his mother after taking a sip of beer. "This tastes like shit." To please his mother, Keith tried college. He lasted three days. "I told you he was a moron," his father said. "Let's hope he's tough." Keith followed his father into ironwork.

Keith's father was a hard man. When Keith fell into the hole on one of his first jobs, a drop of about 30 feet that ended, fortunately, in a pile of sand, he wiped the sand from his eyes and looked up to see his father glaring down at him from above. "You no good bastard, get up here!" his father shouted. "You're embarrassing me." Then there was that time his father swung a maul at a lintel and missed, landing the blow on Keith's kneecap. It made a pop so loud men could hear it on the other side of the building. "Ah, get up, you sissy," scolded his father when Keith fell back in pain. "That didn't hurt."

Keith's father may have shouted louder than some of the ironworkers of his generation, and he may have been tougher on his son, but not by much. A lot of the old timers handled their novice sons much as they handled steel, with force and diligence. They woke them up at four in the morning and got them to the job site an hour early, because that was the ironworkers' way. Some made their sons wear connecting belts all day long so they'd get used to the weight of the clanging tools, so they'd turn into good connectors and make their fathers proud. When their sons screwed up, the fathers shouted, and when their sons got hurt, they told them to shake off the pain and get back to work.

As an apprentice in those days, you worked hard and did what you were told and hoped no one noticed your mistakes. Keith was so scared of getting shouted at by his father or one of the other older men that he never found time to worry about the height or the danger. In the meantime, the boy who hated the taste of beer had begun to drink it with a convert's passion.

It was drinking that brought him one afternoon in 1982 to a bar near a job site in Parsippany, New Jersey. Keith was an experienced connector by now and was looking for a partner. There at the bar among the other ironworkers sat a quiet young Mohawk with black hair and olive skin, named Marvin Davis. Marvin was not from Kahnawake but from Six Nations, an Iroquois reservation in northwest New York. He'd just spent a few years in San Antonio, Texas, working on office buildings, and had recently boomed up east in search of better wages. The fact that Marvin was a fellow Mohawk was enough to recommend him to Keith. He asked Marvin if he felt like going connecting. Marvin said he did. And so began an extraordinary partnership and friendship that would still be intact 20 years later.

Their shared Mohawk heritage aside, Keith and Marvin were about as different as two men could be. Whereas Keith was verbose and volatile, Marvin was quiet and even-keeled. "By the way, Marvin," Keith would announce to his friend at the end of a workday, "I just quit for us." Marvin was the peacemaker, smoothing things over with foremen or supers whom Keith had told off. Sometimes, too, Marvin was there to break up fights between Keith and his father.

One thing both men had in common: they liked to work hard. "It wasn't just show up and go to work," said Marvin. "We're both guys who wanted to go to work. We looked *forward* to it."

When Keith and Marvin met, Keith was still working out of No. 711, the Canadian local through which many Kahnawake Mohawks came into ironwork. One day he got a call from the business agent of Local 40 in New York inviting him to join, a high honor. "This may sound funny," Keith told the business agent, "but can my partner come in? No disrespect, but if he doesn't come in, I don't want to come in." The business agent consented.

After that it was understood that when Keith Brown and Marvin Davis showed up at the shape hall for work, they went out together. "They don't want both of us," said Keith, "they don't get either of us." In the meantime, Marvin had moved into a house less than a mile away from Keith's in New Jersey. Both men were married to pretty, young Mohawk women and their wives hit it off, and so did their children. Meanwhile, on the steel, Keith and Marvin developed into a superb connecting team. It wasn't just that they liked and trusted each other, it was also a physical chemistry. "Some guys will fight each other on how to make a piece," said Marvin. "Me and him, we just moved forward. It got to the point where we didn't have to look at each other. We knew each other's moves."

Between moves, they drank. Sometimes they drank all day. They started the morning with a shared six-pack on the way to work, then split a few more six-packs at coffee breaks and lunch. After work, they really started in, making a tour of the usual ironworkers' haunts, ending the night at a place in the Port Authority Bus Terminal. By the time they got home, they were often too drunk to remember the alibis they'd contrived for their wives. The next morning, they would start all over again with a six-pack just to straighten out from the night before. They drank extravagantly, but never so much they couldn't do the work. Officially, on-the-job drinking was strictly prohibited; tacitly, it was tolerated. "Back then, they'd just say, 'Keep drinking and keep working,'" said Marvin. "As long as you were doing your job, it was, 'Here, have some more. If that's what makes you go, *go.*' "

There were days Keith Brown drank two cases of beer between morning and night. The boy who hated the taste of beer had grown up to be a full-blown alcoholic.

One day, Marvin announced he'd decided to stop drinking. He wanted nothing more to do with alcohol. "I was getting sick and tired of it," said Marvin. "You get to that point in your life—you gotta grow up sooner or later." Keith kept at it for another year after Marvin stopped, but the pleasure went out of it.

That was the year Keith's father died. It was also the year he and his wife separated. His life had reached a crossroads and he knew it. He was sitting in his house one night, drunk, halfway through a can of beer. He realized that if he wanted custody of his children—and he did—it was now or never. "I said to myself, you gotta make a decision. You're either going to give them away, cause you can't raise no kids drinking, or you put it down and never touch it again." And that was the end of it. Once he made the decision, he never went back.

Keith and Marvin connected together for another eight years. Their last connecting job was a huge Midtown office building for Bear Stearns, the New York financial concern. It was 1998 and they were both on the cusp of forty, generally the age a connector starts thinking about moving on to less strenuous labor. One afternoon the superintendent approached Keith and asked him if he wanted to take over as walking boss. Keith knew that accepting the promotion would mean severing his partnership with Marvin, perhaps forever. Before giving the super an answer, he went to Marvin and spoke to him. "If you don't want me to take it, I won't," he said. "It's your call." Marvin told him to take it. He told Keith he was going to see the job to the end, and then he, too, was going to hang up his connecting belt.

Three years later, in the late summer of 2001, Keith Brown and Marvin Davis were still together, still partners, and still went everywhere together. They were both walking bosses on the Time Warner Center, sharing the building between them. Keith commanded the first phase of erection, the raising gangs, the rigs, the bolter-ups, and the steel deliveries. Marvin took care of the follow-up, the detail crews, the welders. They didn't see as much of each other as they used to. They no longer commuted to and from work together, as they had for years, because Keith had recently started seeing a woman who lived in the East Village. Most afternoons, though, they met up for lunch, usually at a Greek deli on 58th Street where everyone knew them.

"How are my friends today?" the counterman bellowed as they straddled a couple of stools one afternoon.

"Happy as a bowl of fuckin' sunshine," mumbled Keith. "Lemme have a cup of coffee. What are you having, Marv?"

Marvin ordered a grilled cheese. At 43, Marvin was a year older than Keith but looked a couple years younger, his features softer, less weathered. He was still the quiet one, the calmer one, still married to the same woman, still living in the same house.

Both men appeared fairly exhausted as they sat at the counter. Keith's stomach was bothering him this afternoon, squelching his appetite. The stress of management was more difficult than the bodily wear and tear of connecting. It was also, both agreed, less satisfying. Instead of building all day, they were digging through an avalanche of logistics and paperwork—and rules. They both appreciated the irony that they, who had broken all the rules, now found themselves in a position where part of their job was to enforce them.

"That's hard for me," said Keith. "Who am I to tell somebody he can't drink? For me to say no drinking, they just look at me and say, 'Yeah, right, who are you bullshittin'?' But I have to do it. And they all know where it's going."

Where it was going was toward a more bureaucratic kind of steel erection driven not by the quest for speed but by the fear of liability, by the proliferation of rules and regulations. Every small change, the sort of thing ironworkers used to take care of by themselves with a torch and beater, now had to be signed off on by an engineer. Every move the ironworkers made was scrutinized by someone else. Every walk across a beam was nit-picked by a site safety manager. "Now insurance companies are coming looking at the way we've done it for a hundred years and wondering how the hell they let this go on."

Keith didn't miss the drinking but he missed the old days. He missed his father, too, tough as the old man had been. Keith understood now how alike they were, just as his mother had always told him. He also understood now that there was a strange kind of caring behind the shouting. His father had wanted his son to become a good ironworker. And Keith had become one. "If he hadn't busted my balls, I wouldn't have worked so hard. That's one thing I give him credit for. Much as these kids hate me, I see 'em standing still, I yell at 'em. I'm probably the worst of them around, but I'm not half as bad as the old-timers. Christ, I used to want to kill those old bastards. I'm sure these kids feel the same about me. But someday they'll look back, they'll understand what I was shouting about."

Keith drank from his third cup of coffee. "There're a lot of mornings I'd like to say fuck being walking boss and put on my belt and go connecting again."

Marvin nodded.

"These are all good raising gangs on this job," said Keith. "Frankly, though, I think Marv and I would kick any of their asses."

Marvin smiled.

"If our bodies could take it, me and Marvin would go out right now."

"Our bodies can't take it," said Marvin. "That's the problem."

"We abused them too long."

"Yeah, we did."

"But we had a hell of a good time while we were doin' it."

"Oh, yeah," said Marvin. "We had fun."

Keith glanced at his watch. It was 12:30. He poured the rest of the coffee down his throat and stood. "Come on, Marv. Time to go shout at the morons."

## BEAUTIFUL DAYS

The heat lifted over the long Labor Day weekend, and the days that followed were bright and dry and cloudless, a string of September jewels. While most New Yorkers' experience of this perfect weather was muted by sealed office windows and recirculated air, the iron-workers enjoyed every moment firsthand, appreciating it as only people who work outdoors in murderous heat and frigid cold truly can. Adding to their pleasure was the fact that steel suddenly began to appear in abundance, as if freighted down the Hudson Valley on the same Canadian front that brought in the cool dry air. ADF had subcontracted out some of its work to other steel fabricators, and the company's other big job in New York, the Random House building on 56th Street, was complete, freeing up its own mills. A steady stream of trucks arrived at Columbus Circle. Keith Brown had his hands full, cursing the inept drivers and apprentices, grinding burnt-down cigarettes into the pavement.

The fourth raising gang arrived on the Tuesday after Labor Day. This gang was led by a foreman named Danny Doyle and included Mike Emerson—brother of Joe and Tommy Emerson—and a pair of Mohawk connectors, Johnny Diabo and Paul "Punchy" Jacobs. On that first week in September, all four cranes, at last, were running, and all four raising gangs were setting steel, enormous hunks of it jutting out at odd angles to satisfy the complex load distributions of Silvian Marcus' design. On Friday, September 7, Tommy Emerson's gang jumped the northeast crane, lifting it several hundred feet over the derrick floor. Then everybody went home to enjoy one last perfect weekend.

# TEN

# The Towers

The towers rose to a height of 604 feet apiece, taller than all but the tallest skyscrapers. From a distance, they appeared slender, even willowy, but that was an illusion. Their combined 40,000 tons of steel made them stronger than any building. They had to be stronger. Unlike a skyscraper, which supported merely itself and its relatively weightless human burden, these two towers would soon support a third huge thing between them: a 3,500-foot bridge span. This was, in 1929, twice as long as any clear span in the world. "The bridge, in all of its proportions, so completely transcends any bridge ever constructed," reported one of the engineers, "that it is difficult to grasp a sense of its magnitude." Eventually, the great suspension bridge, commissioned by the Port Authority of New York and designed by engineer Othmar Ammann, would be given a name worthy of itself—the George Washington—but in the early summer of 1929 it still had no official name. Nor was it officially a bridge. The towers were nearly complete but they remained unattached twins, separated at birth by the Hudson River, one rising from the banks of northern Manhattan, the other from the shallows beneath the New Jersey palisades.

If you were a self-respecting bridgeman active between the years 1928 and 1931, this was where you wanted to be: on the banks of the lower Hudson or somewhere over the water between. They came from all around the country to raise the bridge and made up one of the most expert and experienced crews of bridgemen ever assembled in one place, having honed their skills on recently built spans like the Delaware River Bridge at Philadelphia and the Ambassador Bridge over the Detroit River. While the slack-jawed public gathered at the base of the Chrysler Building and the Empire State Building to mar-

The towers of the George Washington Bridge under construction,
as seen from the Manhattan shore.
*(Port Authority of New York and New Jersey)*

vel at the ironworkers, these bridgemen, miles from the thick of the city, toiled away unobserved and uncelebrated. But they believed they were up to something far more daring and spectacular than the domesticated "beam jumpers" and "housesmiths," as they dismissed their downtown brethren. These bridgemen were cocky and blithe even by the usual standards of ironworkers, paying "no attention whatever to the line where planks end and the extremely hollow variety of space over the Hudson River begins," according to one reporter who made a trip uptown. Near the base of the Manhattan tower, the bridge company posted a notice on the wall of a construction shack:

IT IS ABSOLUTELY FORBIDDEN FOR PASSENGERS
TO RIDE ON TOP OF ELEVATOR OR TO SLIDE
DOWN ELEVATOR CABLES.

The notice said a lot about the sort of men who worked on the bridge. An Indian had already died on the Jersey tower while attempting to jump onto a moving elevator cab. Other bridgemen were known to dispense with elevator cabs altogether and slide down the elevators' guide beams. "You can get quite a speed coming down five hundred feet on one of them," said H. G. Reynolds, foreman of the New York tower.

McClintock-Marshall Company ran the erection of both towers, but each side of the Hudson was a separate and distinct field operation. Bill Fortune was foreman on the New Jersey tower. Fortune was a Southern gentleman who favored tailored tweeds and polished shoes and played golf at Englewood Country Club on his days off. On the Manhattan side, it was Reynolds, a sharp-tongued Virginian born on a tobacco farm 65 years earlier. Reynolds was a self-proclaimed roughneck who had been working on bridges since he was 15. He had no use for golf or any other recreation. All he cared about was building bridge towers. Tall and lean, with steel-gray hair and bushy gray eyebrows, he even looked like a bridge tower. He was said to possess a fine sense of humor, but at work he was a "driver," a demanding boss who favored the stick over the carrot. "I'll reach right out and break my wrist on your thick head!" he was overheard shouting at a tagline man who was doing a poor job of steering a column.

The "Jerseymen" began their tower in mid-May of 1928. The New Yorkers began theirs in mid-July. "Give me the steel and I'll catch up and pass 'em," Reynolds promised his bosses at McClintock-Marshall. *Impossible,* they told him. *Watch me,* he responded. The rivalry was friendly but intense. Men would cut lunch early to gain a jump on the other tower. They hustled five days a week, eight in the morning until five in the evening, and half a day on Saturday. Erection on both towers paused for lack of steel in the winter of 1929, then resumed in March. By early summer, the New York tower had pulled ahead of the Jersey tower. "You couldn't call it a rivalry," Reynolds boasted afterward in the best ironworking tradition. "It was a walk away for our side."

The towers were complete. The time had now come to join them and make a bridge.

## SPINNING

Suspension bridges are made by drawing many thousands of thin steel wires, each about the diameter of a pencil, back and forth between the banks of a river in a process called "spinning." The wires are slung over the tops of the towers, secured in the "anchorages" on either side, then bunched together into the cables that eventually hold up the road deck. Altogether, 107,000 miles of such wire would go into the four cables of the George Washington Bridge before spinning was complete. This was wire enough to reach halfway to the moon—or, as it happened, to New Jersey and back about 50,000 times.

In early July of 1929, a barge towed a wrist-thick steel rope over the Hudson from New Jersey to New York. Cranes mounted on each tower hoisted the dripping steel rope out of the water and slung it over the tops of the towers. The rope now swooped sharply from the Jersey shore, crested over the 604-foot tower, sloped down 275 feet into a drooping catenary, soared up again to the tip of the Manhattan tower, then plunged down to the Manhattan anchorage. With that first long cursive M, the towers were joined. The bridge was truly a bridge.

The function of this first steel rope, and several dozen that soon followed, was to support the two 22-foot-wide catwalks the bridgemen would use to make the rest of the bridge. These ropes were only a temporary stage, but upon them was played the most spellbinding performance of the bridge's construction. It commenced when a handful of bridgemen ventured onto them in an open craft of wood and metal called a "carriage." They traveled along in fits and starts, laying prefabricated floor sections of steel and wood cross-wise on the rope. The work got interesting when several of the men stepped out of the carriage and slid along the ropes, hundreds of feet over the river, hanging almost literally by the seat of their pants. A glimpse of this astonishing feat is included in a scratchy 12-minute film shot by the Port Authority during the construction of the bridge. A man sits on one of the ropes sidesaddle, scooting down its steep slope, using his hand to pull himself along. His feet are hooked under a parallel rope to keep him from falling backwards. Below is a sheer drop of four or five hundred feet.

The catwalks complete, the wire spinning commenced on the morning of October 18, 1929. The wires were shuttled across the span by narrow grooved wheels—they looked like oversized bicycle wheels—attached to tramway ropes. These ropes were endless loops of a giant motorized pulley, each rope hauling two wheels, so that as one wheel arrived in New Jersey, the other arrived in New York. The wheels flew past each other on their course over the river, spilling out wire in their wake, riding a few feet above the catwalk, where the bridgemen stood at the ready.

The job of the 300 bridgemen was to keep the wire spinning and to gather and bundle it into tight clusters. Some of the men were stationed at the anchorages, those huge hunks of concrete and steel on the banks of the river where the wires were secured to bedrock. When the wheel arrived, the men would grab the loop of wire it delivered, fasten it to one of the "strand shoes" in the anchorage, and reload the wheel with a new loop of wire. Then they would reverse the engine and send the wheel back to the opposite shore. A good gang would have the wheel in and out of the anchorage in fifteen seconds.

Speed was the mantra of every pusher on every bridge: faster, faster, *faster*! And if the booming voice of their pusher was the stick that drove them on to great feats, the carrot was the incomparable pleasure of beating the gangs working the other cables. How many times could they send their wheel across? How many more than the others? A round trip took about 10 minutes, so 50 trips would make a good day, but if one gang made 50, the other gang tried for 51 or 52. Among them, the bridgemen managed to spin out 100 miles of wire per hour, faster than any bridge crew had ever done before.

A second division of bridgemen manned the summit of the towers. "Here she comes," a man would call as the wheel approached, and then they would hear it, whirring and clattering as it climbed the steep slope from the anchorage. A moment later, it crested the tower, and a moment after that, it was gone, swooping down toward the river, leaving the wire behind. The men grabbed the wire and fed it into a groove on one of the four "saddles" from which the cables would hang. They had to grab it fast because, as the wheel descended, paying out more wire, the weight of the wire rapidly increased. A delay of a few seconds could mean they'd have to stop the wheel and jack up the wire and endure their foreman's loud abuse.

The remainder of the bridgemen took up positions at regular intervals along the catwalks. One man, the "appraiser," stood in the center of each catwalk and eyeballed the wire to make sure it had just the right slack and droop. The other men scattered over the sloping catwalk like hillside farmers. They stood several feet under the tramway rope and waited for the wheel. As it passed, they grabbed the wire, still trilling and vibrating, and pulled it in by hand or metal crook, gathering it into sheaves, or "strands." Four hundred thirty-four wires made a strand; 61 strands made a full cable. Once the cables were spun, bridgemen would slowly pass over each with a giant hydraulic "squeezer," a ring-shaped clamp that compressed their 26,474 parallel wires into perfect three-foot-wide cylinders. Then they wrapped the cables with more wire, binding them like a sprain.

Gathering wire could be dangerous work. If the wind caught the wire before a bridgeman did, it could whip up and slap him off the bridge. One of the young men who worked on the bridge that autumn, George Bowers Jr.—his father, George Bowers Sr., also worked on it, as did a brother, Jim—had recently been employed on the Delaware River Bridge, a previous record holding suspension bridge. One afternoon, while spinning over the Delaware, he'd made the mistake of letting the wire get between his legs. When a gust of wind caught it, the wire lifted him off the catwalk, 15 feet into the air, slammed him back down onto the catwalk, then lifted him and slammed him down once more before he managed to dismount. Smoking was strictly forbidden on the wooden catwalks on account of fire hazard, but nobody made a peep when young George pulled out a cigarette and lit it.

Thirteen men had fallen from the Delaware River Bridge. Of those, three survived (including George's brother, Jim). By all expectations, this new bridge over the Hudson, twice the length, should have cost two or three times as many lives, but it did not. Just 12 workers perished on the George Washington Bridge. Three of the dead were caisson diggers who drowned when a cofferdam broke. The other nine died on the towers. Not one man died during the laying of the catwalk or the spinning of the cables.

On the morning of September 30, 1930, as cable spinning wound down, a professional daredevil named Norman Terry slipped past guards at the Manhattan anchorage and climbed the steep catwalk to the tower. From 600 feet, he descended to the lowest point of the catwalk, about 220 feet over the middle of the river. Below, on the water, several photographers and reporters from the *Daily News* waited in a boat, having been tipped off to the stunt by Terry's manager. A film crew was there, too, ready to capture the event. Terry hesitated a moment, as if the view gave him second thoughts. Then, with his arms stretched out and his heels tight together, he sprang out into a perfect dive. He maintained his form until he was about 20 feet over the river, then suddenly seemed to buckle. He landed on his back, badly. Rather than earn himself fame and fortune as the first man to survive a jump from the George Washington Bridge, he obtained a less happy distinction by becoming its thirteenth victim—and the last man to die on the bridge before it opened to traffic on October 25, 1931. By that point, the ironworkers were long gone.

The Depression was a surprisingly fine time to be a bridgeman in America. Privately financed skyscraper construction slowed to a trickle, but a flurry of publicly financed bridge projects kept the ironworkers' heads above water. In New York, the George Washington was soon followed by the Triborough Bridge—actually a trio of bridges envisioned by Robert Moses and designed by Othmar Ammann to thread together the Bronx, Manhattan, and Queens. The Bayonne arch was completed in 1931 and the Bronx Whitestone, yet another Ammann design, in 1939.

The real action for bridgemen in the 1930s was not in New York, though. It was out west: the Conde B. McCullough Memorial Bridge over Coos Bay in Oregon; the Lewis and Clark Bridge over the Columbia River, also in Oregon; the Tacoma Narrows Bridge in Washington State; the San Francisco Bay Bridge in California. And, of course, the Golden Gate.

No bridge would ever achieve quite the astonishing leap in scale that Ammann's George Washington made in 1931, but the Golden Gate was a dramatic follow-up. The total length of this new bridge, end to end, was almost 9,000 feet, with a center clear span of 4,200 feet, 20 percent longer than the G.W.'s. Almost as impressive as its size, at least as far as the ironworkers were concerned, were several safety precautions implemented by its builders during construction. American Bridge Company provided every worker with a leather hard hat, an unprecedented measure at the time. More remarkable, the company strung a cotton fiber safety net under the bridge to catch falling bridgemen. The safety net proved its worth at least 19 times.

While the bridge boom provided jobs to ironworkers, Congress passed two laws that benefited them in other ways. The Davis-Bacon Act of 1931 required contractors on all federally financed construction projects to pay the prevailing wage of the locale where the work occurred. A contractor didn't have to hire union workers, but he had to pay a union wage to the men he did hire. The Wagner Act, passed by Congress in 1935, guaranteed employees the right to organize into unions and seek collective bargaining with their bosses. For the first time in American history, the law forbade employers from firing an employee simply because he belonged to a labor union.

The Wagner Act had an immediate and salubrious impact. U.S. Steel and Bethlehem Steel, the dual Big Steel nemeses that ironworkers had been fighting since the turn of the century, recognized the ironworkers' union for the first time in 30 years. Ten years later, a Republican-controlled Congress would water down the Wagner Act with passage of the Taft-Hartley Act, but relations with Big Steel would never return to their poisoned pre-Depression state. Bethlehem and U.S. Steel were now committed to hiring union labor, while the union, for its part, was content to keep the peace. In New York, the ironworkers would not strike again until 1963. And when they did, the issue would not be one of the old perennials, like money or jurisdiction or power. It would be a safety net under the Verrazano-Narrows Bridge.

## THE LAST GREAT BRIDGE

The Narrows is a mile-wide neck of saltwater joining the Upper Bay of New York Harbor to the Atlantic Ocean. It is the portal to the port of New York. Brooklyn thrusts out into the bay from one side, Staten Island from the other, and between the two washes the sea. The "bridge over the sea," as the Verrazano-Narrows Bridge has been called, was to be the last link in the interborough highway system that Robert Moses had begun with the Triborough Bridge 25 years earlier. Moses, the master-builder of New York, was back to perform one last monumental act of urban planning. Othmar Ammann was back to engineer one last superlative bridge.

Bridge building had slackened after the Depression, pausing for World War II, then picked up again in the late 1940s. Americans demanded automobiles, and automobiles demanded new highways and tunnels and, of course, bridges. In the five boroughs of New York City alone, ironworkers erected 28 bridges in the 28 years between the completion of the George Washington in 1931 and the start of the Verrazano-Narrows in 1959. Those two bridges, the George Washington and the Verrazano-Narrows, were the bookends of the great American age of bridge building. The George Washington was Othmar Ammann's first; the Verrazano-Narrows would be his last.

It would also be the last extraordinary bridge built in America. Its full span, anchorage to anchorage, would stretch 6,690 feet. Its clear span, at 4,260 feet, would be the longest in the world, reaching 760 feet farther than the George Washington's and 60 feet farther than the

Golden Gate's. So great was the distance between the bridge's two towers that Ammann took the curvature of the earth into account in his calculations: each of the 690-foot bridge towers would rise straight up from the earth's surface, but they would be one and five-eighth inches farther apart at their tops than at their foundations.

The towers topped out in the fall of 1962, and spinning began in early spring of the following year. For 6 months, 15 hours a day, 6 days a week, the bicycle wheels raced back and forth over the channel, paying out their wire. The ironworkers split the day into two shifts, one shift spinning by day, the other by night.

Nearly as many people came to watch the work as to do it, for this bridge, unlike the George Washington, had the city's undivided attention. Every day, between a hundred and two hundred spectators, most of them elderly, retired, and male, gathered on the promontory off Bay Ridge to applaud and second-guess the work. In midtown Manhattan, the construction voyeurs who lined up along the edge of building sites and peeked through the plywood were called "sidewalk superintendents." Here they were "seaside superintendents." No plywood blocked their view of the bridge, but since the most interesting work occurred half a mile out to sea and several hundred feet in the air, the experienced ones brought binoculars.

Almost 12,000 tradesmen would work on the bridge before it was done, including concrete masons, electricians, and painters, but it was the ironworkers that the old men came to watch. "Without the structural steel workers," wrote one reporter who trekked out to Bay Ridge to observe the work, "bridgewatching is like Yankee-watching without Mickey Mantle in the lineup."

The writer Gay Talese often made the trip from Manhattan. He came to cover the bridge for the *New York Times* and to gather material for a slim book he later published about its construction. In his articles and his book, Talese wrote about Ammann and the politics of the bridge and the anger of the citizens dispossessed by the bridge, but his real interest, like that of the seaside supers, was the bridgemen. He was especially fascinated by the nomadic, carousing boomers. "They drive into town in big cars, and live in furnished rooms, and drink whiskey with beer chasers, and chase women they will soon forget," he wrote in his unabashedly romantic portrait. "They are part circus, part gypsy—graceful in the air, restless on the ground." Talese quoted a Dr. S. Thomas Coppola, who treated many injured bridgemen during the course of the bridge's construction. "These are the most interesting men I've ever met. They're strong, they can stand all kinds of pain, they're full of pride, and they live it up."

And sometimes, of course, they died. The first man to die on the Verrazano-Narrows fell off an approach ramp and landed on the road below. The second fell inside the Brooklyn tower. The third and last was a soft-spoken 19-year-old named Gerard McKee. He was 200 pounds and well over 6 feet tall, a gentle giant who came from a large family of ironworkers in Red Hook, Brooklyn. He fell on a gloomy Wednesday morning in October of 1963, while attaching suspender cables that would hang down from the cables and hold the road deck. His partner, another young ironworker named Edward Iannielli, heard a shout and turned to see McKee grasping the edge of the catwalk by his fingers, dangling 350 feet over the water. Before Iannielli or anyone else could save him, McKee lost his grip and fell. He was an excellent swimmer, a former Coney Island lifeguard who'd amused himself as a boy by swimming across New York Harbor from Red Hook to the Statue of Liberty. If anyone could have survived a plunge into the Narrows, it was Gerard McKee. But no one could.

Gerard McKee's death triggered an ironworkers' strike, led by Jim Cole, Local 40's Newfoundlander business agent. The ironworkers refused to go back to work until American Bridge agreed to stretch nets under the bridge, just as the company had done 30 years earlier under the Golden Gate. Four days later, American Bridge conceded.

Robert Moses neglected to include ironworkers in the opening ceremonies for the bridge on November 21, 1964, just as he had neglected to include them in the groundbreaking ceremony and the ceremony to mark the commencement of the wire spinning. He did remember to include Othmar Ammann, the bridge's engineer, referring to him in a speech as "one of the significant great men of our time." Unfortunately, he neglected to mention Ammann by name, so when a small old man stood up and lifted his hat, most people in the audience probably had no idea who he was. Ammann died a year later at the age of 86.

As for the other old men, the seaside supers, they had to find something else to do with their free time now. The show was over. They had witnessed the end of an era. Rivets were on the way out, to

Spinning the first cables on the Verrazano-Narrows Bridge. This view is from the top of the Brooklyn tower, 690 feet above water.
*(Port Authority of New York and New Jersey)*

be replaced by high-strength bolts and welding. The rivet gangs would soon be a memory. So, too, would be the sight of the steel wires traveling back and forth across water, because no new suspension bridge would go up in New York again, not in what was left of their lifetimes anyway, and probably not in their children's or grandchildren's lifetimes either. The last great bridge was done. The attention of the city, and of the ironworkers, turned north across the bay to a 16-acre patch of soft ground in lower Manhattan, where two towers were about to rise higher than any structure yet built by man.

## SQUARE ONE

Early on a bright morning in September of 1968, a young ironworker named Jack Doyle descended a long dirt ramp into the huge square hole at the bottom of the city. He was 24 years old. He spoke with a Newfoundlander's brogue and walked with a slight limp, the result of a blow he'd taken to his hip while playing hockey in Conception Bay. The doctor had advised him to seek a sedentary occupation. Instead, Jack Doyle had followed his father and uncles and brothers into ironwork, becoming, of all things, a connector. "Guys would see me up there limping and get worried," he recalled years later. "Well, not to blow my own horn, but I walked steel with the best of them. I was pretty catty."

He was catty—a Newfoundlander term for surefooted—but he was blessed with an equally indispensable ironworkers' talent for luck. He'd fallen three times and gotten away without a scratch. The first time, in Canada, he landed in a snowbank. The second time, in Detroit, he managed to grab a brace on the way down and sustained minor injuries. The third time, just a few months behind him now, he nearly died. He fell just one floor but landed on a table where carpenters were cutting sheets of plywood with a large circular saw. He missed the blade, and bisection, by inches.

Jack arrived at the foundation of the World Trade Center directly from the shape hall. He'd known about these new buildings for years. He'd read a magazine article about the Trade Center back in Canada, how the towers were going to be the tallest in the world, and the idea of working on them had thrilled him even then. And now here he was, 6 stories below ground, in the largest hole ever dug in New York City, a vast basin wide enough to accommodate 16 football fields. Most of the grillages—the pedestals of steel beams that would transfer the weight of columns to the concrete footings—had already been set. A few huge columns rose from the ground at the northwest corner of the hole, the first inklings of the north tower.

Jack had been moving around almost continuously since leaving home five years earlier. He'd worked on skyscrapers in Toronto, then boomed to Detroit for a while, then Philadelphia. He'd been back to Newfoundland, too, where he'd met a girl from the town next to his and gotten himself engaged.

Coming to this hole at the bottom of Manhattan was like coming home. Two of his brothers, Norm and George, were there. His first cousin, Leo Doyle, was superintendent in those early days, and Dick Brady, his fiancée's brother, was there, too, pushing a rig. There were dozens of young men he recognized from the head of the bay, like Joe Lewis and Willie Quinlan and Billy Moore. As he stood there in the cool dampness, he knew he'd arrived exactly where he wanted to be. "I knew when I went down there that morning that I was staying," he said. "I wanted to see the top of it."

In the fall of 1968, as Jack Doyle and his fellow ironworkers were climbing their way out of the ground, the tallest building in the world was the Empire State Building. The second tallest was the Chrysler Building. Both of these buildings were nearly 40 years old.

Hundreds of new skyscrapers had been constructed since the end of World War II, some of them distinguished works of architecture, but the new skyscrapers had little in common with the skyscrapers of the 1920s. Where those had been clad in stone and thick with steel, the new ones were lightly framed and dressed in glass. Where the old skyscrapers had risen in ever ascendant step-backs toward a cupola or a peak, shaped like wedding cakes and rocket ships, the modernist buildings tended to be sheer-walled rectangles, perfect "glass boxes," as they were often called. Where the old buildings had been decorative and brash, the new buildings were steadfastly austere.

And, finally, where the old buildings had striven for height, these new structures aspired only to middling altitude, a mere 50 stories through the 1950s, 60 stories through the 1960s. The Depression had quashed the ambition to go higher. Every developer in town knew that the Empire State Building—the "Empty State Building," as New Yorkers called it—had taken 15 years to reach full occupancy, and none wished to repeat that fiasco.

The new buildings were structurally ill-equipped for great height in any case. It's not that they lacked the strength for it; they were plenty strong. Indeed, their steel was significantly stronger than the steel found in earlier skyscrapers. But because the steel was stronger, engineers put less of it into buildings, which, in turn, made the buildings relatively light. And the absence of all the extra masonry cladding and heavy internal partitions that modernist architects disdained made the buildings even lighter. That incidental heft hadn't made the old buildings stronger, but it had made them more stable, more inert. These new light buildings, in contrast, were highly susceptible to wind; and for every story added to their height, their wind loads increased exponentially. If buildings are going to be tall and light, they must also be somehow rigid. And in the early 1960s, lightness and rigidity seemed to be mutually exclusive.

A young Bangladeshi-born engineer named Fazlur Khan found a way to resolve the contradiction. Before Khan, steel buildings distributed their loads evenly among columns running vertically throughout the area of the building. An early innovation that helped stiffen buildings was to bulk up the steel in the center of the building, in the form of a core; these cores housed the elevator shafts and stairwells and, most important, acted as spines for the building.

Fazlur Khan was the first to seize on the idea of concentrating more steel on the *outside* of the building. He did to buildings what steel manufacturers had long been doing to structural shapes: he moved the steel to where it was needed most, concentrating columns not only around the core, but also around the perimeter. By moving much of the load burden to the external walls, Khan's "framed tubes," as he called them, marked a partial return to the design of old-fashioned masonry buildings. His buildings had both the spine of a vertebrate and shell of a crustacean. They were light, but they were also rigid.

At the same time that Fazlur Khan was improving the technology of tall buildings, American developers were experiencing a new yen to build them. Khan's own 100-story John Hancock Center, begun in Chicago in 1965, was the first of the new tall breed. Meanwhile, in New York, the Port Authority of New York and New Jersey—the same agency, now renamed, that had commissioned the George Washington Bridge 35 years earlier—finalized plans for the World Trade Center. Standing at the center of this vast project would be the two tallest towers in the world.

Architect Minoru Yamasaki, working closely with the Seattle engineering firm of Worthington-Skilling, designed two nearly identical rectangular buildings in which each of the 208-foot-wide walls would be made up of 61 columns. These columns, along with the thick but narrow panes of glass between them, would form the exterior of the buildings. They would also bear its weight in conjunction with the steel core. The design would give the buildings enormous uninterrupted floor spans, 60 feet from core to wall, which would translate into an unusually high ratio of rentable square footage—75 percent of the building's area compared with the 50 percent common in older skyscrapers. And to sweeten the deal, the design would limit the use of steel to an economical minimum. It was true that, at

96,000 tons apiece, the steel in each of the World Trade Center's towers would weigh about 60 percent more than the steel in the Empire State Building. But given the ratio of steel to square footage, this was relatively light. For that 60 percent, each tower would provide 150 percent more rentable space.

The steel did not feel light to Jack Doyle. "Everything we touched in the hole was huge. Every column we hooked onto was forty or fifty tons." Higher up, the steel would slim down considerably, but in the hole it was gargantuan and cumbersome, and six floors of it had to be erected before the ironworkers could lift their necks above the ground.

Jack spent the fall and early winter setting huge columns and girders with Manitowoc crawler cranes. Once the frame finally climbed above ground, he moved into a raising gang pushed by his older brother, George, and connected under a kangaroo crane. The World Trade Center marked the debut of these extraordinary new tower cranes, soon to become a fixture of skyscraper construction in New York, replacing the derricks that had done the job of hoisting iron and steel for a century. None of the ironworkers had ever seen a kangaroo before; now they were working with eight of the largest in the world.

The gangs hung steel in three stages. First, they set a few floors of the core through which the many elevators would run. This was familiar work, fairly standard column-and-post connections. Next they set columns of the perimeter wall. The columns came in racks of three, joined together by horizontal spandrels and alternating in height between 15 and 30 feet. The ironworkers stacked the column racks around the perimeter of the building, bolting and welding them at the bottoms and the tops.

Now came the most unusual part of the operation. Instead of setting standard I-beams horizontally between core and wall, the raising gangs used the kangaroos to hoist huge prefabricated sections of floor panel—60 feet long, 20 feet wide, and about 3 feet deep—and lower them snugly into the gap between core and columns. Structurally speaking, these floor sections killed three birds with one stone. They provided the decking into which concrete would be poured to make the building's floors. They provided the ducts through which air-conditioning and electrical and telephone wires would run. And, most important, they contained the light steel trusses that would transfer lateral forces—wind, mainly—from the exterior walls to the core and make the building act as a single rigid body.

One afternoon, George Backett, the super, called Jack over for a word. He told Jack he'd decided to appoint him foreman of a raising gang under the northeast kangaroo crane. "I want you to push the rig," he said. "I know you can handle it." It was an unexpected and daunting promotion. Jack was in his mid-20s, younger and less experienced than every other man in the gang, and this was the biggest skyscraper job in the world. If George Backett had asked, Jack might have hesitated to assume such responsibility. But George Backett wasn't the type to ask.

Jack took over the crane just as the job moved into a new phase. The heaviest portion of the building was behind them. The gangs had become acquainted with the kangaroos and the peculiarities of the tower's design and were poised to kick up their speed a notch. It had taken them 18 months to get from the hole to the 30th floor. It would take just nine more months to top out at the 110th floor.

As the building rose, legends and tales grew alongside it, some of these even true. There was the time the tugboat operators went on strike, shutting off the delivery of the floor panels, and somebody at the Port Authority had the bright idea of using an enormous helicopter—a skycrane—to make the deliveries. So one Saturday morning, Jack and the rest of his raising gang stood on a pier at the edge of the Hudson River to greet the skycrane and unload the floor panel. "And then we see it," said Jack, still smiling at the memory years later. "It's coming up the river with the piece hanging from underneath. Halfway up the river, all of a sudden we see the piece drop." The panel had started to swing wildly and the pilot had cut it loose, and down it went to the bottom of New York Harbor. The ironworkers got their eight hours overtime and went home. That was the end of transporting floor panels by helicopter.

The building hit another snag around the 44th floor, when the elevator operators went on strike. Now the only way for the ironworkers to get to the top was to climb. Every morning for weeks they humped themselves up the stairs, and when the stairs ran out, they climbed another five or six stories by ladder, and when they got to the top they sat down and caught their breath. A Mohawk pusher named Walter Beauvais decided to get around this inconvenience by hitching a ride from the ground on one of the floor panels. Riding loads was no longer acceptable practice, and had not been for years, but Beauvais—known to his fellow ironworkers either as "Chickenbones" or "Hambone"—jumped on when nobody was looking and secreted himself under an overturned barrel. He grasped the choker, and the load took off. This was not the first time Walter Beauvais had gone around the rules—indeed he was a self-professed risk taker of the highest order—and the union shop steward had his eye on him. As it happened, that same shop steward was standing on top when Beauvais arrived and popped out from under the barrel, ready for work. The shop steward fired him on the spot. "I had to get to the top," Walter Beauvais explained years later with a shrug. "Anyway, I came back after a week. No hard feelings."

## BLOODY FRIDAY

The north tower reached the 70th floor in mid-spring of 1970. The sounds of the city fell away and the view opened up into a remarkable panorama, not of the city below but of the world beyond the city, of the Atlantic Ocean and suburban sprawl, of wooded hills and countryside. On a clear day you could see up to 45 miles. You could see east across Brooklyn and Queens, all the way to Jones Beach and the Atlantic shipping lanes, as far as Asbury Park to the south and Tarrytown to the north.

As vividly as he would later remember the astonishing view on a sunny day, Jack would remember the fog they began to encounter as they rose above the 70th floor. He'd remember how the hook of the kangaroo would drop over the side of the building and plummet into the whiteness. "We'd be on top, waiting for it to come back, and of course we couldn't see the street. That was a ghostly thing, because the cables just went down and disappeared. After four or five minutes you'd just hear the crane engines start whining over your head. You could tell by the sound when they had a heavy load, but sometimes, if they'd just dropped the whip line, you couldn't hear it. All of a sudden, *boom*, this big load of rusty steel would bounce out from the clouds."

They were approaching a thousand feet, but the deck felt as safe and protected as a quiet cove. The perimeter columns buffeted the wind and enclosed the ironworkers. Just how well the columns did their job became apparent when you walked to the edge of the floor, stuck your head out between them, and looked down at the street. The wind nearly blew your head off. The instant you pulled yourself back in, the wind stopped and the air went still.

Standing on the deck, you felt detached from the world down there. You were a thousand feet up but sometimes it felt more like a thousand miles. Of course, this was an illusion. You were in the middle of New York City, in the middle of 1970.

Nineteen-seventy was a pivotal, turbulent year in America. The Kennedys and Dr. King were dead, and the idealism of the 1960s had burnt down to a simmering rage. Nineteen-seventy was the year ironworkers and their fellow tradesmen proved they were as capable of venting rage as anyone else in America.

The two defining political issues of the year were civil rights and Vietnam, and the ironworkers stood squarely on the wrong side of both. Their record on civil rights was weak at best. Neither Brooklyn's Local 361 nor Manhattan's Local 40 had initiated a single black person into their membership until 1964, the year Congress passed the Civil Rights Act. The exclusion of blacks in the union until this point may have been an explicit policy, albeit an unwritten one, but the primary motive behind it was more likely nepotism than racism. Before the Wagner Act of 1935, the union eagerly sought more members. Nowadays, it had many more aspirants than it could possibly accept. It was difficult for anybody, white or black, to get in unless he had a strong connection to someone who already belonged, preferably his father or a close uncle.

The first black union ironworker, a slender 21-year-old named Michael Stewart, joined the New York local in 1964. By 1966, 14 other black men had enrolled in the apprentice training programs for Locals 40 and 361. The union trumpeted this as progress, but civil rights advocates dismissed it as tokenism, a "ruse" to cover up entrenched discrimination. A 1967 report by the New York City Commission on Human Rights found that the city's building trade unions continued to maintain "almost insurmountable barriers to nonwhite journeymen seeking membership." Local 40 was one of nine New York unions singled out for dishonorable mention.

It wasn't their views on race, however, that so effectively seared the image of construction workers as mindless reactionaries into many Americans' minds in 1970. It was their views, and actions, on the Vietnam War.

The Vietnam War was fought overwhelmingly by working-class Americans. Just 20 percent of troops came from white-collar households, while 80 percent had acquired no more than a high school education. They were small-town farmers from rural America and young black men from the inner city. And they were, many of them, the white sons of building tradesmen. To these young men and their families, anti-war protesters were spoiled college kids who wriggled out of the draft and then had the temerity to bad-mouth their country and the military. Throughout the 1960s, as protests against the war grew louder and more rancorous, the "silent majority," as Nixon called his pro-war working-class constituency, bit their lips and seethed. Then, one spring day in 1970, a few blocks from the World Trade Center, a group of ironworkers and other building tradesmen stopped seething and exploded. The event became known as "Bloody Friday."

The seeds of Bloody Friday were probably planted years earlier, but the direct antecedent was a speech President Nixon gave on April 30, 1970. Having repeatedly promised to withdraw troops from Vietnam, Nixon now told America he'd decided, on second thought, to extend the draft and, furthermore, to invade Cambodia and root out Vietcong resistance. Anti-war activists were outraged. Demonstrations flared up at college campuses across the country. On May 4, National Guardsmen opened fire on demonstrators at Kent State University in Ohio, killing 4 students, wounding 11 others, and sending the country into a state of shock.

Four days after Kent State, on Friday, May 8, anti-war demonstrators, mostly students from New York University and Hunter College, staged a rally on the corner of Wall Street and Broad Street, near the base of the World Trade Center. City schools were closed for the day and American flags flew at half mast in honor of the four dead students in Ohio. The rally was progressing peacefully when, just before noon, 200 or so construction workers, including ironworkers from the World Trade Center and the U.S. Steel Building (rising on the former site of the Singer Building) suddenly descended on the demonstrators, pushing through police lines and beating the students with fists, boots, and pipes. The mob then stormed City Hall and ordered officials to restore the flag to full staff. This done, the mob launched into a rousing chorus of "God Bless America."

Seventy people were injured before the riot ended. The police, who tended to share the tradesmen's attitude toward the student demonstrators, did little to intervene. "They came at us like animals," said one 20-year-old student. "You could hear them screaming, 'Kill the commies.' They charged and we ran for our lives."

One of the "animals" was a 29-year-old ironworker, an ex-Marine who worked on the U.S. Steel Building and had recently broken three of his toes when a steel beam fell on his foot. "It was probably the only day my foot didn't hurt me a bit," he told the *New York Post*. "I had other things on my mind."

To a city and country already reeling, Bloody Friday and several successive demonstrations, collectively known as the "hard-hat riots," were one more extraordinary fact to absorb. Liberals, especially, were confounded. Wasn't the proletariat supposed to be on the same team they were on, snuggled up under the inclusive embrace of the Democratic Party? Apparently not. Apparently, the proletariat wished them bodily harm.

Conservatives, for their part, welcomed the hard hats as a much-needed antidote to hippie peaceniks. Nixon could hardly contain his glee, declaring Bloody Friday "a very exciting thing." At a special White House ceremony later that month, the president personally thanked a gathering of trade union representatives for their support. In return, Peter Brennan, president of the Building and Construction Trades Council of New York, presented Nixon with a hard hat of his very own.

But the romance was short-lived. In February of 1971, just 10 months after praising the hard hats at the White House, Nixon bowed to pressure from pro-business lobbying groups and suspended the Davis-Bacon prevailing wage act, a singularly harsh blow to trade unions. Nixon's betrayal came as a shock to the ironworkers and other tradesmen, but nobody felt too sorry for them. They had done far too good a job of tarring themselves as racist warmongers to stir up much support from their old allies, the liberals. As for conservatives, they only had a use for them, it seemed, when they were beating up liberals.

## COLOSSUS

Autumn arrived, heralded by the carcasses of dead birds on the top deck. "They were small birds, little black birds," remembered Jack Doyle. "Probably flying at night and hit the boom." Evidently, the birds were migrating on last year's flight plan and had no idea a building had risen into the winds that carried them south.

Then winter. "One day early that winter," said Jack, "we had one of those silver thaws, where it got mild and wet snow was falling, then turned cold fast, especially at that height. The next morning I went up with the super and the shop steward to have a look at the cranes, to see that everything was fine up there." Jack and the two other men rode the elevator, then climbed the last few floors on ladders, and when they stepped out through the core onto the deck, they found themselves in a place they hardly recognized. "It was like something out of *Doctor Zhivago*," said Jack. "There was an inch of ice all over the crane booms, all over the lacing and the cables, and they were standing there, everything decorated in ice. The heat of the day was starting and you could hear the ice cracking. Up on the boom, every now and again, a small piece would crack and fall, but nothing else, just everything silent and beautiful. It was like the world stood still."

Down below, the carping had already started. Broadcasters worried the towers would block the transmission of television signals from the top of the Empire State Building, leaving black rectangles in the middle of television sets all over the Tristate area. Real estate moguls predicted the towers would glut the market and depress prices throughout the city. Aesthetes objected to the towers because they were ugly—"annoyingly familiar," as Glenn Collins put it in the *New York Times Magazine*, resembling "two shiny new sticks of Arrow staples, standing on end."

"Tall buildings are an outmoded concept—this is Victorian thinking," wrote the renowned critic Lewis Mumford of the towers. "They are not economically sound or efficient—in fact they are ridiculously unprofitable. . . ." The Trade Center's fate, predicted Mumford, "is to be ripped down as nonsensical." This was a fate many seemed to wish upon the World Trade Center in those days. It was, as *BusinessWeek* described it, "the colossus nobody seems to love."

Well, the ironworkers loved it. It was *their* colossus. Many of them had spent two or three years of their lives building it. Not only had the towers provided them with steady employment and ample pride, but they'd kept them safe, too. Those same perimeter columns that carried the load of the building and buffeted the wind had enclosed them and protected them as effectively as palings on a crib. Five men died constructing the Twin Towers, but none of them were ironworkers.

There were injuries, of course, several of these quite serious. Two ironworkers fell and became paralyzed. And at the top of Tower One, George Doyle—Jack's older brother—stepped on a plank that gave way under him, and fell 20 feet. The plank hit his head and cut a gash in it. He recovered but was out for several weeks.

It was George Doyle, not Jack, who was supposed to top out Tower One. Topping out is an ironworkers' tradition marking the setting of the highest piece of steel in a building or bridge. The beam is decorated with an American flag and frequently with a small fir tree as well. Despite the fact that the ceremony had long ago been seized by publicists and financiers as a photo-op, topping out was something ironworkers took seriously. To be the foreman whose gang raised the topping-out flag was an honor.

The day before the topping-out ceremony, George's crane broke down. The honor went instead to Jack.

At 11:30 A.M. on December 23, 1970, a cold gray day, Jack Doyle gave the order to his signalman, who relayed it to the crane operator. As the crowd watched from the deck of the 110th floor, a 4-ton, 36-foot-high column rose into view, paused on the deck for the photographers, then rose again and settled into the core. Months of detail work remained before the ironworkers would leave the building and hand it over to the trades that followed, but the tallest steel frame in the world was now complete. Jack Doyle had made it to the top.

The towers' position as the tallest buildings in the world was challenged almost as soon as they were finished. In October of 1972, the owners of the Empire State Building explored the possibility of

On a foggy December day, Jack Doyle *(right)* tops out the north tower of
the World Trade Center.
*(Courtesy of Jack Doyle)*

adding 11 stories to the building and resurrecting it as the world's tallest. That never panned out. But in 1974, Sears, Roebuck and Company completed the Sears Tower in Chicago, 1,450 feet of steel arranged in tubes by Fazlur Khan. The tallest in the world—for the moment.

On the night of August 7, 1974, a young French highwire walker named Philippe Petit rigged a $^7/_8$-inch steel cable between the tops of the two towers by shooting an arrow across the 200-foot gap. The following morning, as thousands watched from below, he stepped out onto the cable and started across, as catty as a man can be. For one hour that morning, as Petit walked back and forth on the cable, the identical twins of the World Trade Center were combined into a single astonishing structure. They were the towers of the highest suspension bridge in the world.

# ELEVEN

# Burning Steel

Later, of course, everybody would remember exactly what they were doing at 10 minutes to 9 that Tuesday morning. Chad Snow was on 60th Street with Ky Horn, unloading heavy columns from the back of an eighteen-wheeler. Joe Emerson and Kevin Scally were setting steel on top, on the northeastern corner of the Time Warner Center. Mickey Tracy was inside the building directing his gang to cut and weld deck angles onto beams. The news came at them from the street, from some teamsters who'd heard it on the radios of their trucks and shouted it out—*The Trade Center! A plane!*—and simultaneously from the highest point on the building, the cabins of the kangaroo cranes, where some of the operating engineers kept themselves company with small transistor radios.

*They're saying a plane hit the Trade Center,* one of the operators called into his two-way.

Sixty feet below, the signalman looked past the boom of the crane into the clear blue sky. *A plane?*

*A little single-engine job they think. Some idiot.*

The operator reached for a pair of high-powered binoculars he kept on hand inside the cab. The binoculars were a tool of his trade. He was perched so high above the derrick floor that he sometimes needed the lenses to see what the ironworkers were doing below. But in idle moments, when the ironworkers were mucking around with a choker or a turnbuckle and the operator had a few minutes to kill, he amused himself by scanning the faraway windows of neighboring skyscrapers. Extraordinary visions appeared within his grasp. Beautiful women strolled naked through sunlit rooms at the top of the city. Had they never heard of blinds? Had they never heard of high-powered binoculars and idle crane operators?

This morning, the crane operator wasn't looking for beautiful women. He was looking for a flickering television set. He found one almost immediately.

*Jesus Christ*, he said to his signalman. *It's burning. I'm looking at it.*

*You can see it?*

*I'm watching it on the TV. Christ!*

As the facts piled on—second tower hit! Pentagon hit! Tower Two down! Tower One down!—the ironworkers gathered in the dirt courtyard at the front of the building. Joe Kennedy descended the metal staircase from the sidewalk bridge. He spoke gravely. "The Trade Center has collapsed. You're all welcome to stay here if you can't get home. The trains are all stopped. Call your wives, call your families. Tell them you're all right."

The men dispersed slowly. They made their calls. Then, in clusters, they started their long journeys home. The bridges had closed to traffic, the subways and trains were frozen. They walked, like hundreds of thousands of other people that day, over the steel bridges that ringed the city.

Mickey Tracy decided to stay put. He figured there was no sense trying to go home, since he lived an hour and a half north of the city and the roads were already at a standstill. He dialed his wife from the trailer but couldn't get through to his home in Connecticut; the lines were jammed. He tried a few other numbers, eventually reaching his sister-in-law in Massachusetts, who then tracked down Mickey's wife, Karen, at a lawyer's office and gave her Mickey's message: he was alive and well and would be home as soon as possible. Karen had gone to the lawyer that morning to discuss the will Mickey and she were drawing up.

After hanging up the phone, Mickey sat in the trailer with the other men who had stayed behind. They listened to the radio, nobody saying much. Then the phone rang. It was Eddie Walsh, one of Local 40's business agents, calling from the shape hall on 15th Street. The fire department had put out a call for ironworkers. Anybody who wanted to volunteer should get over to the Armory on 68th Street and Park Avenue, Walsh said. The National Guard would take it from there.

Mickey stood up, said good-bye to the men in the trailer, and walked out into the stunning day. The message he had left for his wife—that he was fine and would be coming home as soon as possible—was only half true. He had a hunch, even as he spoke the words, that he wasn't going home anytime soon. A few blocks down Broadway he turned into the lobby of a hotel, a place he'd stayed a few times in the past. After checking in, he returned to the street and found a small store around the corner, where he purchased three pairs of socks, three pairs of underpants, and three T-shirts. With his bag of undergarments, he walked back to 59th Street. He stood by the eastbound lane and stuck out his thumb. A moment later, a van halted. "I'm going to Park and 68th," he told the driver. "Gimme a ride?" The driver nodded, and Mickey climbed in.

Stepping into a stranger's car in the middle of Manhattan on a day the world seemed to be coming apart was not for everyone, but Mickey thought nothing of it. He was blessed with a quick, puckish wit and could always talk his way out of trouble; and where his mouth failed him, he trusted his fists. He was only 5'4" but thickly built and strong. "It doesn't take much," he once explained, "for us ironworkers to crack a guy." Mickey was given to such pronouncements about ironworkers. "We're physical guys, but we take care of people," he would say. "The ironworker is a generous person." Or: "Bad ironworkers have bad ironworker kids." Or: "Ironwork is a series of moves; every day you learn a new move; miss a day, you miss a move."

Mickey was a fourth-generation ironworker and had been at it himself for 22 years. He was Bronx-born but a Newfoundlander by heritage. He had no idea where on the Rock his family originated but he did know a story about three brothers who got drunk one night and stole a boat from Newfoundland and sailed it down to Boston. They sold the boat, drank the proceeds, and took up ironwork to support themselves. One of the three brothers was Mickey's great-grandfather, who later fell and died in Boston. Mickey's grandfather, Jack Tracy, then moved to New York and worked out of Local 40, until he fell, too. As part of the operation to save Jack Tracy, surgeons inserted a metal plate inside his head. "We think maybe it was a lead plate," said Mickey, "'cause he started acting a little strange after that."

By the time the van deposited Mickey at the Armory, the place was crawling with ironworkers. They stood or sat about in clusters, smoking cigarettes and waiting for clearance to go downtown. "There were guys there I hadn't seen in years. There were guys there I used to connect with, men who broke me in when I was a kid. I tell you, there was so much ironworking talent in that room it humbled me."

National Guardsmen swarmed around them nervously. "The G.I. Joes were talking about chemical things, nerve gas, anthrax, smallpox," remembered Mickey. "They couldn't clear us to go because they didn't know what was down there. So we just waited around. A few of us helped load some tents and supplies onto army trucks. We wanted to be busy and do something." The ironworkers had to fill out paperwork while they waited. NEXT OF KIN, read one entry. Mickey wrote down his wife's name and his home address.

Several hours had passed at the armory when it dawned on Mickey and a number of the ironworkers that they were going to spend all afternoon here unless they made a move. Without a word to the G.I. Joes, and lacking proper clearance, they slipped out to Park Avenue, boarded a fleet of pickups and four-by-fours, and took off. The convoy headed west, then sped south along the river. Mickey sat in the back of one of the pickups, trying to anticipate what he was heading into. Fatality statistics of fifty or sixty thousand had been discussed at the Armory. Airborne chemical and biological weaponry had not yet been ruled out. Mickey thought about his wife and son and said a prayer. He was, he later admitted, apprehensive. But he never doubted that he was doing the right thing. "I decided that I was going to try to do something. They needed ironworkers. Cutting steel, moving steel. This is what we do every day. There was nobody more equipped to do it."

The sun dipped over the high-rises across the river. It was a beautiful afternoon, crystal-clear and warm. Then Mickey saw what appeared to be snow swirling up in the breeze, a blizzard of concrete powder and paper. The gray snow covered the ground with a thin dusting at first, but as they drove on it became a blanket, as much as two inches deep. Further on, huge hunks of steel lay scattered over the highway as if they'd fallen from the sky. Which, of course, they had.

Those who went to the site in the first few days kept returning to the same two images to describe it. "It's like a war zone." Or: "It's like a movie." Or they said nothing, they were silent. What television could not convey, they all agreed, was the total overwhelming vastness of the obliteration. "You gotta be able to turn your head around and look," said John White. "I can't even explain it, that's how fucked up it is down there." Mickey, who generally had a word for every occasion, found little to say about his first vision of hell. He just shook his head and grimaced. "It was bad," he said. "I'll tell you that. It was bad."

Black, gritty smoke billowed off the wreckage. Mickey saw a few cops wearing respirators, but the ironworkers had only flimsy paper masks, which proved so useless against the fine particles of smoke and dust that many of the men pulled them off and tossed them aside. A few sections of the external walls of the towers stuck up from the rubble, appearing as fragile as eggshells. The rest was a tangled heap no higher than two or three stories. The most obvious features of the heap—"the pile" as rescue workers would soon name it—were the prefabricated triads of columns jutting out from it at obscene angles. Firemen clambered over the mess, spraying hoses or shoveling or clawing at it.

For all the activity, the place was strangely quiet. The hum of the generators and the engines of cranes and backhoes drowned out voices under a dome of white noise. Nobody was saying much anyway. The men went into a state of numbness and worked quietly for the most part, speaking only when they had to.

Mickey did not get very close to the pile that first night. The immediate critical task was to clear the roads so the cranes and other heavy equipment could gain access to the site. Cranes had been lumbering toward lower Manhattan almost from the moment the first tower collapsed, but until rescue workers cleared a path to the pile, all of the cranes in the world were useless. Mickey fell in with a gang of ironworkers under one of the cranes. They were lifting and removing the crushed fire trucks and ambulances that littered the road, walking the crane in toward the pile one lift at a time. The ironworkers lacked the most basic rigging to do the work until they discovered some cables and other rigging stowed away inside the fire trucks. They used the trucks' own rigging to lift them and set them aside. They slowly worked their way toward the smoking jagged heap where an untold number of people—hundreds?

thousands?—were buried alive, they assumed, and waiting for them.

Mickey tried to keep himself focused on the work and prevent his eyes from wandering. "I did not want to gawk at anything," he said. "I was there to do ironwork, and that's what I did." There were occasional interruptions, as when 7 World Trade Center collapsed around 5:30 P.M. and everybody turned and ran. But as soon as the dust cleared, they got back to work.

Mickey left after midnight, utterly exhausted and depleted. He invited a blond kid named Justin, an apprentice he'd gotten to know at Time Warner Center, to come back to the hotel and crash on the floor. The two men hitched a ride on a garbage truck, Mickey in front with the driver, the kid perched on the fender in back, and jumped off on Broadway near the hotel. They must have been a sight as they came through the revolving door into the hotel lobby. Their arms and faces and shirts were caked in dust. More dust clotted their eyebrows and hair. Their jeans were soaked with water from the firehoses. Their boots were heavy with mud, their socks drenched. Their throats were raw from the smoke and dust they'd been inhaling for hours.

In the room Mickey pulled out a couple of self-heating army rations he'd managed to grab before leaving Ground Zero. They sat on the bed and shoveled the food, a mysterious but edible stew, into their mouths. Their throats hurt when they swallowed, but they were famished. When they were done, Mickey reached into the plastic bag he'd managed to hold onto since early that afternoon. He handed the apprentice a package of clean underpants and socks and a T-shirt, then took one of each for himself. These were the last clean clothes he'd see for a while.

Wednesday was the day tens of thousands of Americans woke up, having never really fallen asleep, possessed of the same powerful urge: to get down to the site of the fallen towers and help. New Yorkers were not alone in fixating on this idea; sheriffs from Maine and home health-care workers from Nebraska, paramedics from Wisconsin, ballerinas from Georgia—people from all over the country shared the obsession. It was as if that grave prediction made by the French savant about the Eiffel Tower over a hundred years ago—that its iron would spontaneously polarize and suck Paris into it—had come to pass at the World Trade Center. Devastation and grief had transformed the towers' steel into a giant magnet.

What distinguished the ironworkers from the masses who responded to the disaster in those early days was the skill they possessed. It was as Mickey said: *There was nobody more equipped to do it.* The most important project of those early days—and indeed for months to come—was the careful but speedy removal of structural steel. Cutting steel. Rigging steel. Hoisting steel. *This is what we do every day.*

If their chosen trade placed a moral obligation on them, it also gave them an intimate connection to the fallen buildings. The dead were not their dead, but the buildings had been *their* buildings. Ironworkers put them up, raised their 192,000 tons of steel, and loved them even when most of the city found them unlovable. "These were buildings you were proud to look at," said Matt, the broad-shouldered ex-Marine fellow ironworkers called Rambo. "They were beautiful buildings. Now it's lying all over the place. You wanna cry ten times a day. And that's not even the human toll. Just looking at the structural damage you wanna start crying."

The ironworkers funneled into lower Manhattan by the hundreds that Wednesday morning. They were structural ironworkers from Local 361 and Local 40, as well as non-structural ironworkers, as well as ironworkers from beyond the New York City jurisdiction. They arrived in torn blue jeans and decal-smothered hard hats, in large groups but also in pairs or alone.

About a hundred men came down from Columbus Circle that morning. They came en masse after convening briefly at the Time

Warner building. A large segment of that group came by subway, while another "hijacked" a city bus, persuading its driver to abandon his assigned route and take them straight to 14th Street. They covered the last two miles on foot, pausing at police checkpoints along the way to flash their union cards. They were still half a mile away when they began to see the dust, the fluttering paper, the smashed cars.

Joe Emerson was among the group that arrived by bus. Joe was a great big lumbering man, 6'2", well over 200 pounds, who turned graceful the moment he stepped onto steel. He was easygoing and good-natured, 32 years old, married to his grade school sweetheart, father of two young children. As they closed in on the site and the smoke thickened and darkened, he drew alongside his two older brothers, Tommy and Mike, and the three of them walked together down Broadway. A fourth brother, Jimmy, the youngest, was already down there with a gang from another job.

The Emersons were bred-in-the-bone New Yorkers. One grandparent came out of Little Italy, another from the old Irish stronghold of Hell's Kitchen. But the Emersons' bloodlines also reached back, on their father's side, to the ironworking dynasty of Kahnawake. Their great-grandfather, Louis Lee, was among the Mohawk riveters who died on the Quebec Bridge in August of 1907. The Emersons had given a lot of themselves to building this city. The three brothers walking down Broadway that morning had set thousands of tons of steel and fallen a dozen times. Their father, a highly regarded connector and pusher in his day, was on early retirement, with two replaced knees, his own having worn out from repetitive stress and too many clashes with steel.

The Emersons passed City Hall and the Woolworth Building. They passed St. Paul's Chapel, its graveyard blanketed in the awful gray snow, then turned west toward the pit—and there it was. Or, rather, was not. "Where in the hell is the building?" said Mike Emerson, second oldest of the brothers. "Where did it go?"

"I just could not believe it," Mike said later. "I couldn't believe that was two hundred and twenty stories of steel."

The Emerson brothers, along with Kevin Scally and a number of other men from the Time Warner job, found their way to one of the cranes on West Street. "Everybody put their game faces on," said Mike Emerson. Again, nobody said much; they just got down to work. The work was tricky and rife with hazards. One of the most hazardous things about it was the surfeit of men. Dozens of ironworkers swarmed around the base of every crane, everyone trying to lend a hand but mainly getting in each other's way. At each crane, 15 men shared a job that required perhaps 5. Crane operators would look out into this riot of good will and see three or four different men giving conflicting hand signals, some of these would-be signalmen obviously not even ironworkers. The operator had to locate an ironworker he knew and trusted and ignore the rest. Gangs from Time Warner and other jobs around the city tended to reconstitute at the site and follow the direction of their pushers, but outside of these small chiefdoms the chain of command was uncertain and inchoate.

"It felt very dangerous," said Mickey Tracy, who had hitched a ride down early that morning in a police car. "Everybody was nervous, trying to do the right thing." But in their ardor to help, said Mickey, "the younger guys were being aggressive, they were fighting for the hook. They weren't even letting the metal land—they wanted to get right on it."

Matt described it more pithily: "It was a big cluster fuck."

After a few hours of grappling with the cranes and trying not to decapitate fellow ironworkers with twisted beams, the Emerson brothers and Kevin Scally decided to move on. "We thought, what the hell, we don't have to be some hero with a crane," said Kevin Scally. "Let's go burn some iron." They found a few acetylene torches and picked their way onto the pile to assist the firemen in a more immediate capacity. The pile may not have been high but it was steep and difficult to scale, a jagged terrain of steel columns, twisted joist, and rebar, all madly knotted together by 50 miles of elevator cable. It took half an hour just to climb out into the middle of it, as the ironworkers tested each foothold, watching for snares and shifting debris, often going down on all fours. Fire smoldered under the surface, making the steel hot to the touch and turning the rubber soles of their boots sticky.

The terrain and the heat were nothing compared to the ghastly vapor—"the nasty fog," John White called it—that vented from the pile and passed easily through the masks the men wore, clawing at the back of the throat and leaving a strange sweet metallic residue on the tongue. The smoke contained molecules of burning plastic and paper, of office furniture upholstery and fiber optic cable, of steel and human remains—of physical things returning to elemental states. "We're used to smoke," said Joe Emerson. "We burn things all the time. But this was different." Later, respirators would be standard equipment for anyone working on the pile, but such precautions were rare in those early days. Many men clambered over the pile lacking even a rudimentary facemask, sucking gobs of potentially toxic fumes and particulates into their lungs. As many as 500 firefighters would eventually consider early retirement as a result of chronic lung problems brought on by that smoke in the early days after the disaster. But nobody was concerned about any of that on Wednesday, September 12. Most of the men were just trying to stay focused on the work, trying not to think too much about what all of it meant.

"It had to be over a hundred degrees out there," said Mike Emerson. "It was hot as hell. And I got out there, and there were a lot of bodies—pretty much unrecognizable body parts—and I took a couple deep breaths, almost like a little panic attack. I didn't know that I could handle it." *Here,* a fireman called. *Over here.* He'd found a crevice under the steel where several dead comrades lay. The ironworkers lit their torches and started to burn.

The work broke down into three distinct stages. The first of these was "burning"—sawing through the steel with the 2,000-degree flame of an acetylene torch to cut out sections, piece by piece. The second step was hooking the cut pieces onto crane cables so they could be hoisted and removed. The third step was loading the steel onto an awaiting truck.

Subtract the heat, smoke, and urgency, each of these steps—burning, hoisting, loading—was rote procedure for an experienced ironworker, albeit in reverse order of the normal work of building. But there was one other critical difference beyond the heat: the ironworkers had little way of judging how a piece of steel would react when it was cut free. Nor could they predict how the pile around it might shift when they extracted it. "When you have iron bent and buried like that," explained Mickey, "you don't know what it's going to do. It stores energy. So how's the energy going to release when you lift it?" Would the piece simply drop or would it pop up? Without knowing what strains the piece was subjected to under the pile—and there was no way to predict this since much of the piece was likely to be covered up—the ironworkers had to guess, then get ready to jump if they guessed wrong.

Before the gang burned a piece, they lassoed it with a choker and hooked it onto a crane. They signaled the crane operator to lift the load a hair, putting enough tension on the line, they hoped, to hold the piece when it broke off but not so much tension that the piece would leap off the pile like an arrow from a bow. It was very important to burn the piece evenly and cleanly. "If you don't know how to burn," said Kevin Scally, "and you leave a sticker"—that is, you don't make the cut clean through—"and you get up on the piece and it's hung up because of that stupid sticker, you're gonna be the nitwit that's gotta go cut it, and it's gonna go flying while you're right there."

In retrospect, the fact that no one died in those early days was a small miracle. Thousands of people flung themselves into one of the most perilous environments imaginable, making it all the more perilous by their teeming presence. But still they came. The Wades and the Doyles and the Jacobses and the Collinses and the Beauvais and the Diabos and the Costellos; the Mohawks from Kahnawake, Akwesasne, and Six Nations; the Newfoundlanders from Conception Bay and Placentia Bay and Brooklyn; the Rebs from down south and the boys from New Jersey—they all came. Some of those who came had started their careers building the towers over 30 years earlier, which made this return visit especially grim and poignant. "I connected that steel there," Willie Quinlan, 54, murmured to his gang one evening on the pile. "I don't believe I'm here cutting it up and taking it apart. It's strange, a strange feeling."

Joe Gaffney had strange feelings of his own down there. Joe Gaffney was an ironworker in his mid-30s who'd worked many months earlier at the Ernst & Young building on Times Square—the ironworker whose mother watched him through binoculars from her office window on Sixth Avenue. After leaving the Ernst & Young building (and his mother's sightlines) in the early winter of 2001, Joe Gaffney had gone to work at the World Trade Center. He'd joined a gang of about a dozen ironworkers to install a radon ice shield around the television antenna atop Tower One. Every night for several months that winter he'd climbed a ladder that ran through a narrow tube inside the 350-foot antenna at the top of the tower, to a point 250 feet or so above the roof. The work had to be done late at night, after Letterman went off the air, to avoid disrupting television signals. The wind whipped fiercely and wind-chill factors dipped into single digits, but in order to squeeze through the narrow mesh tube he had to remove his coat. When he got to the top of the ladder and walked out onto a catwalk at 1,600 feet, nothing above him but dark winter sky, Joe Gaffney was the highest man in Manhattan—the highest earthbound man for miles in any direction—freezing and exhilarated.

But it wasn't upon that experience that Joe dwelt as he worked on the pile in the days after September 11. Nor was it upon the eerie fact that he was meant to have been back at the Trade Center on the morning of September 11, working a new job—a daytime job—that would have placed him on the summit of the north tower when the first plane struck. (The job, by some fluke, had been postponed by several weeks.) Rather, what Joe Gaffney thought about down there now was his dead father. Joe's father was a small-time hood from Bay Ridge who was "into the rackets," as Joe put it. His nickname in the Ridge was "The Enforcer" because he had a knack with his fists and a tendency to use them. "People used to tell me there was no one tougher. When it was time to collect book, he always got his money."

Joe's father had one legitimate job in his life. He was an iron-worker on the World Trade Center. His brother—Joe's uncle—was a Local 40 man who arranged it with the hall. For a few months, it looked as if Joe's father had turned over a new leaf, that he'd put his criminal past behind him and settled into a regular domestic life with his wife and three sons. The illusion lasted only briefly before Joe's father quit work and went back to the rackets. But Joe would never forget what it meant to him as an eight-year-old kid to look up at the Twin Towers from across the river and think: *My Dad. He built those. He built those towers.*

Wednesday was a day of spontaneous heroics at the site, but it was also a day of rampant chaos. And so, on Thursday, two days after the attack, the machines of order, the giant bureaucracies of the city, began to impose a makeshift structure onto Ground Zero. The city divided the site into quadrants and contracted four building compa-nies, including Bovis Lend-Lease (builders of the Time Warner Center) to handle the physical removal of steel. Ironworkers who wanted to work at the site were to report to the union shape hall. Local 40 would limit the number of ironworkers to about 400 men cycled over three shifts: 8–4, 4–12, 12–8. The ironworkers had been working without pay since Tuesday, but starting on Friday they would be compensated at normal union wages. Any man not chosen for Ground Zero was urged to report back to his regular job Friday morning.

Those men tapped to return to Ground Zero enjoyed a peculiar kind of honor. They had the job everyone wanted—and now they were getting paid for it—but it was an increasingly grim job. The sour odor of death wafted over the pile on Thursday. Decay had set in. Everybody still desperately wanted to find survivors, unwilling to accept that there were none. Instead of survivors they found shoes, stuffed animals, wallets, gym bags, photographs, many tons of paper, wedding rings, and lots of small body parts. Most iron-workers of any experience had seen someone die or get severely injured. But there is no preparation for the experience of finding a human foot in the middle of a field of rubble, as Joe Emerson did one afternoon.

Friday was the worst day. Friday was the day it rained. And the day the president came to town.

Mickey Tracy was standing in the basket of a cherry picker, burning a piece of steel under a cold drizzle, when a cop told him to come down at once. No one was permitted to have any height on the president. Mickey was initially reluctant to go anywhere near the commotion attending the president's arrival. He'd noticed that the police were behaving skittishly, "nervous and sweating," and he planned to avoid getting shot by an overwound cop. On the other hand, he had some time on his hands now. He cleaned up his tools, then strolled over toward the sea of police and firemen that had gathered to greet the president.

"Stop right there!" a cop called as Mickey started to slip under the police tape.

"The president's here," said Mickey to the cop. "I'm going to see the president."

"You can't get any closer."

This offended Mickey. "Hey, he's not just the cops' and firemen's president. He happens to be my president, too."

A big burly cop approached Mickey. He glanced at the nametag above the brim of Mickey's hard hat. "You wanna see the president, Mickey?"

"Yeah," said Mickey. "I wanna see the president."

The big cop grabbed Mickey and pulled him into a bear hug. He held Mickey tight for a second, so close Mickey could feel the cop's beard scruffing his cheek, then let him go. "All right," said the cop, "let him in." Only after Mickey was through on the other side of the tape did he realize he'd just been frisked. "But he did it really nice," said Mickey later. "It was a class act."

Mickey, at 5'4", could hardly see a thing over the heads of the firemen. He maneuvered his way into the crowd. A few of the firemen in front of him parted, and there, suddenly, was the president, standing right before him, his hand thrust out. Mickey shook it.

"He says, 'Mickey, thanks for being here.' I said, 'Thank you for coming, Mr. President, I think you needed to see this.' I didn't want to take too much of his time, even though I am a pretty good talker. I didn't want to start crying. I think he was on the brink of crying, to tell you the truth."

The president's visit, while welcome, proved a mixed blessing to the workers at Ground Zero. The Secret Service, in an effort to secure the area, refused to allow a new shift of men to enter the site and replace the men already down there. Which meant that every ironworker had to work a double shift of 16 hours in the cold rain. By the end of the day, the men were shivering and exhausted and accident-prone. After Mickey cut a small piece of steel with an acetylene torch, another ironworker picked up the piece and brushed the burnt end of the steel against Mickey's arm, branding a permanent scar into his bicep. "I could hardly blame the guy," said Mickey. "Still, I had a word with him about it."

That night, after 16 hours of work, Mickey was too exhausted to go anywhere. He fell asleep on a floor between two elevator shafts on the second story of the World Financial Center. The smashed-out windows let a cool breeze flow in from the river, free of the smell of death from the nearby morgue. The next morning he woke up and went back to work, "a bad decision," in retrospect. He was spent, drained, wasted. He'd had enough. That night, after 10 more hours, he left for good. He made his way back to Columbus Circle, paid his hotel bill, and got his car out of the parking garage on 58th Street where it had been sitting for the last five days. He started for home.

"That was a terrible drive, being in the car alone for one and a half hours. I never felt so lonely in my life. I had never been away from my family for five days."

He pulled off the highway and drove down the suburban streets, then turned into his neighborhood. American flags flew on every mailbox. He passed the local firehouse, and waved to a fireman he knew. And then he saw the banner at the end of the street. "Thank You, Mickey. God Bless America." Everybody in the neighborhood had signed it. It took Mickey a second to realize the sign was intended for him. He turned into his driveway and saw a big flag flapping on the front lawn. His wife, Karen, he later learned, had spent the day hunting down the flag. American flags were scarce by the end of the week. She went to the hardware store. The owner told her he was sold out. "Well, you have one in your window," observed Karen.

"Yes, but that one is for the store."

"But I need a flag."

"I'm sorry, I can't give you that flag."

"You don't understand," she pleaded. "My husband is coming home tonight."

The owner finally relented. He let her have the flag. "My wife," said Mickey, "is a very convincing woman."

The dog ran up to greet Mickey as he stepped out of his car. He walked up to the door and opened it, feeling as if he'd been away for months. His wife hugged him, and then his son flung his arms around him. "My son is fifteen years old," said Mickey. "It's hard to get hugs. But he hugged me."

There was a great deal of hugging of ironworkers in the immediate aftermath of 9/11. Ironworkers, like firemen and policemen and other rescue workers, found themselves thrust into the role of heroes, a role they had not played convincingly since the glory days of the late 1920s and early 1930s. The word "heroes" was devalued by overuse after 9/11, but the ironworkers really were heroes of a sort. For no pay (in those early days) and at no benefit to themselves, they risked their lives to help in a very fundamental way. All those qualities that had seemed odious about "hard hats" in 1970—the unreformed maleness, the brawny toughness, the jingoism—were recast overnight as courage, valor, and patriotism. "The men who normally power this city, the lawyers, brokers, financiers, are useless," wrote a New York corespondent for the *Washington Post* that Friday. "The term 'laborers' has earned a new respectability among their fellow citizens. . . . And no one is calling them Larry Lunchpail and Joe Six-pack either."

At the end of every shift, crowds of well-wishers stood along the West Side Highway or at the police barricades and applauded the men as they drove out from Ground Zero in trucks. "All those people out in front when you go past the barricades," said Kevin Scally. "That's why you go back. That's the best feeling I've probably ever had in my life." The Mohawk ironworkers who arrived home at Kahnawake that weekend were hailed as local heroes. As they gathered that Friday night at the Legion hall and the Knights of Columbus and at the bar of Old Malone's Restaurant, people crowded around to hear their stories of Ground Zero. "Even the French are treating us like heroes," said Chad Snow, who went home that weekend after a few days on the pile. "And the French hate us."

In the weeks to come, ironworkers would be lauded almost continuously in the press. People who had no idea what an ironworker was or did before September 11, were suddenly aware of these men in hard hats doing extraordinary things at Ground Zero. On September 25, two Local 40 ironworkers, James Beckett and Mike Grottle, would ring the opening bell at the New York Stock Exchange, a sure indication of ironworkers' new status. Meanwhile, signs of appreciation began appearing in windows near construction sites around the city, including a very large one in a window across from the Time Warner Center: "THANK YOU, IRONWORKERS!" Kevin Scally predicted that all this gratitude and adulation would not last. "We'll be popular for a while," he said without rancor. "And then we're gonna disappear."

## MONDAY REVISITED

That first Monday back at Columbus Circle sucked. It sucked even more than Mondays usually sucked, and no amount of good press could cure that. The men returned to Columbus Circle drained and distracted, many suffering hacking coughs brought on by the smoke at Ground Zero. For the Mohawks, the Sunday night good-byes had been even more difficult than usual. New York had never seemed so dangerous and so far from home.

Many of the ironworkers had broken down over the preceding weekend. The stress and the sadness they'd managed to keep at bay throughout the week let loose in torrents and nightmares. It hit Kevin Scally the night before, Sunday night, after he came back from working on the pile all weekend. Joe Emerson was driving home on the Long Island Expressway when tears began to stream from his eyes. Nearly every ironworker who had spent any time at Ground Zero broke down that weekend. "I think it was knowing that I wasn't going back," said Kevin. "I just lost it."

As it turned out, Kevin and Joe were not done yet. Monday evening they got a call from the hall asking them to return to

Ground Zero that night. This would entail putting in a full shift overnight—having already worked a full day—then going straight to work at Columbus Circle the next morning to put in another full shift. They both accepted without hesitation. "You hate it when you're there," Kevin explained, "but you hate it more when you're not."

What pulled the ironworkers at the Time Warner Center out of their collective funk was the work. Almost immediately the job hit a new stride. Those four days the building stood stock-still had given the steel fabricators a chance to produce a backlog of shapes for the first time. After a miserly midsummer trickle of five or six trucks of steel per day, trucks now began arriving at a rate of 15 or 17 per day. To make up for lost time, Bovis decided to bump the ironworkers up to 10-hour days.

In September, two kangaroo cranes, working in tandem, lifted 10 parallel, 92-foot headers over the courtyard to form a portico over the main entrance. Jerry and Matt on one side, Kevin and Joe on the other, the connectors bolted the headers in, then walked out onto the steel to join them crosswise with narrow beams. The headers were about a foot and a half wide, veritable turnpikes, and a safety crew had already hung a net about 30 feet below them. But net or no net, going out onto a strip of steel 70 feet over the ground and 45 feet from the nearest structure was dizzying. The strange part wasn't looking down—looking down was nothing—but rather standing out in the middle of the header and looking straight up at the sky as a load of beams floated in from above. "That was a little hairy," allowed Jerry.

The raising gangs turned their attention to the jazz center at the end of the month. The jazz center was a proscenium-style auditorium that would roost in the middle of the Time Warner building, between the haunches of the two towers. When complete, it would be one of the premium music venues in the city, acoustically, ergonomically, and visually. But the pleasures of the future jazz fans would come at the cost of great effort and peril to the ironworkers. The steel in the jazz center was light but it was also extremely narrow, some beams barely wider than a man's boot. It wowed and wiggled underfoot as the men set it. The connectors spent days walking around on this steel, often 60 feet over the floor, a trial of focus and nerves for the most hardened ironworker.

One day in November, Jerry and Matt set a couple of cantilevered beams at the southeastern corner of the building, where it tapered into a sharp prow. The first beam stuck out 15 feet from the body of the building, parallel to 58th Street. Matt stepped onto it and walked halfway across it to where the crane hook attached to the choker. Seventy feet below to his right a cement truck idled on 58th Street, waiting for the light to change. Matt unbuckled the choker, slung it over the hook, made a cutting motion with his hands, and the crane hook shot off.

Once the hook cleared, Matt walked on to the far (unsupported) end of the beam, where he stepped down onto the lower flange and sat. He pulled out a pack of Marlboros and tried to light one. The wind blew out the first match, but the second took, and Matt perched at the end of the beam, looking out over Central Park, holding smoke in his lungs.

Jerry, meanwhile, had crossed a short beam that lay perpendicular to Matt's. He stood and waited for the next piece of steel that would complete the prow—the third leg of the triangle. Matt exhaled, then turned and called to Jerry. *What?* Matt pointed at his bolt bag. Jerry reached into his own bolt bag, pulled out a bolt, and tossed it underhand to Matt, who swiped it from the air with one hand. (Had he missed, the bolt would have sailed out over 58th Street, a lethal missile, and probably taken out a windshield—or worse.) He dropped the bolt into his bolt bag, then got back up on his feet. The third leg was descending. Both men stood on the steel, looking up, waiting for it. Neither was tied off.

As the pace of the job increased, little accidents and near calamities began to accumulate. A beam rolled over the foot of a tagline man. A young African-American apprentice fell off a ladder and injured his back. In mid-October, Johnny Diabo, one of the connectors recently arrived from the Random House building, caught the tip of a finger between two pieces of steel and snipped it off. "It's funny," said Johnny as he regarded his damaged hand. "Just a couple weeks ago a few of us were sitting in a bar and saying how none of us had ever lost any fingers or toes." Johnny took the fingertip home with him to Kahnawake that weekend and buried it in his backyard—an old Mohawk custom, he said—then returned to work on Monday, the finger bandaged in gauze and black tape.

On a very windy afternoon in early November, Tommy, the operator of crane No. 3—Matt and Jerry's crane—was lifting a beam off the derrick floor when an updraft got under his 180-foot boom and pushed it skyward. Jerry lunged and grabbed the tagline hanging off the beam. He quickly wrapped it around a column, trying to prevent the boom from riding any higher. For a moment, this arrested the upward thrust of the boom, but then the tagline snapped and the boom shot off. Everybody who saw this understood what would happen the instant the gust let up: the boom would fall, and the beam dangling under it would hammer down onto the building. More precisely, it would hammer down onto the head of an unsuspecting young ironworker from Buffalo, New York, who sat on the steel frame directly under it, obliviously bolting up.

"Buffy—watch out!"

Buffy, as the young man was known to his fellow ironworkers, did not look up to see what was the matter. He heard his nickname, discerned the urgency behind it, and leaped as if significant voltage had been applied to his backside. He leaped the way people leap in cartoons, flying over the beam to a column and grabbing hold of it. *SLAM!* The beam cracked onto the very spot where Buffy had been sitting an instant earlier. The collision made a loud noise and sent vibrations whipping through the frame of the building.

Later, as a number of ironworkers unwound at Smith's Bar on Eighth Avenue, they agreed that if Buffy hadn't been so young and so scared, he'd be dead now. "If it had been an older guy, he'd just sit there," said David Levy, a bolter-up in his early 40s who had watched the event unfold. "I probably would have just sat there on my ass."

"Buffy was scared shitless," said Jerry. "I've never seen a man move faster in my life."

"I was scared," agreed Buffy. "It was pretty funny."

"I'd definitely be dead," said David Levy, who had the distinction of being one of a handful of Jewish ironworkers in New York and whose nickname was simply Jew.

"So, if somebody shouted, '*Watch out, Jew!*'—"

"—I wouldn't move." He shrugged. "I'd be like, *What the fuck is wrong with you? Don't bother me, asshole.* That's the problem with getting old in this business. It takes more to scare you. "

## JACK GOES BACK

Jack Doyle stepped out of a cab on the corner of Broadway and Liberty Street. It was a damp morning in mid-November. He wore a trenchcoat and pressed suit pants and a pair of two-tone leather bucks. The rain had ended, but the streets remained slick and the air misty and chilly, causing Jack's hip to ache a little. Favoring it, he approached the police barricade. He fished into his coat pocket for his pass, which he flashed before the police officer standing beside the barricade.

"Wrong pass," said the cop. "Brown was last week. This week is orange."

"Orange?"

"Yeah. They changed it."

"Is that right? Well, this is the one they gave me."

One of the ironworkers' foremen walked up to greet Jack, then had a quiet word with the cop. The cop finally relented: Jack was free to pass. Thirty-four years after the morning he first arrived in 1968, a catty young connector from Conception Bay, Jack Doyle walked down Liberty Street, back to where his journey to the top began.

All told, Jack had spent seven years of his life down here on the 16 acres of the World Trade Center. After topping out the north tower in 1970, he'd gone on to push a rig at 3 World Trade—the 22-story Marriott Hotel—then later became walking boss at 7 World Trade, a 47-story office building erected in the late 1980s. He'd worked in one capacity or another on every one of the seven buildings in the World Trade Center complex. And every one of them was gone now.

"Hey there, Jack." Several ironworkers greeted him as he walked west on Liberty Street. "Jack Doyle! Hello!"

Ironwork had been good to Jack. Other than a few missing fingers, he'd gotten through his years on the steel without much damage. He and his wife had raised a family of three kids in the house on Staten Island he bought back in 1970, while pushing his rig on Tower One. He'd sent the kids to good colleges and seen his son, Kevin, make Law Review at Seton Hall. He'd worked his way up through the ranks from pusher to walking boss, from walking boss to superintendent, and now, at the age of 58, he was president and business agent of Local 40 of the ironworkers union, which made him one of the top building trade executives in the city.

Jack approached the eastern edge of the site and looked out over the wreckage. Just two months had passed since the attacks, but already an astonishing 56,000 tons of debris had been trucked away, and the pile had been transformed into a pit. The pit still smoldered, exhaling a vapor of carbon monoxide, benzene, propylene, and several other possible carcinogens, but other than the odor, which was off-putting, Ground Zero seemed well controlled. The frenetic urgency that had characterized it for many weeks was gone, replaced by a trimmer and more efficient operation. From 300 ironworkers a few weeks earlier, the number had dropped to about 180.

Danny Robbins, a broad-shouldered, blond-haired ironworker, joined Jack at the edge of the pit. "Housewreckers still talking about taking down the Customs House with a wrecking ball."

"Smash it down? Sounds like a mess." They started walking north on Church Street, skirting the edge of the pit.

"Yeah, then our guys have to go in there and crawl all over it and burn it out and get hurt. It's stupid. We oughta go in there with a crane and take it apart."

"That makes more sense," agreed Jack. "I'll have a word."

"That'd be great."

They turned west, onto Vesey Street, and passed the blackened and gutted Customs House. This had recently been a busy paved street cast in perpetual shade by the tall buildings surrounding it. Now it was a swath of sloppy mud, as empty as a country lane. A dirt field spread to the west and north, where pickups and SUVs were haphazardly parked. Jack stopped walking.

"That was 7 World Trade. That was a forty-seven-story sky-scraper. I can't get over that. Look at that, it's a parking lot."

He stood there for a moment, gazing across the expanse of mud. 7 World Trade had never achieved quite the renown of the Twin Towers, but the job of building it was one that ironworkers talked about for years afterward. It was a big, complex job that involved hoisting and joining enormous members of steel, and a lot of men got badly hurt on it. One of the worst accidents befell a good friend of Jack's, Pat Kennedy, who lost his leg under a grillage of steel one morning while the building was still in the hole.

Danny Robbins led the way over rough ground, over beams and rebar. They came around the edge of the Customs House. The mud was thick and sloppy here. Jack, still catty after all the years, stepped lightly between patches of hard pan. A rim of mud formed at the soles of his bucks but he didn't seem to notice or care. Straight ahead, two men stood in ankle-deep sludge, shoveling around the edges of a recumbent column. One of the pair was a white-haired man who looked to be a few years older than Jack. The other was a young man with a couple days' growth of beard. This was Mike Emerson.

"Hey, if it ain't Jack Doyle!" called the older man.

"What is this?" called Jack, grinning. "Since when do ironworkers carry shovels?"

"They've turned us into laborers here," said Mike Emerson with a laugh. "We're digging it out so we can get a chain under it."

Mike Emerson had been down here every day since he first arrived with his brothers on the morning of September 12. He'd worked 12 hours a day, seven days a week—a pace he would maintain for 10 months, straight through to end of the cleanup. Many tough ironworkers had spent a few weeks down here and called it quits, understandably finding the grimness of the site, the dead bodies, and foul smoke too much to bear. But others got energized by it. They found it weirdly sustaining. Mike Emerson, after his initial panic attack on the pile that first Wednesday, turned out to be one of these, much to his own surprise. "I found I had a knack for this kind of work," is how he put it. "The rugged work. Being in that environment. The burning, being out there in that big cloud of smoke and cutting pieces, hooking them up—it just came natural to me."

The work had taken a toll on his personal life. A week before the terrorist attacks, Mike's wife had given birth to a baby girl. Mike had barely seen the baby, or his wife, since the birth. He left home at 5 in the morning and returned at 10 in the evening. Nearly all of his waking hours were spent at Ground Zero or on the train commuting between there and his house 50 miles north of the city. He knew that he could quit at any time. And yet, for reasons he didn't quite understand himself, he also knew he had to keep going. "I gotta say, my wife, she's a tough girl. There were guys I worked with, their wives just couldn't take it. Mine never complained. She knew it was where I wanted to be. It was like I had a drive. Once I started there, I was hell-bent. It was just something I had to do." Sitting on the train after a long shift, Mike would close his eyes and count his blessings. He felt like the luckiest man in the world to be returning home to his family. But then, next morning, he'd wake up feeling an urgent need to get back to Ground Zero. As of mid-November, he'd yet to take a single day off since the attack. And when he finally did take one off—Christmas Day—he'd feel restless and guilty being home. "I thought a lot about all the kids that were left behind. 'Cause I used to see them down there, the families. Sometimes they'd come down. You knew how many lives were just friggin' wrecked."

In the early weeks, after most of the ironworkers had gone back to their regular jobs, and long after they really had any good reason to hope, Mike and the other rescuers at Ground Zero searched for the living. "We really all believed that there were people down there in air pockets, hanging on, waiting for us to uncover a hole. I'd been in that building nine million times. I knew there was a lot of underground, all these different levels. You really logically thought somebody could have made it out alive. But then, after two or three weeks, we were like *Man, I can't believe we didn't find anyone alive.*"

Now it was about finding the dead. Before 9/11, Mike had seen guys get badly hurt on jobs, but he had never seen a dead body. In the months since, he'd seen a great many of them in various states of disorder. The discovery of a corpse had become a familiar, even welcome, occurrence. It meant that a grieving family would have a body to bury; a sort of closure, if not exactly peace.

The work had become a regular job in many respects, albeit a regular job unlike any other on earth. It continued to be enormously dangerous. Ironworkers still pulled out cherry-red beams, the steel so fragile it could snap as they lifted it. Many of the men at Ground Zero had suffered minor injuries. As of early November, there had been 34 broken bones, 441 lacerations, more than 1,000 eye injuries, and hundreds of burns and sprains and smashed fingers. And plenty of dangerous work remained, for the further they dug, the more unstable the steel would be.

But for all the danger, those who had the knack for the work enjoyed a deep satisfaction in accomplishing it. You knew you were doing something important. And you were treated like an important person. The perks included round-the-clock free food and coffee, warm shelter in which to rest, and a constant stream of celebrity visitors who came to gawk. Ground Zero was hallowed ground but it was also—this being New York—*exclusive* ground, and the blue police barricades were the velvet ropes of the moment. Susan Sarandon and Brooke Shields and Jack Nicholson and Miss USA and Derek Jeter—they all came to see the disaster and to ogle the heroes. For the ironworkers, this was an unfamiliar though not unpleasant sensation: being the object of a star's gaze.

Jack Doyle walked onward, greeting ironworkers. No one seemed particularly surprised to see him out here in the mud. A man brought over a photograph of the World Trade Center and asked Jack to sign it. As Jack handed the photograph back, a puff of black smoke drew his attention back to the pile. The firemen turned their hose on the smoke. "Something just caught fire out there," said Jack. He squinted at the pile for a moment, then his eyes drifted to a husk of columns still standing near the Customs House. These columns were almost 10 stories high and had once belonged to the lower floors of Tower One. They were all that remained of it now. In a few weeks, they would come down, too, and nothing would be left. The columns had formed the northeast corner of the building, where Jack had pushed his rig 33 years earlier.

"Every piece of that steel I know," Jack said now. "I touched it all with these hands. And look, it's still standing." He smiled. "I'd say we did a pretty good job."

Mike Emerson in front of
the remains of the north tower.
*(Courtesy of Mike Emerson)*

## CHRISTMAS

On the Wednesday before Christmas, Keith Brown rang in the holidays by slugging the project manager for ADF. The chance of Keith Brown, the walking boss, hauling off and taking a swing at somebody had always seemed high, and ever higher as the work at Time Warner Center sped up and Keith's impatience and irritability waxed accordingly. But still—*the project manager?* The man was ostensibly Keith's boss, several ranks above him. Nobody slugs the project manager.

The fight was on everybody's lips at the Coliseum that evening. Some of the ironworkers had overheard the two men arguing over an open frequency two-way radio shortly before the fight. They heard the project manager yell at Keith, upset that certain pieces of steel had not yet been bolted up on the 12th floor. They heard Keith yell back, suggesting that the project manager refrain from shouting. They heard the project manager shout again, something to the effect of *This work is fucked up and you better get the fuck up here and get it done right.* In retrospect, the project manager probably wished he'd chosen his words more carefully.

"Sure," Keith responded into the two-way. "You stay there. I'll be right up."

The radio went silent. Everybody waited, including, to his credit, the project manager. Several minutes passed, as Keith rode the elevator, then climbed to the 12th floor on ladders. When he stepped out onto the derrick floor, he saw the project manager waiting for him. The conversation went something like this:

"Keith, listen—"

"Shut the fuck up—"

"Keith, I'm your friend."

"Bullshit." *Smack.* Keith hit him.

"Keith, come on—"

*Smack.* Keith hit him again. "Don't you ever fucking raise your voice to me again."

"Jesus, Keith—" *Smack.*

At this point, two ironworkers grabbed Keith and pulled him away from the project manager. "If it weren't for them, I'd throw you off the side of the building," shouted Keith at the project manager as the two men restrained him. "You should send these guys Christmas cards."

The ironworkers who gathered in the Coliseum that evening generally agreed that while perhaps Keith Brown had acted rashly in slugging the project manager, he had also been within his rights. "It's one thing when one ironworker shouts at another. That's in the family. But this guy, he's not an ironworker."

"I'll tell you this," added another man, "he sure as hell shouted at the *wrong* ironworker."

The details of the fight having been duly parsed, and the chances of Keith Brown getting fired fairly weighed (the betting was that he would be, but the betting would turn out to be wrong), attention turned to more important matters, like the $500 pool of cash raised among the four raising gangs and the four crane operators. Each Wednesday the men put in a certain stake, usually $10 apiece, bumped up to $20 this week in honor of the holidays, then played for it with the poker hand in the serial numbers on their paychecks.

"I plan on taking it," said David "Chappie" Charles, slumped over the bar, his eyes crinkled into a smile. "I'm just saying it's mine."

"No, I believe this one is mine," said Frank Kirby, looking deadly serious.

While the men discussed their respective chances of getting lucky, Christmas lights flickered in the window and on the wall behind the bar, over a glittering array of bottles. John the bartender cracked open beers five or six at a time. Down near the jukebox the free buffet steamed in stainless steel troughs, and several ironworkers grazed over the buffalo wings and baked ziti. The place was crowded, and the beer and the food cast a warm glow over the men. In another hour or so, the young professionals of the Upper West Side would start to arrive and there would be an awkward overlap of clientele—the pivotal half hour or so when John had to be on his toes to break anything up before it started. For the moment, though, the bar belonged to the 30 or so ironworkers who were there, and the atmosphere was convivial but subdued. Johnny Diabo and his connecting partner, Paul "Punchy" Jacobs, were sitting at a table together, and so were Matt and Jerry, talking about what ironworkers always talk about at bars: ironwork. From across the bar came Joe Emerson's booming voice, shouting something at Matt—"Yo,

NBC"—which was Joe's nickname for Matt. It meant Nothing But Connect, and it was Joe's way of ribbing Matt for his vow that, henceforth, he planned to do "nothing but connect." Matt responded by giving Joe the finger. Kevin Scally glanced at his watch. He'd gotten married in October and had a wife waiting for him back home. Somebody handed him a new beer and suggested to Kevin that he might as well put any ideas of leaving out of his mind.

Mickey Tracy was still there, too. It was time for him to start his long journey home to Connecticut, where his wife and son would be waiting for him. He took a sip of Heineken and scratched his jaw. "You know, I've been thinking," he said. "I've had a good life. Iron-work has been good to me. You're part of something bigger. You changed the skyline. I'm 5'4", but I stand tall, understand? You can't take that away from me, baby. This business gave me a great life."

"So would you like your son to be an ironworker?"

"My son," said Mickey, "is going to be a lawyer."

## TWELVE

# Topping Out

On a cold and gray November afternoon in 1951, John McMahon, a young ironworker for American Bridge Company, stood over the Monongahela River near Pittsburgh, deep in the heart of Big Steel country. He was working in a gang of bridgemen rehabilitating an old steel bridge that crossed the river between U.S. Steel's blast furnaces on one side and its open-hearth furnaces on the other. Half a century later, McMahon still recalls the moment his 20-year-old self grasped the enormity of Big Steel. "It was the day before Thanksgiving and I was packing up to go home, standing up on top of the truss, and I was looking down the river and I said, 'Good God Almighty, this is some outfit I'm working for.' Everything we used belonged to them. The rivets and the paints, and everything you could see—the barges, the trains, the factories—and every stack had smoke pouring out of it and all hell was breaking loose, and there was fifty or sixty thousand people working in there and it was just a-goin' Jesse, twenty-four hours a day seven days a week. And I thought, 'Hell, we'll never run out of work.'

"Now it's all gone. And I'm still here. It's all barren ground, they've torn it all down. They got waterfront property for sale."

No one in the middle of the twentieth century could reasonably have predicted the precipitous decline of American steel over the latter half of the century. The view that John McMahon took in from that truss over the Monongahela was one most Americans shared of the steel industry in 1951. It was a vast and inviolably American enterprise. Since its founding in 1901, U.S. Steel Corporation had controlled 30 percent of the world steel market, while the American steel industry as a whole had claimed as much as 60 percent of the world market. This advantage remained unchallenged through the first half of the twentieth century. Coming out of the war at midcentury—around the same time that John McMahon was marveling from the bridge over the Monongahela—the United States still produced half the raw steel in the world. In 1953, U.S. Steel would have its biggest year ever, producing 35.8 million tons of product. The company would never match that number again.

The seeds of Big Steel's demise were sown in its success. Postwar profits were so generous that Big Steel lapsed into complacency. The genius and drive that allowed Andrew Carnegie to anticipate the future was sorely lacking in the modern steel executives. They kept making steel almost exactly as they'd been making it the previous 50 years, in antiquated open-hearth furnaces. Postwar Europe and Japan, meanwhile, were rebuilding with new technology, most significantly the BOF (Basic Oxygen Furnace) that would make steel production more efficient and less expensive, and that would shortly help those countries take a huge bite out of America's share of the world steel market.

The decline was swift. In 1960, America produced just 25 percent of the world's steel—a 50 percent loss of market share in 10 years. By 1970, as Jack Doyle was topping out Tower One of the World Trade Center (to which Big Steel contributed not an ingot), the number had fallen to 20 percent, and by the mid-eighties it was just over 10 percent, where it has been parked, with slight variation, ever since.

At the start of the twenty-first century America produced less steel than China, Japan, or the European Union. U.S. Steel Corporation—known now as USX—produced a tiny fraction of the world's raw steel, and none of it was structural. Bethlehem Steel, whose wide flange H-columns had had a profound impact on the construction of early skyscrapers, was also out of the structural steel business and filing for bankruptcy. American Bridge Company, once the most formidable steel erection company in the world, still existed, but barely. McClintock-Marshall and Post & McCord were gone entirely.

The largest American producer of structural shapes at the start of the new century was Nucor Corporation, which made its steel from recycled scrap, including junked auto bodies, old refrigerators, and demolished steel-frame buildings. The scrap steel was melted down in electric arc furnaces, recast, then sent back out into the world as new shapes and products. The 192,000 tons of steel that had once supported the World Trade Center were destined for just such a fate. If the towers' steel would not end up in one of Nucor's electric arc furnaces—most of it had been shipped to steel manufacturers overseas—the result would be the same: melted, recast, reincarnated. Some of the new steel would probably return to these shores and find its way into a skyscraper of the future. This assumed, of course, that skyscrapers of the future were going to be made of steel and not, for instance, of reinforced concrete. Once this would have been a safe assumption. No longer. The demise of the American steel skyscraper was already well under way before September 11, 2001. The fall of the Twin Towers was bound to hasten it.

Why did the towers fall? Journalists, engineers, politicians, and the bereaved families of victims began asking the question almost immediately after the collapse. No fewer than three major studies—two federal, one private—have been devoted to answering it. It's tempting to dismiss all of this inquiry as speculation into the obvious. Any seven-year-old knows why the towers fell: because planes traveling over 500 miles per hour and loaded with 10,000 gallons of jet fuel slammed into them. The very question—why did they fall?—assumes the towers could have done otherwise, that somehow they *failed* when they fell. But as one of those federal studies (commissioned by FEMA) declared in its final report, "The structural damage sustained by each of the two buildings as a result of the terrorist attacks was massive. The fact that the structures were able to sustain this level of damage and remain standing for an extended period of time is remarkable and is the reason that most building occupants were able to evacuate safely."

The exact sequence of events that led to the collapse of the towers will probably remain a mystery, since much of the forensic evidence turned to dust in the collapse. From such evidence as exists, though, most engineers agree that the initial impact of the planes, destructive as it was, had little, if anything, to do with the towers' collapse. The buildings absorbed the force of the planes quite easily. The structure was so strong that, by one estimate, columns as close as 20 feet to the impact zone barely registered the strain.

It was not the initial impact that brought the buildings down but the fire that came afterwards. First fed by the conflagration of jet fuel, then by ignited paper, carpet, and furniture, the fire weakened the steel and made it unable to support the building. Steel doesn't melt until temperatures reach about 2,500 degrees Fahrenheit—the temperature at which it is smelted—but it softens and distends at much lower temperatures, around 1,100 degrees Fahrenheit. The temperatures in the Twin Towers in their last hours were far higher than that, perhaps as high as 2,000 degrees in some areas. New York City fire code requires contractors to spray steel components with a thin coat of fireproof material, but apparently this material chipped off the steel when the planes hit the buildings, leaving the metal bare and vulnerable.

The most vulnerable steel of all happened to be in the floor trusses. Those trusses, 60 feet long in most cases, spanned the gap between the core of the building and the exterior columns. They not only carried the weight of the floors, but also provided the all-important lateral support between the perimeter and the core. They kept the perimeter walls from caving and buckling. A study by FEMA surmises that as the trusses heated up, they began to "lose rigidity and sag into catenary action"—they began, in other words, to droop. As they drooped, they lost their function as lateral braces for the columns. The angle brackets that held them to the columns, relatively small pieces of steel, probably sheared. The floors broke free of the columns and began to cascade, in a vertical domino effect, one on top of the other, the weight of the higher floors tearing through the lower floors. The columns, lacking lateral support, buckled and followed the floors to the ground.

The theory of the falling trusses has been disputed in a study commissioned by Larry A. Silverstein, leaseholder of the World Trade Center. This study suggests that it was not the floor trusses but the towers' columns that gave way under the intense heat. If so, the towers behaved much as any other steel building would have behaved under similar circumstances and were not uniquely vulnerable. This conclusion happens to benefit Silverstein, for the more like other buildings the Twin Towers behaved, the less liable Silverstein will be to legal claims made by victims' families. In the end, whatever the reason for the towers' collapse, one thing seems certain: it was a body blow to the reputation of steel.

A few weeks after the disaster, in a television interview, Barbara Walters asked Donald Trump what lessons builders of the future might learn from the Trade Center. "More concrete," said Trump. Concrete would not have melted as the steel did; it is more heat resistant than steel. Trump's view was echoed widely in the months after the attack. "It's better to build in reinforced concrete," Dr. Mir M. Ali, a professor of architecture at the University of Illinois, told the *New York Times*. "If there is an impact, crash, or explosion, it can absorb the energy better. That makes the building less vulnerable."

The technology of concrete had improved greatly in recent years, said Dr. Mir, and an all-concrete structure would have lasted longer than a steel structure. "The trend is toward more concrete."

Charles Thorton, founding partner of Thorton-Tomasetti Group, perhaps the most prestigious structural engineering firm in the world, soon added his voice to this consensus. He suggested that his Petronas Towers in Malaysia, now the tallest buildings in the world, could have withstood the attack better than the Twin Towers, in part because they were made mostly of reinforced concrete.

A more fundamental question to come out of 9/11 was whether very tall buildings were still viable structures. Who wants to work or live in a potential terrorist target? A *USA Today* Gallup poll taken soon after the attack found that while 70 percent of Americans still favored construction of skyscrapers, 35 percent admitted they were less likely to enter one. A 900-foot skyscraper planned in downtown New York was quickly scrapped, as were Donald Trump's plans to build the world's tallest building in Chicago. If very tall buildings were to remain a part of the urban landscape, they would exist under different circumstances, composed, probably, of different ingredients. The symbolic power of the skyscraper—the Great American Steel Skyscraper, anyway—was defunct.

## WINTER

This was not good news for American structural ironworkers. Certainly not for New York's ironworkers, for whom steel-frame skyscrapers were the bread and butter of their trade. It was true that, in the short term, the events of 9/11 had put ironworkers in the spotlight as they had not been for 70 years. This had no real practical benefit, but it felt good. It was also true that the rebuilding of the now barren 16-acre site would probably provide a great deal of work over the next several years. But whatever replaced the World Trade Center would probably contain less structural steel (and more reinforced concrete) than what had been there.

If ironworkers at Time Warner Center spent a lot of time fretting about the future of their trade, they did it privately and quietly. There wasn't much opportunity for fretting that winter in any case. The days at Columbus Circle were long and busy, as the steel, oblivious to its own newfound frailty, continued to rise. The building stepped in at the eighth floor, narrowing considerably, so the floors required less steel and went up faster. By the start of January, the south side of the building had reached the 20th floor. It was up to the 26th floor by the middle of the month.

The higher the building rose, the colder the weather up top. The wind whipped in from the river and the ironworkers could do little to stay warm but keep moving. There were days the temperature dipped into the low 20s and the wind chill dropped into the teens and the steel felt like ice. At lunch, some men took refuge in the Coliseum or at the tables in the back of the Rich and Famous Deli on 60th Street, but many didn't even bother trying to warm up. What was the point? They ate their lunch sitting on the sidewalk, watching the pedestrians scurry by.

Then the temperature rose above freezing and winter rain came, days of it, a steady, damp-nose, flu-inflicting rain. The ironworkers reported for work at the usual time, hung around the cold shanty to see what the weather would do, then Joe Kennedy came out of his trailer and dismissed them.

Rain days were a mixed blessing to the ironworkers. They were holidays—sort of. Exactly how much of a holiday depended on a man's pay scale. Foremen worked on straight time and got paid no matter what the weather did, so rain, from their point of view, was all good. Connectors usually made a deal for one paid rain day per week, so they didn't mind the occasional soak either. The rest of the ironworkers had to make do with an hour of "show up pay" they got for showing up on time and waiting around while the bosses listened to the weather report and decided what to do.

A day of rain now and then was a respite; a week of it began to feel like unemployment. The men went back home or dispersed to one of the established rain-day watering holes, like Smith's on Eighth Avenue and 44th Street. The Mohawks usually returned to Bay Ridge and took refuge in the Snook Inn, a spacious and handsome tavern on Fourth Avenue, or the cozier confines of the Killarney on Fifth. Most of the men who boarded in Bay Ridge had never seen their home-away-from-home except in the dark or in the rain. If it wasn't night or wet, they were likely to be working, or up north in Kahnawake.

A Friday afternoon in early February found the raising gangs on the south tower erecting the trusses under a dazzle of false spring. Most of the truss pieces had been fabricated in an old steel mill near Montreal (directly across the St. Lawrence River from Kahnawake, as it happened) but looked as if they came straight out of the Mesozoic. They were gargantuan and ugly, sprouting fins and ridges and tusks. Once they were bolted together on the 18th floor of the north tower and the 23rd floor on the south tower, the truss pieces would top-out the steel frames and serve as foundations from which the concrete towers would rise, transferring the towers' weight to the foundation through the enormous steel "boomer" columns. Other than the boomers, these truss pieces were the largest steel components in the building.

On this sunny but bracing February afternoon, a few triangles of the truss rose already complete along the southern edge of the tower. George's gang worked on the eastern edge of the tower, lifting steel from the ground and setting it on huge timber skids on the deck, a staging area between earth and air. On the southwestern corner, the other raising gang—Pat Hartley's gang—was busy setting steel. They had already lowered a hulking diagonal column to the perimeter of the floor and were attaching its base to a lower column. This new column would make up one side of an isosceles triangle in the diagonal zigzag of the truss. In a move that would have made a safety inspector blanch, had there been one up here to observe it, Punchy Jacobs ducked under the safety wire and hung out over the edge of the building, holding on to the diagonal with one hand, banging a bolt through it with the other. As he swung the beater, a strange shrill sound slowly crescendoed over the hum of the crane, something like a gull's call—the song of vibrating steel. Johnny Diabo stood near Punchy, ready to take the maul when Punchy tired. Johnny's missing finger had knocked him out of connecting for a while, but now he was at it again. His fingertip—the one that he'd buried in his backyard at Kahnawake—had grown back, good as new. When the bolt was in and the nut tight, Johnny climbed the slanted column to the top, silhouetted against the sun, and unlatched the choker.

The day was perfect for physical labor. For several hours the men worked quietly and intensely, laying in the diagonals. Then it was break time. An apprentice arrived at the top of the ladder with a box of snacks and refreshments. The men sat on columns and beams laid out on the floor and rested, talking quietly. A few of the ironworkers drank tallboys from brown paper bags. They were up high now and there were no safety inspectors to bother them, no contractors to reprimand them—nobody at all watching over them. They were on their own, which was exactly how they liked it.

## UNFINISHED BUSINESS

The steel frame of the building officially topped out on February 27. The date reflected the schedules of invited dignitaries more accurately than it reflected the state of the building. The steel frame would not in fact be complete for another few months. The steel portion of the building would not be *truly* complete until more than

Time Warner Center, winter 2002. On the south tower *(left)* the ironwork-ers use the kangaroo cranes to set the truss. The steel portion of the north tower *(right)* is complete for the moment. The ironworkers will return a year later to crown the building, at 700 feet, with more steel. *(Photo by the author)*

a year later, when ironworkers returned to crown the building's summit in steel. So much for details.

The celebration, held in the steel cage of the jazz center, was a star-studded affair. The mayor gave a speech. Wynton Marsalis played trumpet. In late morning, on cue, the ceremonial beam, American flag and small fir tree attached to its flank, floated by the jazz center on its ascent to the top of the building, and everyone turned to applaud as if it bore some actual significance. A few moments later, out of sight from the crowd, the crane laid the beam on the 22nd floor of the south tower, where it would rest and rust and await removal to its final berth on the 24th floor. For the moment, there was no 24th floor.

In all the many speeches made that morning, no one mentioned the astonishing decline of AOL Time Warner's stock over the last year. Attendees politely skipped over the fact that the company had lost about half its value since AOL and Time Warner merged the previous winter, and that the merger, barely a year old, was already looking like a colossal debacle. (The company would eventually concede as much, deleting AOL's acronym from its name, and from the building once intended to bear it.)

A couple of months after the topping-out party, *The New Yorker* would capture the change that had occurred in the country's economic mood on the cover of its annual "Money Issue." Two years earlier, at the height of the Wall Street boom, the cover of the Money Issue had featured an illustration of a money tree, and three men standing under it gathering dollars by the bushel. Getting rich quick with minimal effort—that pretty much captured the mood of the country then. Now the cover showed a very different image: a pair of brawny ironworkers hanging off the edge of a steel skyscraper, one man riding a derrick hook, the other perched on a cantilevered beam, applying a rivet gun to the steel. The image was a surprising choice for the cover of an issue devoted to finance, but of course that was the point: it celebrated the old-fashioned virtue of hard physical work performed for a daily wage; of constructing something solid and real—a steel building—rather than a house of cards. The editors of the magazine seemed to be acknowledging that, as much as the meaning of work had changed over the previous century, there remained a raw physical element in the work of some people, an element, even, of daring and courage, and that these long-neglected virtues were as valuable now as ever.

Mickey Tracy still recalled the topping-out party two years earlier at the Condé Nast Building on Times Square, where *The New Yorker* now published. He remembered how the beautiful magazine people applauded the completion of a building the ironworkers had built, enjoying a ceremony the ironworkers had invented, while the ironworkers themselves were cordoned off, segregated under the watchful eyes of security guards, almost as if they presented a physical threat to the glossy crowd. "We got fed up," said Mickey. "Who needs that? So we left." The party at Time Warner was a far more inclusive affair, another reflection, perhaps, of the ironworkers' enhanced status after 9/11. Ironworkers were free to mingle as they pleased.

As the men celebrated at Columbus Circle that morning, Brett Conklin sat in his house in Suffern, surfing the doldrums of daytime television and waiting to get better. Almost exactly a year had passed since his fall from the Ernst & Young building on Times Square. Brett was still out of work, still in pain, and still fighting depression brought on by idleness and limited options. Squeezing by on $400 a week in workers' compensation, he had too little money and too much time. It had devastated him to watch his fellow ironworkers, many of them friends, working at Ground Zero after 9/11 and to be unable to contribute himself. "That sucked," he said. "To be honest, everything sucks. The biggest thing now is coping with it. It changed the rest of my life—the rest of my life is changed. I don't know how to look at it anymore."

He was due to go in for surgery in March to repair his foot. He would have to learn to walk all over again but at the least the pain in his ankle would diminish—that was the hope, anyway. He'd already had one surgery, but it hadn't relieved the pain. The new surgery meant he would certainly never work on steel again. The nerves would be severed, the bones fused so his foot would have no lateral give to it anymore. He would lie in bed for two weeks with his foot elevated, then wear a cast for twelve weeks. It would take three to five years for him to learn to walk properly again. After his foot was repaired, he would probably go in for another surgery to repair the crushed vertebrae in his back.

Brett looked forward to enjoying a normal life someday, to getting married and starting a family. "I just gotta get through this first.

My girlfriend's pressuring me now. She's like, 'Come on, come on, let's get engaged,' and I'm like, 'I can't afford to buy you a wedding ring—I can't afford *nothin'* right now.'" He planned to start school again in the fall and complete his credits toward a college degree. "I might go into some kind of computer business. I don't know yet. Maybe marketing, something like that. I don't know if I'm a sit-behind-the-desk type of guy. I really don't know yet." For all the grief ironwork had brought him, he missed it terribly. "It was the best. There was nothing better."

Earlier that winter, an all-steel skyscraper had started to rise on Times Square, directly across Seventh Avenue from the now completed Ernst & Young building, where Brett had fallen a year earlier. This new building was going to closely mimic the Ernst & Young building, not only in appearance but also in use. It was to be corporate headquarters for Arthur Andersen, the *other* major accounting firm in New York. (A few months later Arthur Andersen, derailed by its involvement in the Enron scandal, would drop out as anchor tenant of the building.)

The new skyscraper had gotten off to a good start, and by early spring the raising gangs had climbed their way out of the hole and up to the fifth floor. As the building rose, the men in the raising gang on the south side could not help noticing the young women working in the offices across 41st Street. The women were employees of Liz Claiborne, the apparel company. Sealed behind plate glass, they were fetching, fashionable, and perfectly unattainable.

When poets court women, they use a pen and parchment; when ironworkers court women, they make do with a can of spray paint and a rusty beam. "GOOD MORNING, GIRLS. YOU LOOK GREAT," one of the men wrote in orange paint on the web of a beam. Then, a few days later: "HI, PRETTY LADY." The young women across the street pretended to be oblivious to the ironworkers' missives but the ironworkers were used to that.

One of the men working in the raising gang on the southern side of the building was Jeff Martin. That was his real name, though few of the men working alongside him knew it. Everybody called him by his nickname, J. Kid. He was in his early 40s and still unmarried, a man's man. His two great loves were riding motorcycles and hunting. He'd been to Ground Zero in the early days after the attack and had worked hard alongside the other ironworkers. He was one of those rare men everybody liked.

J. Kid fell from a column on the southern edge of the building early on a Wednesday morning in May. He was coming down off the top of the column, having gone up to remove a hoisting hitch. He wasn't doing anything daring or careless. On the contrary, he'd gone out of his way to take precautions, climbing a ladder rather than scaling the column or jumping a ride on the crane hook, as he might have done in the old days. The accident occurred when he was trying to set his feet back down on the top rung of the ladder. Somehow the ladder kicked out from under him, and he lost it and fell. He glanced off the edge of the floor, then slipped out under the safety wires and dropped more than 50 feet to the street corner below.

Over the next few days, his fellow ironworkers put together a makeshift memorial at the corner of 41st and Seventh, where J. Kid died. Somebody nailed together a wooden cross. Scattered around the base of the cross were mementos of J. Kid's life: a set of deer antlers, a cap, a pocketknife. A turquoise bracelet. A bouquet of flowers lay there on the ground as well. They had been sent over by the women across the street.

"GIRLS AT LIZ C.," somebody wrote on a south-facing beam a few days later, "THANKS FOR YOUR KINDNESS."

J. Kid was the first of several construction fatalities on New York skyscrapers that year. A few weeks after his death, a young Newfoundlander was fatally injured while jumping a kangaroo crane in Brooklyn. Two elevator workers would plunge to their deaths on Madison Avenue. Another young man, working as a surveyor for a steel erection company, would also die before the year was out.

It was an odd coincidence that 2002, the first year of OSHA's Subpart R (which had gone into effect in January), would turn out to be the most lethal year in recent memory for high-steel construction workers in New York. You couldn't blame OSHA, though. There were always a lot of accidents when a construction boom was on. Accidents happened. There was only so much that OSHA could do about it.

"Nobody wants their kid to do this," said Joe Gaffney, the man whose mother had watched him through binoculars when he worked at Ernst & Young—and whose father had briefly interrupted his career of crime to work on the World Trade Center. Joe loved ironwork but he appreciated its risks keenly. "You need to have a little fear. A little fear's a good thing or you stop being careful. If you're not aware of what you're doing, you're gonna wind up in the hole. You don't get a second chance."

In September of 2002, a few days before the anniversary of the terrorist attack on the World Trade Center, Joe Gaffney would fall from the 22nd to the 20th floor of a skyscraper on Madison Avenue—the same building where the elevator workers had died a couple of weeks earlier. He would fracture his spine and spend a few days in the hospital in critical condition. His was one of those accidents that some men fear more than death, the sort of accident that puts a man in a wheelchair for the rest of his life. But Joe was lucky. His spine was fractured but not broken. He would heal. He got a second chance after all.

## GOD KNOWS

Jerry Soberanes sat on a concrete stoop next door to the Coliseum. The day was warm and sunny, and the Coliseum was filled with ironworkers slaking their thirst. Jerry preferred to be out here, alone on the stoop, eating a salad. "It's too crowded in there now," he said. "I liked it better when it was just the raising gang."

Fifteen months had passed since Jerry and Matt and Bunny and John and Chett showed up and looked into the enormous hole. Across the street, the south tower rose 24 stories over Columbus Circle. The lower floors were clad in glass façade, the upper floors still bare. The ironworkers had set 28,000 tons of steel. Jerry, as one of eight connectors, had personally set about 3,500 tons of it, give or take a few. Another year from now, Jerry and Matt would return to top out the building with a steel crown at 700 feet. For now, though, their work was nearly done.

No one died. No one got badly hurt. There was that to be thankful for. On the other hand, the job hadn't been much fun, either. Nothing like the great sport the raising gangs had anticipated coming in. The steel had sputtered in for so many months, and even when there was finally steel, getting it up in the air had been a painstaking process. The competition was a dud. "We blew everybody out of the water," Kevin Scally bragged once, but he didn't say it with any conviction. The truth, as Kevin admitted, was that the gangs could not compare themselves. For one thing, they worked too far apart from each other to keep track of each other's progress. And there were other complicating factors. Matt and Jerry's gang, for instance, had done a lot of heavy lifting for Johnny and Punchy's since their tower crane happened to have a greater lifting capacity. Time spent lifting another gang's steel was time spent not setting your own.

The job put a sour taste in the men's mouths for reasons that had nothing to do with sport or competition. For most of them, the Time Warner Center marked their first experience of the new world of ironwork: the rules, the oversight, the abridgements of autonomy. The lesson the ironworkers learned at Time Warner was that their work would be (presumably) safer, but that it would also be more regimented and considerably duller. Even Matt, who had been so zealous about connecting a year ago, had lost some of his enthusiasm for this job. "It's become drudgery," he admitted one day in early May. At least, now, the end of the drudgery was in sight. By the end of May, it was done.

Jack Doyle returned once more to the site of the World Trade Center at the end of May. He arrived on the evening of May 28 to witness the removal of the last piece of the steel from the hole. The mayor was there, alongside a bugler and a brigade of bagpipers. The event was the opposite of a topping-out ceremony: they were here to pull out a piece of steel, not set one. They came to mourn, not celebrate.

Jack came in his official capacity, as president of Local 40. But he also came as the young man from Conception Bay who'd showed up here long ago determined to make it to the top. As he walked down the ramp into the deep hole, he was flooded with déjà vu. He knew this hole. He'd been here before. "That was an eerie feeling for me," he said. "I never thought that I would look at those walls again. We filled it up with steel, they filled it up with concrete—they covered it over. We put buildings all around. And now here I am walking back into square one after thirty-odd years. Just the same as if nothing was ever there."

Much had changed since 1968, of course—in the world at large and in the world, more specifically, of ironworkers. Most of the young ironworkers gathered in the hole with Jack that evening had never caught a rivet or pushed the bullstick of a derrick; never taken a ride on the ball of the crane or even, some of them, experienced the keen thrill of walking a beam high above the ground with nothing to keep you there but your own guts and balance. And as the work had changed, so had the ironworkers. Jack could see the change reflected in the faces of the men, 13 percent now African-American, another 5 percent Hispanic. Even a couple women had joined Local 40; neither had been seen around the hall for a while, but others, surely, would come. Jack was not a sentimental man. You could welcome some changes and you could object to others, but there was not a damn thing—short of standing in a hole in the ground under the spell of déjà vu—that you could do to halt the future.

The last column stood under what had once been the south tower. It weighed 58 tons, one of the enormous pieces that Jack had grappled with 34 years earlier. As a crowd watched, an ironworker lit a torch and began to cut through the steel. Shortly before 8:30, under the glow of floodlights, a crane hooked the column and lifted it, laying it on the back of a flatbed waiting nearby. The workers shouted "U.S.A.! U.S.A.! U.S.A.!" and "Union! Union! Union!" but nobody complained about jingoism or featherbedding, or any of the sins often laid on union tradesmen. The job had come in three months ahead of schedule and well under budget, an achievement that owed a lot to the hard work of hard hats. "The construction workers who have dedicated themselves to this effort are on the verge of completing an enormous job, and in many ways this is their night to reflect and remember," said Mayor Bloomberg. Afterward, as the ironworkers and other construction personnel filed up the ramp, saluted by firemen and police, the mayor shook their hands, one by one.

It was a moment of high praise for the ironworkers and other laborers who worked at Ground Zero, but it would not last. Gradually, maybe inevitably, the prediction that Kevin Scally had made a few days after 9/11—*We'll be popular for a while, and then we're gonna disappear*—came to pass. The new status of the ironworkers and other tradesmen subsided; the attention faded. The fact that the press and public seemed to forget their contribution so easily upset some of the men, but most took it in stride. "God knows what we did down there," said Mickey Tracy. "That's good enough for me."

Mike Emerson returned to his family. He and Danny Doyle, the foreman with whom he'd come down from Columbus Circle on

September 12, went on to another job together, along with several other men they'd worked closely with at Ground Zero. They had spent as much time down there as anyone; unlike the firemen and policemen, who generally worked leapfrog shifts, three days on, three days off, the ironworkers worked straight shifts, seven days on, no days off. It said something about the mentality of ironworkers that a year after 9/11, while 500 firemen were claiming disability due to smoke inhalation and psychological trauma, not a single iron-worker had made such a claim. "We could try," said Mike. "It's just, I don't think anyone would listen to us."

Joe Lewis shuttled back and forth between the row house in Brook-lyn and his home in Conception Harbour that summer. He talked often about getting back to work, but the doctors' prognosis of the nerve damage in his arm was not encouraging, so he made the best of it, spending as much time in Newfoundland as he could between the obligatory appointments with doctors and lawyers. He contin-ued to play music whenever the opportunity arose, and what he could not play, he sang.

Newfoundland turned out to be not quite as distant from the event of September 11 as one might have supposed. Hundreds of overseas flights had been grounded there when American airspace closed in the wake of the terrorist attack. Newfoundlanders took in the stranded passengers and fed them for several days, showering the wayfarers with hospitality. On his last trip to Newfoundland, Joe noticed that the ferry to Argentia was packed with foreigners. People who had been stranded in Newfoundland were returning as tourists to revisit the place they'd fallen in love with. What cod could not provide—a decent economy—perhaps tourists could.

Keith McComber—Bunny Eyes—dropped out of ironwork for a time after leaving the Time Warner job. He passed a few months at a rustic Mohawk hunting lodge in the woods a hundred miles north of Kahnawake, then returned to New York that winter. He became a foreman of his own raising gang, a natural step for a connector. He put on a little weight, also a natural step for a man who quits the action of connecting for the more sedentary life of pushing. He seemed entirely content with where he'd landed.

Many of the men who had worked at Columbus Circle moved due east that summer to begin building an enormous skyscraper on 59th Street and Lexington Avenue. It was another Bovis job, and Joe Kennedy was superintendent. He brought over three of the raising gangs from Columbus Circle to work under the three cranes. This new building—it would become home to Bloomberg Media, the company founded by the city's billionaire mayor—shared a number of important features with Time Warner Center. It began as another huge hole, one of the biggest in the city, and combined a steel podium with reinforced concrete towers.

The safety measures that had been applied so vigorously at Columbus Circle turned out to be even stricter here, and the iron-workers balked. One afternoon, a connector stepped off a column onto the hook of the crane and swung out like Tarzan over the hole, then rode the hook down into it. It was an exhilarating sight, not because it looked like fun—though it did—but because it was about the most outrageously illicit thing an ironworker could do in 2002, and he did it in broad daylight in front of dozens of people. The task of reprimanding the connector fell to Keith Brown, who had recently come over to Lexington Avenue to serve (with Marvin Davis, of course) as walking boss. It gave Keith no pleasure to tell the connector that if he ever rode a hook again he'd be fired on the spot.

As it happened, cattycorner to the Bloomberg Media building, on the ground floor of an old red brick walk-up at Third Avenue and 59th Street, was a bright and expensive sandwich shop. The floors were slate, the walls lime green, the patrons well dressed in white-collar garb. The ironworkers never went there for lunch, preferring the plainer, more affordable deli on the other side of the building, but a hundred years earlier the place had crawled with ironworkers. It was Lynch's saloon, Sam Parks' old haunt—the very spot where Parks and his underlings drank and plotted and "entertained" their rivals. No sign of that sawdust saloon remained in the overpriced sandwich shop. Too much had changed. Sam Parks was dead, vanished, removed one spring morning early in the last century to parts unknown. But he was not gone entirely. A wisp of his reckless, scrappy spirit had been released into the atmosphere by the smoke of the burning towers. It was visible down there in the hole with Jack Doyle in the smoke of the torch cutting the final column, and now, through the windows of this sandwich shop on 59th Street, in the smoke of Matt's cigarette as he walked a beam 80 feet over Third Avenue, and in the clouds rushing across the blue sky as a chunk of steel floated under them, into the outstretched hands of Kevin Scally and Joe Emerson.

Whatever rose downtown could not be what was there before. The Great American Steel Skyscraper had been forever demoted from an icon of strength to a symbol of vulnerability. But it could stand for an idea every bit as compelling as what the old towers stood for: *Defiance*. It would take a certain amount of defiance to plan and inhabit a skyscraper on the site where two had been turned to rubble, and it would take defiance to build it. How much structural steel it would take—well, that remained to be seen. With any justice, the answer would be many thousands of tons, all of it hoisted and bolted in the sky by ironworkers. They would shove it, prod it, whack it, ream it, kick it, shove it some more, swear at it, straddle it, pound it mercilessly, and then rivet it or weld it or bolt it up and go home. On a good day.

# SOURCES

## CHAPTER 1: SOME LUCK

Brett's fall:

*New York Times*: February 25, 2001; "Iron in the Blood, Misfortune on the Mind."

Ironworker injuries:

"Insurance: Workers' Comp Rates Ready to Take Off." *ENR*. August 30, 2002.

U.S. Department of Health and Human Services. *Worker Deaths By Falls: A Summary of Surveillance Findings and Investigative Case Reports.* September 2000.

U.S. Department of Labor. Bureau of Labor Statistics. *Compensation and Working Conditions.* Spring 2000.

U.S. Department of Labor. Occupational Safety and Health Administration. *Federal Register/Vol. 63, No. 156.* August 13, 1998.

U.S. Department of Labor. Occupational Safety and Health Administration. *Federal Register/Vol. 66, No. 12.* January 18, 2001.

Men who fell:
Norris, Margaret. *Heroes and Hazards.* 1932.
Thomas, Lowell. *Men of Danger.* 1936.
*New York Times:*
    July 16, 1903; "Workmen Fall . . ."
    September 10, 1903; "Fell From Bridge; Lives."
Childe, Cromwell. "The Structural Iron Workers." *Frank Leslie's Popular Monthly.* July 1901.

## CHAPTER 2: THE MAN ON TOP (1901)

Early history of skyscrapers:
"The Attractiveness of M. Eiffel's Proposed Tower." *Scientific American.* August 21, 1886.
Birkmire, William H. *The Planning and Construction of High Office Buildings.* 1898.
Bossom, Alfred C. *Building to the Skies: The Romance of the Skyscraper.* 1934.
*Brochure Advertising Retail Space* (re: Flatiron). 1902.
Burrows, Edwin G. and Mike Wallace. *Gotham: A History of New York City to 1898.* 1999.
Douglas, George H. *Skyscrapers: A Social History of the Very Tall Building in America.* 1996.
Freitag, Joseph Kendall. *Architectural Engineering: With Especial Reference to High Building Construction, Including Many Examples of Prominent Office Buildings.* 1906.
Horowitz, Louis J. and Boyden Sparks. *Towers of New York.* 1937.
James, Henry. *The American Scene.* 1907.
Landau, Sarah Bradford and Carl W. Condit. *Rise of the New York Skyscraper, 1865–1913.* 1996.
*New York Times:*
    July 14, 1895; "Limit of High Buildings."
    September 27, 1896; "Fatalities to Workmen."

Saliga, Pauline A. *The Sky's the Limit: A Century of Chicago Skyscrapers.* 1990.

Shultz, Earle and Walter Simmons. *Offices in the Sky.* 1959.

Starrett, Paul. *Changing the Skyline: An Autobiography.* 1938.

Starrett, W. A. *Skyscrapers and the Men Who Build Them.* 1928.

Union History Company. *History of Architecture and the Building Trades of Greater New York.* 1899.

**Early bridges:**

Cooper, Theodore. *American Railroad Bridges.* 1898.

Curtis-Clarke, Thomas. *An Account of the Iron Railway Bridge Across the Mississippi River at Quincy, Illinois.* 1869.

Curtis-Clarke, Thomas. "European and American Bridge Building Practice." *The Engineering Magazine.* 1901.

Detroit Bridge & Iron Works. *Memoir of the Iron Bridge Over the Missouri River, at St. Joseph, MO, Built in 1871-2-3.*

Kemp, Emory L. "The Fabric of Historic Bridges." *The Journal of the Society for Industrial Archeology.* 1989.

MacQueen, P. "Bridges and Bridge Builders." *Cosmopolitan, A Monthly Illustrated Magazine.* Vol. 13, 1892.

McCullough, David. *The Great Bridge: The Epic Story of the Building of the Brooklyn Bridge.* 1972.

Passfield, Robert W. "The Turcot Riveted Arch-Truss Bridge." *The Journal of the Society for Industrial Archeology.* 1997.

Vose, George L. "Safety in Railroad Travel." *The North American Review.* October 1882.

**Early ironworkers:**

*The Bridgemen's Magazine.* 1901–1903 (all issues).

Childe, Cromwell. "The Structural Workers." *Frank Leslie's Popular Monthly.* July 1901.

Grant, Luke (for the United States Commission on Industrial Relations). *The National Erectors' Association and The International Association of Bridge and Structural Ironworkers.* 1915.

Moffett, Cleveland. *Careers of Danger and Daring.* 1913.
Poole, Ernest. "Cowboys of the Skies." *Everybody's Magazine.* November 1908.

## CHAPTER 3: THE NEW WORLD

Drinking:
Sonnenstuhl, William J. *Working Sober: The Transformation of an Occupational Drinking Culture.* 1996.

Workforce statistics:
Shifflett, Crandall. *Almanac of American Life: Victorian America 1876–1913.* 1996.
Caplow, Hicks, and Wattenberg. *The First Measured Century: An Illustrated Guide to Trends in America, 1900–2000.* 2000.

Definition of skyscraper:
Tallmadge, Thomas E. (ed.). *The Origin of the Skyscraper: Report of the Committee Appointed by the Trustees of the Estate of Marshal Field for the Examination of the Structure of the Home Insurance Building.* 1939.

## CHAPTER 4: THE WALKING DELEGATE (1903)

Sam Parks [The narrative of Parks' rise and fall is mainly drawn from approximately 100 newspaper articles published between April 1903 and May 1904]:
*Commercial Advertiser*
*New York Daily News*
*New-York Daily Tribune*
*New York Herald*
*New York Post*
*New York Press*
*New York Times*
*The Sun*

**More Sam Parks:**
Baker, Ray Stannard. "The Trust's New Tool—The Labor Boss." *McClure's Magazine.* November 1903.
*The Bridgemen's Magazine.* 1901–1904 (all issues).
Clarkin, Franklin. "The Daily Walk of the Walking Delegate." *The Century Illustrated Monthly Magazine.* December 1903.
International Association of Bridge, Structural and Ornamental Iron Workers. *A History of the Iron Workers Union.* 1996.
Lardner, James and Thomas Reppetto. *NYPD: A City and Its Police.* 2000.
Lewis, Henry Harrison. "Sam Parks: Grafter and Blackmailer." *Harper's Weekly.* October 17, 1903.
Scott, Leroy. *The Walking Delegate.* 1905.
Starrett, W.A. *Skyscrapers and the Men who Build Them.* 1928.

# CHAPTER 5: MONDAYS (2001)

**Ironwork:**
Cherry, Mike. *On High Steel: The Education of an Ironworker.* 1974.

**Spacing out:**
Moffett, Cleveland. *Careers of Danger and Daring.* 1913.
*New York Times:* September 29, 1900; "Fell 85 Feet . . ."
Thomas, Lowell. *Men of Danger.* 1936.

# CHAPTER 6: KAHNAWAKE

**Early history of Kahnawake Mohawks:**
Blanchard, David S. *Kahnawake: A Historical Sketch.* 1980.
*The Catholic Encyclopedia, Volume III.* 1908.
Snow, Dean R. *The Iroquois.* 1994.

**Quebec Bridge:**
*The Bridgemen's Magazine.* July–September 1907.
Canada. Royal Commission. *Quebec Bridge Inquiry Report.* 1908.
Middleton, William D. *The Bridge at Quebec.* 2001.
*New York Times:*
    August 30, 1907; "Bridge Falls, Drowning 80."
    August 31, 1907; "Had Warned Men On Bridge."
    September 1, 1907; "Bridge Warning Was Just Too Late."
    September 2, 1907; "Engineer Found Flaw."
    September 5, 1907; "The Quebec Disaster."
    November 21, 1907; "Charges Against Cooper."
Petroski, Henry. *Engineers of Dreams.* 1995.
"A Portentous Bridge Disaster." *Scientific American.* September 14, 1907.
"The Quebec Bridge Disaster." *Scientific American.* September 7, 1907.
Whalen, James M. "A Bridge with Two Tragedies." *Legion Magazine.* November/December 2000.

**Mohawk ironworkers:**
"American Indians in High Places." *Parade.* January 31, 1982.
Conly, Robert L. "The Mohawks Scape the Sky." *National Geographic.* July 1952.
Freilich, Morris. "Cultural Persistence Among the Modern Iroquois." *Anthropos.* 1958.
Freilich, Morris. "Scientific Possibilities in Iroquoian Studies: An Example of Mohawks Past and Present." *Anthropologica.* 1963.
Hill, Richard. *Skywalkers: A History of Indian Ironworkers.* 1987.
Katzner, Bruce. "The Caughnawaga Mohawks: the Other Side of Iron Work." *Journal of Ethnic Studies.* Winter 1988, v. 15, n. 4.
Mitchell, Joseph. "The Mohawks in High Steel." *The New Yorker.* September 17, 1949.
"Mohawks Like High Steel." *Bethlehem Review.* Circa 1966.

"Reds Uncle Sam Can't Keep Out." *The Literary Digest*. May 1927.

Rose, William T. "Mohawk Indians Are World Famous for Their Skill in 'High Steel.'" *Industrial Bulletin 40*. October 1961.

Wilson, Edmund. *Apologies to the Iroquois*. 1960.


## CHAPTER 7: COWBOYS OF THE SKIES

Mid-air murder:

*New York Times*:

July 12, 1906; "Murder in Mid-Air by Union Workers."

July 13, 1906; "No Further Arrests for Mid-Air Murder."

July 15, 1906; "Seven Ironworkers Held."

July 17, 1906; "The Murderous Housesmiths."

Dynamite and McNamaras:

Adamic, Louis. *Dynamite*. 1934.

Caesar, Gene. *Incredible Detective: The Biography of William J. Burns*. 1968.

Fine, Sidney. *Without Blare of Trumpets: Walter Drew, the National Erectors' Association, and the Open Shop Movement, 1903–1957*. 1995.

Grant, Luke (for the United States Commission on Industrial Relations). *The National Erectors' Association and The International Association of Bridge and Structural Ironworkers*. 1915.

Hunt, William R. *Front-page Detective: William J. Burns and the Detective Profession 1880–1930*. 1990.

McDougal, Dennis. *Privileged Son: Otis Chandler and the Rise and Fall of the L.A. Times Dynasty*. 2001.

McManigal, Ortie E. *The National Dynamite Plot*. 1913.

*New York Times*:

April 23, 1911; "Union Leaders Arrested. . . ."

"Other Cases of Dynamiting."

"J.J. McNamara's Career."

April 24, 1911; "Strong Guard for McNamara."
April 27, 1911; "Dynamite Prisoners in Los Angeles Jail."
December 2, 1911; "James B. McNamara's Confession."
"How Suspicion Fell on the M'Namaras."
"Mother Won't Believe It."
December 3, 1911; "Get Ironworkers' Records."
December 4, 1911; "Gompers Cries: 'I Did Not Know.' "
October 13, 1913; "Dynamiter Owns to Many Crimes."

**Into the ether:**
Cochran, Edwin A. *The Cathedral of Commerce.* 1916.
"The Erection of the 612-foot Singer Building." *Scientific American.*
    September 7, 1907.
"Facing Death on a Four-inch Beam." *The Literary Digest.* May 30, 1914.
"The Industrial Daredevil." *Scientific American.* November 30, 1912.
Johnston, William Allen. "Sky-scrapers While You Wait." *Harper's*
    *Weekly.* June 11, 1910.
*New York Times:*
    September 30, 1911; "Giant Fears His Wife."
    January 27, 1912; "Hammers Six Men, Gets Back his $28."
    July 2, 1915; "Buried by Steel, Directs Rescue."
Poole, Ernest. "Cowboys of the Sky." *Everybody's Magazine.* November
    1908.
"The Tallest Office Building in the World." *Scientific American.*
    March 8, 1913.

**Golden age:**
Davenport, Walter. "High and Mighty." *Collier's.* March 1, 1930.
Fistere, John Cushman. "No Timid Man Could Hold This Job." *The*
    *American Magazine.* June 1931.
Hine, Lewis W. *Men at Work: Photographic Studies of Modern Men*
    *and Machines.* 1932.
Littell, Edmund. "Men Wanted." *The American Magazine.* April 1930.

*New York Times:*
   August 25, 1925; "Risks Life for $1; Loses It as a Fine."
   April 9, 1928; "Iron Workers Aloft."
   September 23, 1929; "Subdues Crazed Man High Up on Bridge."
Norris, Margaret. *Heroes and Hazards.* 1932.
Poore, C. G. "The Riveter's Panorama of New York." *The New York Times Magazine.* January 5, 1930.
Saunders, John Monk. "It's a Tough Job, but Somebody's Got to Swing It." *The American Magazine.* May 1925.
"Sky Boys Who 'Rode the Ball' on Empire State." *Literary Digest.* May 23, 1931.
Tauranac, John. *The Empire State Building: the Making of a Landmark.* 1995.
Thomas, Lowell. *Men of Danger.* 1936.
"Why Boys Shun the Building Trades." From *The Building Age;* reprinted in *Literary Digest.* December 8, 1923.

## CHAPTER 8: FISH

Newfoundland history and ironworkers:
Brown, Cassie with Harold Horwood. *Death on the Ice: The Great Newfoundland Sealing Disaster of 1914.* 1972.
Conception Harbour Heritage Committee. *Conception Harbour: Our Story.* 2000.
Kurlansky, Mark. *Cod: A Biography of the Fish That Changed the World.* 1997.
*New York Times:*
   May 25, 1974; "Newfoundland, Butt of Canadian Jokes . . ."
   August 3, 1979; "Newfoundland, Long Poor and Laggard . . ."
   July 13, 1980; "Suddenly, Newfoundland . . ."
O'Driscoll, Richard and Elizabeth Elliot (eds.). *Atlantis Again: the Story of a Family.* 1993.
Thurston, Harry. "The Fish Gang." *Equinox.* September/October 1985.

## CHAPTER 9: THE OLD SCHOOL

**Happiness:**

Sheldon, Kennon M. et al. "What Is Satisfying About Satisfying Events? Testing 10 Candidate Psychological Needs." *Journal of Personality and Social Psychology.* February 2001.

**Working class:**

Zweig, Michael. *The Working Class Majority: America's Best Kept Secret.* 2000.

**Safety standards:**

U.S. Department of Labor. Occupational Safety and Health Administration. *Federal Register Vol. 66, No. 12; Safety Standard for Steel Erection; Final Rule.* January 18, 2001.

## CHAPTER 10: THE TOWERS

**George Washington Bridge:**

Ammann, O. H. *Second Progress Report of Hudson River Bridge at New York Between Fort Washington and Fort Lee.* 1929.

Bounden, E. W. and H. R. Seely. "George Washington Bridge: Construction of the Steel Superstructure." *Transaction of the American Society of Civil Engineers.*

*Construction of the George Washington Bridge over the Hudson River.* Silent film in possession of Port Authority of New York and New Jersey. Circa 1931.

*New York Times:*

March 27, 1927; "Huge Hudson Bridge is a Five-year Task."

March 24, 1929; "Work Is Speeded on Hudson Bridge."

July 10, 1929; "The Bridge Builders."

July 14, 1929; "Weaving Bridge Cables High Above. . . ."

September 15, 1929; "A Dizzy Task for Men Without Nerves."

April 11, 1930; "Describes Hudson Bridge."

May 14, 1930; "New Hudson Bridge is 55% Complete."

May 25, 1930; "Weaving a Great Span over the Hudson. . . ."

September 22, 1930; "Dies in Stunt Dive from Ft. Lee Bridge."

September 6, 1931; "A Span That Symbolizes the Steel Age."

October 18, 1931; "How the Bridge Was Built."

December 6, 1959; "The Big Bridge Grows Bigger."

Norris, Margaret. *Heroes and Hazards.* 1932.

Rastorfer, Darl. *Six Bridges: The Legacy of Othmar H. Ammann.* 2000.

Stearns, Edward W. *Constructing the Hudson River Bridge at Fort Lee.* (Talk delivered to the American Institute of Steel Construction.) Circa 1931.

**Verrazano-Narrows Bridge:**

*New York Times:*

September 18, 1962; "Towers Topped Out on Narrows Bridge."

December 6, 1963; "Negotiations Fail in Strike on Bridge"

December 7, 1963; "Bridgemen to Get Nets on Narrows."

January 23, 1964; "Bridge Delights 'Seaside Supers.' "

October 24, 1964; "Verrazano Bridge Getting Coat of Gray . . ."

November 19, 1964; "Bridge Workers Will Boycott Opening . . ."

November 21, 1964; "Staten Island Link . . ."

November 22, 1964; "New Landmark Greeted with Fanfare . . ."

November 22, 1964; "Web Across the Narrows was 5 Years . . ."

O'Neill, Richard W. *High Steel, Hard Rock, and Deep Water: The Exciting World of Construction.* 1965.

Talese, Gay. *The Bridge.* 1964.

**World Trade Center:**

Collins, Glenn. "Notes on a Revolutionary Dinosaur." *The New York Times Magazine.* August 6, 1972.

"The Colossus Nobody Seems to Love." *Business Week.* April 3, 1971.

Gannon, Robert. "Topping Out the World's Tallest Building." *Popular Science.* May 1971.

Gillespie, Angus Kress. *Twin Towers: The Life of New York City's World Trade Center.* 1999.

Koch, Karl with Richard Firstman. *Men of Steel: The Story of the Family That Built the World Trade Center.* 2002.

*New York Times:*
October 20, 1970; "World Trade Center Becomes ..."
December 24, 1970; "Trade Center 'Topped Out' With Steel ..."

**Hard Hats, race, and Vietnam:**

Appy, Christian G. *Working Class War: American Combat Soldiers and Vietnam.* 1993.

Linder, Marc. *Wars of Attrition: Vietnam, the Business Roundtable, and the Decline of Construction Unions.* 1999.

*New York Post:*
May 9, 1970; "They Came at Us Like Animals."
May 12, 1970; "Hard Hats and Cops."
May 16, 1970; "Construction Workers—Who They Are ..."

*New York Times:*
September 3, 1964; "Quiet Negro Pioneer ..."
April 1, 1965; "Negro Hiring Up in Building Jobs."
September 28, 1966; "Negroes Get Opening to Building Jobs."
June 1, 1967; "Trade Union Bias Found Unchecked."
April 13, 1968; "Ironworkers Union Charged ..."
August 28, 1969; "Negro Groups Step Up Militancy ..."
May 9, 1970; "War Foes Here Attacked ..."
May 16, 1970; "Thousands in City March ..."
May 24, 1970; "Workers for Nixon and Flag Come Out ..."
February 28, 1971; "Hard Hats Seethe Over Wage Curb."

## CHAPTER 11: BURNING STEEL

**Ironworkers as heroes:**

*Washington Post:* September 15, 2001; "New York's Men of Steel: Hard Hats, Soft Hearts."

## CHAPTER 12: TOPPING OUT

American steel:

Hoerr, John P. *And the Wolf Finally Came: The Decline of the American Steel Industry.* 1988.

Strohmey, John. *Crisis in Bethlehem.* 1986.

Warren, Kenneth. *Big Steel: The First Century of the United States Steel Corporation 1901–2001.* 2001.

Why the towers fell:

*The Associated Press:* May 1, 2002; "Report: Fire Brought Down WTC Towers."

Hamburger, Ronald et al. *World Trade Center Building Performance Study.* Federal Emergency Management Agency. 2002.

*National Public Radio.* Transcript of interview with Abolhassan Astaneh-Asl. October 16, 2001.

*New York Times:*
November 11, 2001; "In Collapsing Towers, a Cascade . . ."
March 29, 2002; "Towers Fell as Intense Fire . . ."
May 1, 2002; "Report of Towers' Collapse Ends . . ."
August 22, 2002; "U.S. Announces New, Tougher Look . . ."
October 22, 2002; "Expert Report Disputes U.S. on Collapse."

*NOVA.* Transcript of interview with Dr. Thomas Eagar. June 13, 2002.

Concrete:

"Concrete Cores Combat Collapse." *Construction Industry Times.* November 5, 2001.

*New York Post:* October 13, 2001; " 'Tough' Talk from Trump . . ."

*New York Times:*
September 18, 2001; "Defending Skyscrapers Against Terror."
September 9, 2002; "9/11 Prompts New Caution . . ."
October 23, 2002; "Comparing 2 Sets of Twin Towers."

"The Right Stuff." *Popular Science.* April 9, 2002.

**Future of skyscrapers:**
*New York Times:*
  November 12, 2001; "Skyscrapers Are Here to Stay . . ."
  December 9, 2001; "The Future of Up."
*USA Today:* September 19, 2001; "Skyscrapers' Popularity . . ."

**Last column:**
*New York Daily News:* May 29, 2002; "Final Girder Taken Down."

# ACKNOWLEDGMENTS

This book evolved from an article I wrote for the City section of the *New York Times* in the winter of 2001. The editor of that section, Constance Rosenblum, encouraged me to write the article, then edited it superbly. Two and half years later, Connie read this book in manuscript and once again blessed me with her editorial gifts. This book would be far less than what it is—would not exist at all, in fact—were it not for Connie's support.

Once launched, I depended in large part on the kindness and patience of people who had no particular reason to grant it to me, but did anyway. I'm indebted to every ironworker featured between these covers, and to many who are not, for putting up with my inquisitive intrusions. A special word of thanks to Jack Doyle, Jack and Kitty Costello, J. R. Phillips, Keith McComber, Joe Gaffney, Joe Lewis, and Brett Conklin. The latter three—Joe, Joe, and Brett—were injured as I was writing the book and proved, each of them, as persevering in their recoveries as they'd been brave on the steel.

In researching the historical portions of this book, I relied on the remarkable collections—and staffs—of the New York Historical

Society Library, the New York Public Library, the New York City Municipal Archives, and the Wirtz Labor Library of the U.S. Department of Labor. The librarians at the Kanien'kehaka Raotitiohkwa Cultural Centre at Kahnawake helped me learn more in a concentrated period of time than I thought possible. Constance Nardella of the Port Authority of New York and New Jersey was good enough to assist me even as her agency struggled back onto its feet after the events of 9/11 (in which much of the Port Authority's archival material was lost).

My understanding of Newfoundland would be a good deal foggier (make that *mauzier*) were it not for the hospitality and guidance of Marg and Paul O'Driscoll, Tilley Costello, and of many others who welcomed me to Conception Bay. George Cross generously shared with me his research into the early history of the ironworkers' union. John McMahon, retired executive director of the Institute of the Ironworking Industry—and a former bridgeman—connected some of the dots for me with his wide-ranging knowledge of structural ironwork and his salty eloquence. Bill Liddy of the American Institute of Steel Construction enlightened me on matters pertaining to steel and put me in touch with several fine tutors, including David Rees and Ronald Flucker. I am grateful also to Silvian Marcus, Ysrael Seinuk, David Worsley, Larry Howard, and Dr. Bernard Cohen. And let me not forget Steelcase Inc., for granting me access to its fine balcony with a view.

My friend Deborah Hellman interrupted new motherhood and a sabbatical in Italy to read this book in manuscript and give me the benefit of her keen intelligence and judgment. My father, Ray Rasenberger, also read sections of this book in manuscript and saved me from committing numerous ill-chosen words to print. My mother, Nancy, colored the entire project with her love of history—and was the first person to speak to me, very long ago, about ironworkers. I gained much, meanwhile, from the counsel of Eugene Linden and the support of Jim and Ruth Varney.

I am extraordinarily grateful to Kris Dahl at ICM, who saw the book in the material and supplied many great ideas on how to shape it. She knew just the man to edit it, too—which brings me to Dan Conaway at HarperCollins. Dan belies the notion that book editors don't edit books anymore. He saw things in mine that eluded me and helped me separate the wheat from the chafe (a cliché he'd never let stand). His scribbles, once deciphered, were illuminating. Dan's assistant, Jill Schwartzman, made the editing process as delightful as it could possibly be with her enthusiasm, utter competence, and many helpful suggestions.

Though this book deals with some sobering material, delight was never far from me as I wrote it. It was, in fact, just down the hall in the form of Willy and Jack, my sons, whose boundless energy and curiosity inspired me throughout. Ann Varney, my wife, has made this endeavor possible in countless ways, but mainly as my first and most trusted reader, which is about the most important ally a writer can have. I owe her more than I can say.

# INDEX